Performance Modeling and Engineering

Performance Modeling and Engineering

Edited by

Zhen Liu and Cathy H. Xia

 Springer

Editors:

Zhen Liu
IBM T. J. Watson Research Center
19 Skyline Drive
Hawthorne, NY 10533
zhenl@us.ibm.com

Cathy H. Xia
IBM T. J. Watson Research Center
19 Skyline Drive
Hawthorne, NY 10533
cathyx@us.ibm.com

ISBN-13: 978-1-4419-4633-1   e-ISBN-13: 978-0-387-79361-0

9 8 7 6 5 4 3 2 1

springer.com

Preface

With the fast development of networking and software technologies, information processing infrastructure and applications have been growing at an impressive rate in both size and complexity, to such a degree that the design and development of high performance and scalable data processing systems and networks have become an ever-challenging issue. As a result, the use of performance modeling and measurement techniques as a critical step in design and development has become a common practice. Research and development on methodology and tools of performance modeling and performance engineering have gained further importance in order to improve the performance and scalability of these systems.

Since the seminal work of A. K. Erlang almost a century ago on the modeling of telephone traffic, performance modeling and measurement have grown into a discipline and have been evolving both in their methodologies and in the areas in which they are applied. It is noteworthy that various mathematical techniques were brought into this field, including in particular probability theory, stochastic processes, statistics, complex analysis, stochastic calculus, stochastic comparison, optimization, control theory, machine learning and information theory. The application areas extended from telephone networks to Internet and Web applications, from computer systems to computer software, from manufacturing systems to supply chain, from call centers to workforce management.

The aim of this book is to bring together the latest advances in methodology and techniques of performance modeling and engineering, ranging from theoretical advances to system and architecture developments, from technology to economics, from academic innovations to engineering processes, from statistical analysis to system control, and from enterprise systems to computer networks. The purpose for this collection is to promote innovative research in these emerging topics, to bridge the gap between theory and practice, and to stimulate the use of these new developments.

The book is organized in two parts. Part I focuses on performance design and engineering, introducing new methodologies and considerations including machine learning, network economics, online advertising and performance engineering. Part II concentrates on scheduling and control, covering new developments in Internet traffic routing, network scheduling, and modeling and control of computer systems. Each chapter is self-contained, including both a broad survey of the topic and the technical challenges and solutions. Below we briefly summarize the content of each part.

Part I on performance design and engineering comprises four chapters. Alina Beygelzimer, John Langford and Bianca Zadrozny present in Chapter 1 an overview of machine learning methods that can be applied to performance prediction. Specifically they focus on reduction techniques that transform practical problems into well-studied machine learning problems, which can then be solved using existing base-learning algorithms.

In Chapter 2, Dave Jewell presents an introduction to Performance Engineering and Management Method (PEMM), a process and a methodology that integrates many useful performance modeling and engineering techniques and provides a holistic approach to addressing the risks related to information technology performance, capacity and scalability.

Jean Walrand discusses economic models of communication networks in Chapter 3. By exploring the interaction of network designs and economics and by discussing a number of concrete models of network neutrality, service differentiation, and security, he illustrates the importance of the economic impact on design choices.

In Chapter 4, Jon Feldman and S. Muthukrishnan provide a comprehensive overview of the auction system for sponsored search advertising. They show examples of research in algorithmic, optimization and game-theoretic issues in bidding, pricing, and market design of such systems. They further describe the mathematical and algorithmic issues and challenges in sponsored search advertising.

Part II on scheduling and control comprises three chapters. In Chapter 5, M. Kodialam, T.V. Lakshman and Sudipta Sengupta provide a survey on recent developments in oblivious routing of Internet traffic. They describe two broadly used oblivious routing schemes and discuss the deployment, performance guarantee, and various routing architecture and protocol issues in today's Internet.

Devavrat Shah presents in Chapter 6 a survey on some of the latest results on design methods and analysis techniques of distributed scheduling algorithms in networks. He argues that a canonical way to design network algorithms is through a message-passing paradigm, through which the various approaches such as randomization, belief propagation, heavy traffic theory, flow-level modeling can be unified.

In Chapter 7, Tarek Abdelzaher, Yixin Diao, Joseph L. Hellerstein, Chenyang Lu and Xiaoyun Zhu provide an introduction to control theory for computing practitioners, and illustrate a number of recent successes in applying control theory to managing applications in the areas of database systems, real-time systems, virtualized servers and power management.

In summary, this book provides new perspectives of performance modeling and engineering. It allows the reader to understand both theoretical and practical issues, and to develop both mathematical frameworks and engineering processes. It also establishes a connection between market mechanisms and the Internet and Internet applications. It provides new insights in the application of control theory and optimization techniques on computer systems and computer networks.

This book is used as the textbook for the ACM SIGMETRICS 2008 Tutorial program. We believe that the book can provide the larger SIGMETRICS community and networking and systems communities theories and techniques that can help improve the performance of computer systems and networks. The book will introduce practitioners to new methodologies and techniques and pose practical problems to researchers from both the theoretical and applied communities.

We sincerely thank all authors and tutorial presenters for their contributions to this book and to the ACM SIGMETRICS 2008 Tutorial program. We also would like to thank our colleagues, Fred Douglis and Srinivasan Parthasarathy for their timely assistance.in reviewing the book chapters. Without all of the work and support from both groups of people, this book would not have been possible. Last but not least, we are grateful to ACM and IBM Research for sponsoring the tutorial program of the SIGMETRICS 2008 Conference.

Zhen Liu
Cathy H. Xia

About the Editors

Zhen Liu received the Ph.D. degree in Computer Science from the University of Orsay (Paris XI), France. He was with France Telecom R&D and then with INRIA (the French national research center on information and automation). He is now with IBM T. J. Watson Research Center and is the senior manager of the Next Generation Distributed Systems Department. Zhen Liu is a fellow of IEEE, a member of the IFIP W.G. 7.3 on performance modeling and a master inventor at IBM. He has served NSF Panels and a number of conference program committees. Zhen Liu is the general chair of ACM Sigmetrics 2008, and was the program co-chair of the Joint Conference of ACM Sigmetrics and IFIP Performance 2004. Zhen's current research interests are in distributed and networked systems, stream processing systems, sensor networks, performance modeling, distributed optimization and control.

Cathy H. Xia received her Ph.D. in Engineering-Economic Systems and Operations Research from Stanford University. She then joined IBM T.J. Watson Research Center as a research scientist. She is currently the chair of the Performance Modeling and Analysis research community at IBM Research. Cathy Xia is the tutorial chair of ACM Sigmetrics 2008. She has served in a number of conference program committees including SIGMETRICS and Performance 2004-2008. Her research interests are in optimal and distributed control of stochastic networks, stream processing systems, sensor networks, Web services, pricing and outsourcing strategies, stochastic processes, queuing theory, and performance modeling and analysis of parallel and distributed systems.

Contents

List of Contributors

Tarek Abdelzaher
Department of Computer Science, University of Illinois at Urbana Champaign, Urbana, IL 61801, e-mail: zaher@cs.uiuc.edu

Alina Beygelzimer
IBM Thomas J. Watson Research Center, 19 Skyline Drive, Hawthorne, NY 10532, e-mail: beygel@us.ibm.com

Yixin Diao
IBM T.J. Watson Research Center, Hawthorne, NY 10532, USA, e-mail: diao@us.ibm.com

Jon Feldman
Google, Inc., 76 9th Avenue, 4th Floor, New York, NY, 10011, e-mail: jonfeld@google.com

Joseph L. Hellerstein
Developer Division, Microsoft Corp, Redmond, WA, e-mail: joehe@microsoft.com

Dave Jewell
Performance Engineering practice, Systems Engineering, Architecture & Test (SEA&T), IBM Global Business Services, e-mail: jewell@us.ibm.com

M. Kodialam
Bell Laboratories, Alcatel-Lucent, Murray Hill, NJ, USA e-mail: muralik@alcatel-lucent.com

T. V. Lakshman
Bell Laboratories, Alcatel-Lucent, Murray Hill, NJ, USA e-mail: lakshman@alcatel-lucent.com

John Langford
Yahoo! Research, New York, NY, e-mail: jl@yahoo-inc.com

Chenyang Lu
Department of Computer Science and Engineering, Washington University in St. Louis, e-mail: lu@cse.wustl.edu

S. Muthukrishnan
Google, Inc., 76 9th Avenue, 4th Floor, New York, NY, 10011, e-mail: muthu@google.com

Sudipta Sengupta
Microsoft Research, Redmond, WA, USA, e-mail: sudipta@microsoft.com

Devavrat Shah
Department of EECS, Massachusetts Institute of Technology, Cambridge, MA 02139, e-mail: devavrat@mit.edu

Jean Walrand
Department of EECS, University of California at Berkeley, e-mail: wlr@eecs.berkeley.edu

Bianca Zadrozny
Fluminense Federal University, Brazil, e-mail: bianca@ic.uff.br

Xiaoyun Zhu
Hewlett Packard Laboratories, Hewlett Packard Corp., Palo Alto, CA, e-mail: xiaoyun.zhu@hp.com

Part I
Performance Design and Engineering

Chapter 1
Machine Learning Techniques—Reductions Between Prediction Quality Metrics

Alina Beygelzimer, John Langford, and Bianca Zadrozny

Abstract Machine learning involves optimizing a loss function on unlabeled data points given examples of labeled data points, where the loss function measures the performance of a learning algorithm. We give an overview of techniques, called reductions, for converting a problem of minimizing one loss function into a problem of minimizing another, simpler loss function. This tutorial discusses how to create robust reductions that perform well in practice. The reductions discussed here can be used to solve any supervised learning problem with a standard binary classification or regression algorithm available in any machine learning toolkit. We also discuss common design flaws in folklore reductions.

1.1 Introduction

Machine learning is about learning to make predictions from examples of desired behavior or past observations. Learning methods have found numerous applications in performance modeling and evaluation (see, for example, [33, 22, 37, 41, 43, 39]). One natural example of a machine learning application is fault diagnosis: based on various observations about a system, we may want to predict whether the system is in its normal state or in one of several fault states. Machine learning techniques are preferred in situations where engineering approaches like hand-crafted models simply can not cope with the complexity of the problem. In the fault diagnosis prob-

Alina Beygelzimer
IBM Thomas J. Watson Research Center, 19 Skyline Drive, Hawthorne, NY 10532 e-mail: beygel@us.ibm.com

John Langford
Yahoo! Research, New York, NY e-mail: jl@yahoo-inc.com

Bianca Zadrozny
Fluminense Federal University, Brazil e-mail: bianca@ic.uff.br

lem, it is reasonably easy to collect examples of resolved faults, but writing robust diagnosis rules is very difficult.

A basic difficulty in applying machine learning in practice is that we often need to solve problems that don't quite match the problems solved by standard machine learning algorithms. In fault diagnosis, for example, the cost of misclassifying a faulty state as a normal state is sometimes much higher than the cost of misclassifying a normal state as a faulty state. Thus binary classification algorithms, which don't take misclassification costs into account, do not perform well on this problem.

Reductions are techniques that transform practical problems into well-studied machine learning problems. These can then be solved using any existing base learning algorithm whose solution can, in turn, be used to solve the original problem. Reductions have several desirable properties.

- They yield highly automated learning algorithms. Reductions convert *any* learner for the base problem into a learning algorithm for the new problem. Any future progress on the base problem immediately translates to the new problem.
- Reductions are modular and composable. A single reduction applied to N base learners gives N new learning algorithms for the new problem. Simple reductions can be composed to solve more complicated problems.
- The theory of learning has focused mostly on binary classification and regression. Reductions transfer existing learning theory to the new problem.
- Reductions help us organize and understand the relationship between different learning problems.

An alternative to reductions is designing new learning algorithms or modifying existing ones for each new problem. While this approach is quite attractive to learning algorithm designers, it is undesirable in some situations. For example, some algorithms cannot be easily modified to handle different learning problems, as evidenced, for example, by inconsistent proposals for extending Support Vector Machines to multiclass classification (see [30]). More generally, we can expect that people encountering new learning problems may not have the expertise or time for such adaption (or simply don't have access to the source code of the algorithm), implying that a reduction approach may be more desirable.

A critical question when comparing the two approaches is performance. Our experience is that both approaches can be made to work well. There is fairly strong empirical evidence that reductions analysis produces learning algorithms that perform well in practice (see, for example, [18, 10, 47, 13, 38]). This tutorial shows how reductions can be easily used by nonexperts.

1.2 Basic Definitions

Data points, called *examples*, are typically described by their values on some set of *features*. In fault diagnosis, for example, each event can be represented as a binary vector describing which observations have been made (ping latency from one node to another, for example). The space that examples live in is called the *feature space*, and is typically denoted by X.

The *label* of an example is what we are trying to predict. The space of possible labels is denoted by Y. In fault diagnosis, Y corresponds to the set of system states.

A *learning problem* is some unknown data distribution D over $X \times Y$, coupled with a loss function $\ell(y', y)$ measuring the loss of predicting y' when the true label is y. (In some problems below, the loss function also depends on additional information about the example.)

A *learning algorithm* takes a set of labeled training examples of the form $(x, y) \in X \times Y$ and produces a predictor $f : X \to Y$. The goal of the algorithm is to find f minimizing the expected loss $\mathbf{E}_{(x,y) \sim D} \, \ell(f(x), y)$.

There are two base learning problems, defined for any feature space X. In binary classification, we want to classify examples into two categories.

Definition 1.1. A *binary classification* problem is defined by a distribution D over $X \times Y$, where $Y = \{0, 1\}$. The goal is to find a *classifier* $h : X \to Y$ minimizing the *error rate* on D,

$$e(h, D) = \mathbf{Pr}_{(x,y) \sim D}[h(x) \neq y].$$

By fixing an unlabeled example $x \in X$, we get a *conditional distribution* $D|x$ over Y.

Regression is another basic learning problem, where the goal is to predict a real-valued label Y. The loss function typically used in regression is the squared error loss between the predicted and actual labels.

Definition 1.2. A *regression problem* is defined by a distribution D over $X \times \mathbb{R}$. The goal is to find a function $f : X \to \mathbb{R}$ minimizing the *squared loss*

$$\ell(f, D) = \mathbf{E}_{(x,y) \sim D}(f(x) - y)^2.$$

Organization: Section 1.3 shows how to solve binary classification problems where some examples are more important to classify correctly than others. It covers problems where false positives and false negatives have different costs as a special case. Section 1.4 demonstrates how regression algorithms can be used to choose among more than two alternatives. Section 1.5 covers a very board set of learning problems, where a decision is not only over multiple choices, but each prediction has a different associated cost. In Section 1.6, we discuss how to compute quantiles with binary classifier learners. Section 1.7 closes with the problem of reducing ranking, as measured by the Area Under the Receiver Operating Characteristic Curve (AUC), to binary classification.

1.3 Importance-Weighted Classification

Standard classification algorithms are designed to minimize the probability of making an incorrect prediction, treating all errors as equally costly. In practice, however, some errors are typically much more costly than others. For example, in credit card fraud detection the cost of an undetected fraud is much higher than the cost of an extra security check. The problem is complicated by the fact fraud is very rare. Ignoring the misclassification costs may produce a classifier that misses all the fraud by classifying every example as belonging to the more frequent non-fraud case. This classifier would be doing very well in terms of not making many mistakes, but it would have a very high cost. Thus a good metric is essential when training and evaluating a cost-sensitive learner.

Current techniques for cost-sensitive decision making fall into three categories: The first approach is to make particular classification algorithms cost-sensitive (see, for example, [15]). Doing this well is often nontrivial and requires considerable knowledge of the algorithm. The second approach uses Bayes risk theory to assign each example to its lowest risk class [14, 46, 32]. This requires estimating conditional class probabilities and, if costs are stochastic, estimating expected costs [46]. The third category concerns black-box reductions for converting arbitrary classification learning algorithms into importance-weighted algorithms [14, 47]. Meta-Cost [14] (implemented in Weka [45]), estimates conditional probability distributions, and thus also belongs to the Bayes risk minimization category above.

Before describing concrete methods for importance-weighted decision making, it is instructive to look at a simple theorem described below.

Motivating Theory

An *importance-weighted classification* problem is defined by a distribution D over $X \times Y \times C$, where X is some feature space, $Y = \{0,1\}$ is the label space, and $C \subset [0,\infty)$ is the importance (or cost) associated with mislabeling the corresponding example. The goal is to learn a classifier $h : X \to Y$ minimizing the *expected cost*

$$\mathbf{E}_{(x,y,c) \sim D}[c \cdot \mathbf{1}(h(x) \neq y)],$$

given training examples of the form $(x,y,c) \in X \times Y \times C$. Here $\mathbf{1}(\cdot)$ is the indicator function which evaluates to 1 if its argument is true, and to 0 otherwise. Since cost information is typically not available at prediction time, this is reflected in the model. If the cost is available, it can be included in the set of features.

When the output space is binary, this formulation of cost-sensitive learning in terms of one number per example is more general than the commonly used cost matrix formulation [16, 14]. A cost matrix specifies the cost c_{ij} of predicting label i when the true label is j. If the label is binary, the costs are associated with false negatives (c_{01}), false positives (c_{10}), true negatives (c_{00}), and true positives (c_{11}). Given a cost matrix and an example (x,y), only two cost entries (c_{1y}, c_{0y}) are relevant for that example. These two numbers can be further reduced to one, $|c_{1y} - c_{0y}|$, because it is the difference in costs which controls the importance of correct classification. This difference is the importance c we use here. The formulation we use is more general because it allows the costs to be example dependent. For example, the cost of a fraudulent charge can depend on the transaction amount. The multilabel case is covered by the more general cost-sensitive classification in Section 1.5. This section covers the binary case.

The following simple theorem is quite instructive.

Theorem 1.1. (Translation Theorem [47]) *For any importance-weighted distribution D, there exists a constant $\langle c \rangle = \mathbf{E}_{(x,y,c) \sim D}[c]$ such that for any classifier h,*

$$\mathbf{E}_{(x,y,c) \sim D'}[\mathbf{1}(h(x) \neq y)] = \frac{1}{\langle c \rangle} \mathbf{E}_{(x,y,c) \sim D}[c \cdot \mathbf{1}(h(x) \neq y)],$$

where D' is defined by $D'(x,y,c) = \frac{c}{\langle c \rangle} D(x,y,c)$.

Proof. Assuming for simplicity that X is finite,

$$\mathbf{E}_{(x,y,c) \sim D}[c \cdot \mathbf{1}(h(x) \neq y)] = \sum_{x,y,c} D(x,y,c) \cdot c \cdot \mathbf{1}(h(x) \neq y)$$

$$= \langle c \rangle \sum_{x,y,c} D'(x,y,c) \cdot \mathbf{1}(h(x) \neq y)$$

$$= \langle c \rangle \, \mathbf{E}_{(x,y,c) \sim D'}[\mathbf{1}(h(x) \neq y)]. \qquad \blacksquare$$

Despite its simplicity, this theorem is very useful because the right-hand side expresses the expected cost we want to control via the choice of h, and the left-hand side is the error rate of h under a related distribution D'. Thus choosing h to minimize the error rate under D' is equivalent to choosing h to minimize the expected cost under D.

The prescription for coping with cost-sensitive problems is now straightforward: re-weight the distribution in your training set according to the importances, so that the training set is effectively drawn from D'. Doing this in a correct and general manner is more challenging than it may seem.

There are two basic methods: (1) Transparent Box: supply the costs of the training data as example weights to the classifier learning algorithm; (2) Black Box: resample the training data according to these same weights.

The transparent box approach cannot be applied to arbitrary classifier learners, but it can be applied to those which use the data only to estimate expectations of the form $\mathbf{E}_{x,y \sim D}[f(x,y)]$ for some query function $f : X \times Y \rightarrow \{0,1\}$. Whenever a learning algorithm can be rewritten to fit this statistical query model [24], there is a simple recipe for using the weights directly. To get an unbiased estimate of the expectation with respect to D', one can use

$$\frac{1}{\sum_{(x,y,c) \in S} c} \sum_{(x,y,c) \in S} cf(x,y),$$

instead of using the sample mean of $f(x,y)$, where S is a set of training examples drawn independently from D. Such mechanisms for realizing the transparent box approach have been used for a number of weak learners used in boosting [18].

Neural networks, decision trees and Naive Bayes can all be expressed in this model, although it may require some understanding of the algorithms to see that. Support vector machines do not fit the model, because the produced classifier is explicitly dependent upon individual examples rather than on statistics derived from the entire sample. But there are still ways to incorporate importance weights directly (see, for example, [47]).

The black box approach has the advantage that it can be applied to any classifier learner, without requiring any knowledge of the learning algorithm.

Black Box: Sampling methods

Suppose that we do not have transparent box access to the learner. In this case, sampling is the obvious method to alter the distribution of examples, in order to use Theorem 1.1.

Simple sampling strategies: Sampling with replacement is a sampling scheme where each example (x,y,c) is drawn according to the distribution $p(x,y,c) = c/\sum_{(x,y,c)\in S} c$. A number of examples are drawn to create a new dataset S'. It may seem at first that this method is useful because every example is effectively drawn from the distribution D'. In fact, it can result in severe overfitting due to the fact that examples in S' are not drawn *independently* from D'. Also, as shown in Elkan [16], creating duplicate examples has little effect on classifiers produced by standard Bayesian and decision tree algorithms.

Sampling without replacement is also not a solution to this problem. In this scheme, an example (x,y,c) is drawn from the distribution $p(x,y,c) = c/\sum_{(x,y,c)\in S} c$, and the drawn example is removed from S. This process is repeated, drawing from an increasingly smaller set according to the weights of the examples remaining in the set. To see how this method fails, simply note that sampling m examples from a set of size m results in the original set, which by assumption is drawn from the distribution D, instead of D' as desired.

Cost-proportionate rejection sampling: We will present another sampling scheme based on rejection sampling [34], which allows one to draw examples independently from the distribution D' given examples drawn independently from D. In rejection sampling, examples from D' are obtained by first drawing examples from D, and then keeping the example with probability proportional to D'/D. In our case, $D'/D \propto c$, so we accept each c-important example with probability c/Z, where Z is a normalizing constant satisfying $\max_{(x,y,c)\in S} c \leq Z$. [1] Rejection sampling results in

---

[1] In practice, we choose $Z = \max_{(x,y,w)\in S} c$ so as to maximize the size of S'. A data-dependent choice of Z is not formally allowed for rejection sampling, but the introduced bias appears small when $|S| \gg 1$.

a set S' which is generally smaller than S. Notice that if examples in S are drawn independently from D, then examples in S' are going to be distributed independently according to D'.

A simple corollary of Theorem 1.1 says that any classifier achieving approximate error rate minimization on D' is guaranteed to produce approximate cost-minimization on D.

Corollary 1.1. *For all importance-weighted distributions D and all binary classifiers h, if*

$$\mathbf{E}_{(x,y,c)\sim D'}[\mathbf{1}(h(x) \neq y)] \leq \varepsilon,$$

then

$$\mathbf{E}_{(x,y,c)\sim D}[c \cdot \mathbf{1}(h(x) \neq y)] \leq \langle c \rangle \varepsilon,$$

where $\langle c \rangle = \mathbf{E}_{(x,y,c)\sim D}[c]$.

Proof. Follows immediately from Theorem 1.1. ∎

Cost-proportionate rejection sampling with aggregation (Costing): Given the same original training sample, different runs of cost-proportionate rejection sampling will produce different training subsamples. Since rejection sampling produces small subsamples allowing us to learn quickly, we can take advantage of the runtime savings to run the base learner on multiple draws of subsamples and average over the resulting classifiers. This method is called Costing [47].

Algorithm 1: Costing (learning algorithm A, training set S, count t)

---

for $i = 1$ *to* t **do**
  S' rejection sample from S with acceptance probability c/Z.
  Let $h_i = A(S')$
return $h(x) = \text{sign}\left(\sum_{i=1}^{t} h_i(x)\right)$

The goal in averaging is to improve performance. There is significant empirical evidence that averaging can considerably reduce overfitting suffered by the learning algorithm, despite throwing away a fraction of the samples. There are also several theoretical explanations of the empirical success of averaging methods (see, for example, [17]). In fact, Bagging [10] and Boosting [18] can both be viewed as reductions. Boosting algorithms [18, 23] reduce from classification with a small error rate to importance weighted classification with a loss rate of nearly $\frac{1}{2}$. Bagging [10] is a self-reduction of classification to classification, which turns learning algorithms with high variance (i.e., dependence on the exact examples seen) into a classifier with lower variance.

Since most learning algorithms have running times that are superlinear in the number of examples, the overall computational time of costing is generally much smaller than that of a learning algorithm using the original sample set S. Costing was shown to have excellent predictive performance and dramatic savings of computational resources (see [47]), which is especially important in applications that involve massive amount of data such as fraud and intrusion detection, and targeted marketing.

1.4 Multiclass Classification

Multiclass classification is just like binary classification, except that there are more than two choices available. Naturally, there are many applied problems where a decision over more than two possibilities is necessary, with such examples as optical character recognition, textual topic classification, and phoneme recognition.

Formally, a *k-class classification problem* is defined by a distribution D over $X \times Y$, where X is some feature space and $Y = \{1, \dots, k\}$ is the set of possible labels. The goal is to find a *classifier* $h : X \to Y$ minimizing the *error rate* on D, $e(h, D) = \mathbf{Pr}_{(x,y) \sim D}[h(x) \neq y]$.

There are several methods for solving multiclass classification problems directly [42, 44, 9, 11, 30, 31, 19]. These approaches *can* be made to work well, but the corresponding optimization problems are often fairly involved.

Given that we have many good binary learning algorithms and many multiclass problems, it is tempting to create meta-algorithms which use binary classifiers to make multiclass predictions.

1.4.1 One-Against-All

Perhaps the simplest such scheme is *one-against-all* (OAA). The OAA reduction creates a binary classification problem for each of the k classes. The classifier for class i is trained to predict whether the label is i or not, distinguishing class i from all other classes (Algorithm 2).

Algorithm 2: OAA-TRAIN (set of k-class training examples S, binary classifier learning algorithm A)

Set $S' = \emptyset$
for *all* $(x, y) \in S$ **do**
  for *all* $i \in \{1, \dots, k\}$ **do**
    add a binary example $(\langle x, i \rangle, \mathbf{1}(y = i))$ to S'
return $h = A(S')$.

Predictions are done by evaluating each binary classifier and randomizing over those which predict "yes," or over all k labels if all answers are "no" (Algorithm 3).

Algorithm 3: OAA-TEST (binary classifier h, test example x)

---

output $\arg\max_i h(\langle x,i \rangle)$ for $i \in \{1,\ldots,k\}$, breaking ties randomly

---

Notice that we do not actually have to learn k separate classifiers in Algorithm 2. We can simply augment the feature space with the index of the classifier and then learn a single combined classifier on the union of all training data. The implication of this observation is that we can view the reduction as a machine that maps multiclass examples to binary examples, transforming the original multiclass distribution D into an *induced* binary distribution D'. To draw a sample from D', we simply draw a multiclass example (x,y) from D and a random index $i \in \{1,\ldots,n\}$, and output $(\langle x,i \rangle, \mathbf{1}(y = i))$.

The lemma below bounds the error rate of Algorithm 3 on D in terms of the error rate of h on D'. Such a statement is called an *error transformation* of a reduction.

Lemma 1.1. (One-against-all error efficiency [2, 20, 8]) *For all k-class distributions D and binary classifiers h, $e(\text{OAA}_h,D) \leq (k-1)e(h,D')$, where OAA_h is the multiclass classifier produced by OAA using h.*

Proof. We analyze how false negatives and false positives produced by the binary classifier lead to errors in the multiclass classifier. A false negative produces an error in the multiclass classifier a $\frac{k-1}{k}$ fraction of the time (assuming that all the other classifiers are correctly outputting 0), because we are choosing randomly between k labels and only one is correct. The other error modes to consider involve (possibly multiple) false positives. If there are m false positives, the error probability is either $\frac{m}{m+1}$ or 1 if there is also a false negative. The efficiency of these three modes in creating errors (i.e., the maximum ratio of the probability of a multiclass error to the fraction of binary errors) is $k-1$, $\frac{k}{m+1}$, and $\frac{k}{m+1}$, respectively. Taking the maximum, $k-1$, we get the result. ∎

The proof actually shows that the multiclass error can be as high as $(k-1)e(h,D')$. By noticing that a false negative is more disastrous than a false positive, we can put more importance on positive examples, first reducing the multiclass problem to an importance-weighted binary problem, and then composing this reduction with the Costing reduction from Section 1.3 to remove the importances. As shown in [8], doing this halves the worst-case error theoretically, and improves over OAA empirically. This gives an example of a practical improvement directly influenced by analysis.

Inconsistency and Regret Transforms

There is an essential problem with OAA.

Definition 1.3. A reduction is said to be *inconsistent* if for some distribution D, the reduction does not produce $\arg\min_f e(f,D)$ given an optimal base predictor $\arg\min_h e(h,D')$ for the induced distribution D'.

Consistency is a very natural and desirable property of any reduction. If the auxiliary problems are solved optimally, the reduction should in turn yield an optimal predictor for the original problem. Unfortunately, OAA is inconsistent.

Theorem 1.2. *The One-Against-All reduction is inconsistent.*

The proof is simple and illustrative. A similar theorem statement and proof applies to ECOC reductions [13].

Proof. Consider a distribution D which puts all the probability mass on some example x. Let $k = 3$ and define the conditional probability as $D(y = 1 \mid x) = 0.5 - \gamma$ and $D(y = 2 \mid x) = D(y = 3 \mid x) = 0.25 + \frac{\gamma}{2}$, for some $0 < \gamma < 1/4$. Thus there is no majority class occurring at least half the time. OAA creates a binary problem for each class $y \in \{1,2,3\}$, distinguishing y (binary label 1) from the two remaining classes (binary label 0). The probability of label 1 for the three binary problems is $0.5 - \gamma$, $0.25 + \frac{\gamma}{2}$, and $0.25 + \frac{\gamma}{2}$ respectively, which implies that the optimal prediction is 0 for each binary problem. When every binary predictor predicts 0, the induced multiclass predictor can't do better than randomize among the three possible classes, resulting in an error rate of $\frac{2}{3}(0.5 - \gamma) + \frac{4}{3}(0.25 + \frac{\gamma}{2}) = \frac{2}{3}$. However, the optimal multiclass predictor always chooses class 1 achieving the error rate of $0.55 < 2/3$. ∎

Practical implications of the inconsistency theorem 1.2 are known and understood by practitioners. It is one of the reasons why practical implementations of one-against-all reductions use internal prediction quantities such as the margin of a predictor rather than the actual binary classification. A basic question is whether such soft versions of OAA work. Some do and some don't. Ideal soft quantities are good class probability estimates, but for many classifiers, these estimates are very poor. For example, the efficacy of Platt scaling [35] (i.e., fitting a sigmoid to a margin to get a probabilistic prediction) can be thought of as strong empirical evidence of the deficiency of margins as probability estimates. Rifkin and Klautau [38] argue that the soft version OAA can be made to work as well as other techniques, if some effort is put into optimizing the binary classifiers.

Regret reductions   The fundamental noise in the distribution D may make optimal performance not be equivalent to zero error rate, motivating the notion of regret.

Definition 1.4. The *regret* of a classifier h on distribution D is defined as

$$r(h,D) = e(h,D) - \min_{h^*} e(h^*,D),$$

where the minimum is taken over all classifiers h^* (of the same type as h).

Thus *regret* is the difference between the incurred loss and the lowest achievable loss on the same problem. Regret can be defined with respect to any loss function. A statement showing how the regret of the base classifier on the induced problem controls the regret of the resulting predictor on the original problem is called a *regret transformation* of the reduction. Regret statements are more desirable than statements relating error rates, because regret analysis separates excess loss from the unavoidable noise in the problem, making the statement nontrivial even for noisy problems. For example, if the binary error rate is 10% due to noise and 5% due to the errors made by the classifier, then the multiclass error rate depends only on the 5%. Any reduction with a multiplicative regret transform is consistent.

1.4.2 Error-Correcting Coding (ECOC) Approaches

Another obvious problem with the OAA reduction is the lack of robustness. If just one out of k binary classifiers errs, the multiclass classifier errs. This section presents approaches based on error correcting codes, where we can even have a constant fraction of classifiers err (independent of k) without mispredicting the multiclass label.

The ECOC approach, popularized by Dietterich and Bakiri [13], learns binary classifiers for deciding membership in different subsets of the labels. The reduction can be specified by a binary-valued matrix C with n rows and k columns, where n is the number of binary problems created by the reduction. Each row i in the matrix defines a binary classification problem: predict $C(i, y)$, where y is the correct label given input x. Given C, each label corresponds to a binary string defined by the inclusion of this label in the sequence of subsets.

For two n-bit binary vectors, the *Hamming distance* between them is the number of bit positions on which they differ. A multiclass prediction is made by finding the codeword closest in Hamming distance to the sequence of binary predictions on the test example.

For the ECOC reduction, a basic statement can be made [20]: with a good code, the error rate of the multiclass classifier is at most 4 times the average error rate of the individual binary classifiers. The proof of this statement is essentially the observation that there exist codes in which the distance between any two codewords is at least $\frac{1}{2}$. Consequently, at least $\frac{1}{4}$ of the classifiers must err to induce a multiclass classification error, implying the theorem. In general, if d is the smallest distance between any pair of columns in C, the loss rate for this reduction is at most $2n\varepsilon/d$, where ε is the average loss rate of the n binary classifiers.

We mention several coding matrices of particular interest. The first is when the columns form a subset of the columns of a Hadamard matrix, an $n \times n$ binary matrix with any two columns differing in exactly $n/2$ places. Such matrices are easy to construct recursively when $n = 2^m$ is a power of 2:

$$C_1 = \begin{pmatrix} 0 & 0 \\ 0 & 1 \end{pmatrix}, \qquad C_{m+1} = \begin{pmatrix} C_m & C_m \\ C_m & \overline{C}_m \end{pmatrix},$$

where $\overline{C}_m$ is C_m with 0s and 1s exchanged. It is clear from the construction that all columns are at the same distance 2^m. Notice that the distance property is preserved when any column or row is complemented. We will use this code in our constructions. Thus, for Hadamard codes, the number of classifiers needed is less than $2k$ (since a power of 2 exists between k and $2k$), and the loss rate is at most 4ε.

If the codewords form the $k \times k$ identity matrix, the ECOC reduction corresponds to the one-against-all reduction.

As OAA, ECOC was modified [2] to consider margins of the binary classifiers, numbers internal to some classification algorithms that provide a measure of confidence in a binary prediction. Decoding proceeds in the same way as for ECOC except a loss-based distance is used instead of the Hamming distance, where the loss is defined by the optimization function used internally by the binary learning algorithm. Instead of working with margins, we define binary classification problems for which the optimal solution computes the relative expected cost (rather than the margin) of choices. This approach can be applied to arbitrary classifier learners rather than margin-based learners. Finally, we can generalize the approach to tackle all cost-sensitive problems rather than just multiclass problems (see Section 1.5). While we talk about predefined, data-independent output codes here, there are methods that *learn* coding matrices based on training data [12].

Probabilistic ECOC

Unfortunately, the ECOC reduction is inconsistent [26]. We describe a probabilistic variant of ECOC [26], which deals with the inconsistency problem by reducing to squared loss regression rather than binary classification. (The same approach can be applied to OAA, but the resulting solution would still not be robust.) If a reduction to binary classification is desired, this approach can be composed with the Probing reduction [28] from squared loss regression to binary classification.

As ECOC, the PECOC reduction is defined by a binary coding matrix C with k columns corresponding to multiclass labels and n rows corresponding to prediction problems. For each row, we form a squared-loss regression problem to predict the probability that the label is in one subset or the other. We write $\mathbf{E}_i$ to denote an expectation over i drawn uniformly from the rows of C.

There are two ways to use the reduction: either for estimating the probability of a class label as in Algorithm 5 or for hard prediction of a class label as in Algorithm 6.

PECOC Theorem

As in earlier reductions, Algorithm 4 transforms the original multiclass distribution D into an induced distribution D' over real-valued examples. As in OAA, we can

---

Algorithm 4: PECOC-Train (set of k-class multiclass examples S, squared loss regressor B)

---

for *each subset i defined by the rows of C* **do**
$\quad$ Let $S_i = \{(x, C(i, y)) : (x, y) \in S\}$
$\quad$ Let $b_i = B(S_i)$.
return $\{b_i\}$

Algorithm 5: PECOC-Predict (classifiers $\{b_i\}$, example $x \in X$, label y whose probability we want to predict)

---

return $\mathrm{ppecoc}_b(x, y) = 2\mathbf{E}_i[C(i, y)b_i(x) + (1 - C(i, y))(1 - b_i(x))] - 1$

Algorithm 6: PECOC-Hard-Predict (classifiers $\{b_i\}$, example $x \in X$)

---

return $\mathrm{pecoc}_b(x) = \arg\max_{y \in \{1,\ldots,k\}} \text{PECOC-Predict}(\{b_i\}, x, y)$

---

assume that we have a single combined regressor $b(x, i) = b_i(x)$ by augmenting the feature space with the index of the classifier. The theorem below is quantified for all regressors, including b learned in Algorithm 4.

Theorem 1.3. (PECOC Regret Transform [26]) *For any k-class distribution D, any regressors b, and any label $y \in \{1, \ldots, k\}$*

$$\mathbf{E}_{x \sim D}\left(\mathrm{ppecoc}_b(x, y) - D(y|x)\right)^2 \leq 4r(D', b),$$

where ppecoc_b is as defined in Algorithm 5.

This theorem relates the average regret of the created regressors to the relative estimation error.

Proof. We first analyze what happens when no regret is suffered, and then analyze the case with regret. For any i, let $D(i)$ be the distribution on $X \times \{0, 1\}$ induced by drawing (x, y) from D and outputting $(x, C(i, y))$. For any choice of i, the optimal squared loss regressor is given by

$$b_i^* = \arg\min_b \mathbf{E}_{(x, y') \sim D(i)}\left[(b(x) - y')^2\right]$$

$$= \arg\min_b \mathbf{E}_{(x, y') \sim D(i)}\left[b(x)^2\right] - 2\mathbf{E}_{(x, y') \sim D(i)}\left[y'b(x)\right]$$

$$= \arg\min_{x, b}\left(b(x)^2 - 2\mathbf{E}_{y' \sim D(i|x)}\left[y'b(x)\right]\right).$$

For each x, the optimal value of $b(x)$ can be found by taking the derivative and setting it equal to zero, because squared loss is convex. This yields $b(x) = \mathbf{E}_{y' \sim D(i|x)}[y']$ which can also be written as

$$b_i(x) = \mathbf{Pr}_{y \sim D|x}[C(i,y) = 1].$$

Since decoding is symmetric with respect to all labels, we need analyze only one label y. Furthermore, since complementing all subsets not containing y does not change the decoding properties of the code, we can assume that y is in every subset. Consequently,

$$\mathbf{E}_i\left[b_i^*(x)\right] = \mathbf{E}_i\mathbf{Pr}_{y' \sim D|x}[C(i,y') = 1] = \frac{1}{2}(D(y|x)+1),$$

where the third equality follows from the fact that every label y' other than y appears in i half the time, in expectation over i. Consequently, $\mathrm{ppecoc}_b(x,y) = D(y|x)$ for each x and y, when the classifiers are optimal.

Now we analyze the regret transformation properties. The remainder of this proof characterizes the most efficient way that any adversary can induce estimation regret with a fixed budget of squared loss regret.

First, notice that PECOC-predict (Algorithm 5) is linear in the base predictions $b_i(x)$, but the squared loss regret of bad predictions is quadratic, according to $(b_i(x) - b_i^*(x))^2$. Consequently, it is cheapest for the adversary to have a small equal disturbance for each i rather than a large disturbance for a single i. (The cost any adversary pays for disturbing the overall expectation can be monotonically decreased by spreading errors uniformly over subsets i.) Thus the optimal strategy for an adversary wanting to disturb the output of PECOC-Predict by Δ is to disturb the expectation for each i by $\Delta/2$. The regret of the base regressors is given by $\Delta^2/4$, implying the theorem. ∎

Hard Prediction

We can use Algorithm 6 to make hard multiclass predictions. For this special case, a simple corollary of the soft prediction analysis holds.

Corollary 1.2. (Multiclass Classification Regret Transform) *For any k-class distribution D and any regressor b,*

$$r(D, \mathrm{pecoc}_b(x)) \le 4\sqrt{r(D',b)},$$

where pecoc_b *is defined as in Algorithm 6.*

Proof. The regret of a multiclass prediction is proportional to the difference in probability of the best prediction and the prediction made. Weakening Theorem 1.3 gives, for all y,

$$\mathbf{E}_{(x,y) \sim D}|\mathrm{ppecoc}_b(x,y) - D(y|x)| \le 2\sqrt{r(D',b)},$$

since for all Z, $\sqrt{E(Z)} \ge E\sqrt{Z}$. When doing a hard prediction according to these outputs, our regret at most doubles because the probability estimate of the correct

class can be reduced by the same amount that the probability estimate of the wrong
class increases.   ∎

As shown in [26], PECOC consistently performs better (or as well) as ECOC and
OAA, across different datasets and base learners.

1.4.3 Approaches Based on Pairwise Comparisons

Another class of multiclass to binary reductions are based on comparing only pairs
of classes [21, 36, 5, 6, 7].

The All-Pairs reduction [21] starts by constructing $\binom{k}{2}$ binary classifiers, one for
every pair of classes. Given a training dataset $S = \{(x,y)\}$, the binary classifier for
the (i,j)-class pair is trained with dataset $\{(x,\mathbf{1}(y=i)) : (x,y) \in S$ and $y=i$ or $y=j\}$
to discriminate between classes i and j. Given a test example, each of the binary
classifiers predicts a winner amongst its two classes, and the class with the highest
number of wins is chosen as the multiclass prediction, with ties broken randomly.

The All-Pairs reduction *is* consistent (as an application of a theorem in [2]).
It is frail theoretically, but it works fairly well in practice. Platt, Cristianini, and
Shawe-Taylor [36] proposed a DAG method which is identical to All-pairs at training time. At test time, the labels play a sequential single-elimination tournament, requiring only $k-1$ classifier evaluations instead of $k(k-1)/2$, making the approach
substantially faster. Error-correcting tournament approaches [7] perform multiple-
elimination tournaments over the labels, yielding robust regret transforms, independent of k. A computational advantage of pairwise reductions, which is especially
important in applications that involve massive amounts of data, is that individual
classifiers are run on datasets that are smaller than the original dataset (unlike OAA
and ECOC approaches).

1.5 Cost-Sensitive Classification

This section presents a reduction from cost-sensitive classification to binary classification. Cost-sensitive k-class classification is just like k-class classification, only
each prediction now has an associated cost.

Definition 1.5. A *cost-sensitive k-class classification* problem is defined by a distribution D over $X \times [0,\infty)^k$. The goal is to find a classifier $h : X \to \{1,...,k\}$ minimizing the expected cost $e(h,D) = \mathbf{E}_{(x,c)\sim D}\left[c_{h(x)}\right]$. Here $c \in [0,\infty)^k$ gives the cost of
each of the k choices for x.

Since cost-sensitive classification can express any bounded-loss finite-choice supervised learning task, the reduction shows that *any* such task can be solved using a
binary classification oracle.

We present a reduction, Weighted All-Pairs (WAP) [5], which reduces k-class cost-sensitive classification to importance weighted binary classification. It can be composed with the Costing reduction from Section 1.3 to yield a reduction to binary classification.

Weighted All Pairs: The Algorithm

WAP is a weighted version of the All-Pairs reduction [21] discussed above. The algorithms specifying the reduction are given below.

Algorithm 7: WAP-Train (set of k-class cost sensitive examples S, importance weighed binary classifier learning algorithm B)

Set $S' = \emptyset$
for *all examples* $(x, c_1, \ldots, c_k) \in S$ **do**
    for *all pairs* (i, j) *with* $1 \le i < j \le k$ **do**
        Add an importance weighted example $(\langle x, i, j \rangle, I(c_i < c_j), |v_j - v_i|)$ to
        S'.
return $h = B(S')$

The values v_i used by the reduction are defined as follows: For a given cost-sensitive example $(x, c_1, \ldots, c_k)$, let $L(t)$ be the function $L(t) = |\{j \mid c_j \le t\}|$, for $t \in [0, \infty)$. By shifting, we may assume that the minimum cost is 0, so that $t \ge 0$ implies $L(t) \ge 1$. Optimizing the loss of the shifted problem is equivalent to optimizing the loss of the original problem. The values v_i are defined as $v_i = \int_0^{c_i} 1/L(t)dt$. Note that the values are order-preserving: $c_i < c_j$ iff $v_i < v_j$ for all i and j.

We say that label i *beats* label j for input x if either $i < j$ and $h(\langle x, i, j \rangle) = 1$, or $i > j$ and $h(\langle x, j, i \rangle) = 0$.

Algorithm 8: WAP-Test (classifier h, example x)

---

for *all pairs* (i, j) *with* $1 \le i < j \le k$ **do**
    Evaluate $h(\langle x, i, j \rangle)$
output $\text{wap}_h(x) = \text{argmax}_i |\{j \mid i \text{ beats } j\}|$

Note that if h makes no errors and $c_i \ne c_j$, then label i beats label j exactly when $c_i < c_j$. WAP-Test outputs the label which beats the maximum number of other labels, with ties broken arbitrarily.

Before stating the error transform, we define the importance-weighted binary distribution D' induced by the reduction. To draw a sample from this distribution, we first draw a cost sensitive sample $(x, c_1, \ldots, c_k)$ from the input distribution D and then apply WAP-Train to the singleton set $\{(x,c_1,\ldots,c_k)\}$ to get a sequence of $\binom{r}{2}$ examples for the binary classifier. Now we just sample uniformly from this set.

Theorem 1.4. (WAP error efficiency [5]) *For any cost-sensitive distribution D and any importance-weighted classifier h,*

$$e(\text{wap}_h, D) \leq 2e(h, D'),$$

where wap$_h$ *is defined in Algorithm 8.*

This theorem states that the cost sensitive loss is bounded by twice the importance weighted loss on the induced importance weighted learning problem.

For notational simplicity, assume that $c_1 \leq \cdots \leq c_k$. Note that no generality is lost since the algorithm does not distinguish between the labels. The following lemma (from [5]) is the key to the proof.

Lemma 1.2. *Suppose label i is the winner. Then, for every $j \in \{1,\ldots,i-1\}$, there must be at least $\lceil j/2 \rceil$ pairs (a,b), where $a \leq j < b$, and b beats a.*

Proof. Consider the restricted tournament on $\{1,\ldots,j\}$.
Case 1: Suppose that some w beats at least $\lceil j/2 \rceil$ of the others. If no label $b > j$ beats any label $a \leq j$, then w would beat at least $\lceil j/2 \rceil + 1$ more labels than any $b > j$; in particular, w would beat at least $\lceil j/2 \rceil + 1$ more labels than i. Thus, in order to have label i beat as many labels as w, at least $\lceil j/2 \rceil$ edges of the form $(w,b), b > j$ or $(a,i), a \leq j$ must be reversed.
Case 2: There is no label $w \in \{1,\ldots,j\}$ beating $\lceil j/2 \rceil$ of the rest of $\{1,\ldots,j\}$. This can only happen if j is odd and there is a j-way tie with $(j-1)/2$ losses per label in $\{1,\ldots,j\}$. In this case, although every label beats $(j+1)/2$ more labels than any $b > j$, in particular i, it is still necessary to reverse at least $(j+1)/2 \geq \lceil j/2 \rceil$ edges, in order to ensure that $i > j$ beats as many labels as each of $\{1,\ldots,j\}$. ∎

Proof. (Theorem 1.4) Suppose that our algorithm chooses the wrong label i for a particular example $(x,c_1,\ldots,c_k)$. We show that this requires the adversary to incur a comparable loss.

Lemma 1.2 and the definition of v_i imply that the penalty incurred to make label i win is at least

$$\int_0^{c_i} \frac{\lceil L(t)/2 \rceil}{L(t)} dt \geq \int_0^{c_i} \frac{1}{2} dt = \frac{c_i}{2}.$$

On the other hand, the total importance assigned to queries for this instance equals

$$\sum_{i<j} v_j - v_i = \sum_{i<j} \int_{c_i}^{c_j} \frac{1}{L(t)} dt = \int_0^{c_k} \frac{L(t)R(t)}{L(t)} dt$$

$$= \int_0^{c_k} R(t) dt = \sum_{i=1}^k \int_0^{c_i} dt = \sum_{i=1}^k c_i,$$

where $R(t) = k - L(t)$ is the number of labels whose value is greater than t and the second equality follows from switching the order of summation and counting the number of times a pair (i,j) satisfies $i < t < j$. The second to last equality follows by writing $R(t)$ as a sum of the k indicator functions for the events $\{c_j > t\}$, and then switching the order of summation.

Consequently, for every example $(x, c_1, \ldots, c_k)$, the total importance assigned to queries for x equals $\sum_i c_i$, and the cost incurred by our algorithm on instance x is at most twice the importance of errors made by the binary classifier on instance x. Averaging over the choice of x shows that the cost is at most 2. ∎

This method of assigning importances is provably near-optimal, as shown in [5].

Theorem 1.5. (Lower bound) *For any other assignments of importances $w_{i,j}$ to the points (x, i, j) in the above algorithm, there exists a distribution with expected cost $\varepsilon/2$.*

Proof. Consider examples $\left(x, 0, \frac{1}{r-1}, \ldots, \frac{1}{k-1}\right)$. Suppose that we run our algorithm using some $w_{i,j}$ as the importance for the query (x, i, j). Any classifier which errs on $(x, 1, i)$ and $(x, 1, j)$, where $i \neq j$, causes our algorithm to choose label 2 as the winner, thereby giving a cost of $1/(r-1)$, out of the total cost of 1. The importance of these two errors is $w_{1,i} + w_{1,j}$, out of the total importance of $\sum_{i,j} w_{i,j}$. Choosing i and j so that $w_{1,i} + w_{1,j}$ is minimal, the adversary's penalty is at most $2\sum_{i=2}^{k} w_{1,i}/(k-1)$, and hence less than $2/(k-1)$ times the total importance for x. This shows that the cost of the reduction cannot be reduced below $1/2$ merely by improving the choice of weights. ∎

The PECOC reduction from Section 1.4.2 can be extended to cost-sensitive classification [26]. Tournaments reductions [6, 7] give the tightest known analysis, with dependence on the expected sum of cost differences instead of the sum of costs as in the cost-sensitive variant of PECOC and WAP.

1.6 Predicting Conditional Quantiles

Recall the definition of a regression problem.

Definition 1.6. A *(least squares) regression* problem is defined by a distribution D over $X \times Y$, where $Y = \mathbb{R}$. The goal is to find a *predictor* $f : X \rightarrow Y$ minimizing the expected *squared error loss*

$$e(f, D) = \mathbf{E}_{(x,y) \sim D}\left[(y - f(x))^2\right].$$

One standard justification for this choice is that the minimizer $f^* = \arg\min_f e(f, D)$ is the conditional mean (conditioned on x): $f^*(x) = \mathbf{E}_{y \sim D|x}[y]$. However, there are many important applications for which mean estimates are either irrelevant or insufficient, and *quantiles* (also known as general order statistics) are the main quantities of interest. For instance, consider trying to assess the risk of a business proposal.

Estimates of the lower quantiles of the conditional return distribution would give a better indication of how worthwhile the proposal is than a simple estimate of the mean return (which could be too high because of very unlikely high profits).

The process of estimating the quantiles of a conditional distribution is known as *quantile regression*. More specifically, the goal of quantile regression is to obtain estimates of the q-quantiles of the conditional distribution $D|x$. Intuitively, q-quantiles for different q describe different segments of the conditional distribution $D|x$ and thus offer more refined information about the data at hand.

Definition 1.7. (Conditional q-quantile, $0 \leq q \leq 1$). The *conditional q-quantile* (or *conditional q-order statistic*) for a distribution D is a function $f = f(x)$ such that for every $x \in X$, $D(y \leq f(x) \mid x) \geq q$ and $D(y \geq f(x) \mid x) \geq 1 - q$. The $1/2$-quantile is also known as the *median*.

Note that the q-quantile may not be unique when the conditional distribution has regions with zero mass.

It is well-known that the optimal estimator for the absolute-error loss is the median [25]. In other words, for every distribution D over $X \times \mathbb{R}$,

$$\arg\min_f \mathbf{E}_{(x,y)\sim D}|y - f(x)| \text{ is the (conditional) median.}$$

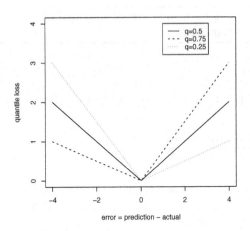

Fig. 1.1 Loss functions which induce quantile regression.

The generalization of absolute-error loss for arbitrary order statistics is the quantile loss function, also known as the pinball loss [40]. Pictorially, this is a tilted absolute loss as in figure 1.1. Mathematically, this is $\mathbf{E}_{(x,y)\sim D}\ell_q(y, f(x))$, where

$$\ell_q(y, f(x)) = q(y - f(x))\mathbf{1}(y \geq f(x)) + (1 - q)(f(x) - y)\mathbf{1}(y < f(x)),$$

where $\mathbf{1}(\cdot) = 1$ if its argument is true and 0 otherwise.

Definition 1.8. A *quantile regression* problem is defined by a distribution D over $X \times Y$, where $Y = \mathbb{R}$, and $0 \leq q \leq 1$. The goal is to find a *predictor* $f : X \rightarrow Y$ minimizing $\mathbf{E}_{(x,y) \sim D} \ell_q(y, f(x))$.

The Quanting Reduction

We show that the quantile regression problem can be reduced to standard binary classification via an algorithm called Quanting [27]. For any $q \in [0, 1]$, the Quanting algorithm estimates the q-th quantile of the conditional distribution $D|x$ using any importance weighted classification algorithm A. Using the costing reduction from Section 1.3, we can also do Quanting via any binary classification algorithm.

The Quanting algorithm has two parts. Given a set of training examples S of the form (x, y) with $y \in [0, 1]$ (we can always renormalize S so that all labels are in $[0, 1]$), Algorithm 9 uses any given importance-weighted binary classification algorithm A to learn a family of classifiers, parameterized by a threshold $t \in [0, 1]$. Each classifier h_t attempts to answer the question "Is the q-quantile above or below t?" To train each h_t, Algorithm 9 creates an importance-weighted training set by adding a weight w to each example in S. Positive examples with $y \geq t$ receive weight q, while negative examples with $y < t$ receive weight $(1 - q)$.

Algorithm 9: Quanting-train (importance-weighted classifier learning algorithm A, training set S, quantile q)

---

for $t \in [0, 1]$ **do**
    $S_t = \emptyset$
    for *each* $(x, y) \in S$ **do**
        $S_t = S_t \cup \{(x, \mathbf{1}(y \geq t), q \cdot \mathbf{1}(y \geq t) + (1 - q)\mathbf{1}(y < t))\}$
    $h_t = A(S_t)$
return the set of classifiers $\{h_t\}$

In reality, of course, one cannot find a different classifier for each $t \in [0, 1]$. Constructing classifiers h_t for t in a discrete mesh $\{0, 1/n, 2/n, \ldots, (n-1)/n, 1\}$ will add a $1/n$ term to the error bound.

Using the learned classifiers, Algorithm 10 produces a prediction of the q-quantile for each x in a given test set S'.

Algorithm 10: Quanting-test (set of classifiers $\{h_t\}$, test set S')

---

for *each* $x \in S'$ **do**
    $Q(x) = \mathbf{E}_{t \sim U(0,1)}[h_t(x)]$

In the (idealized) scenario where A is perfect, one would have $h_t(x) = 1$ if and only if $t \le q(x)$ for a q-quantile $q(x)$, hence Algorithm 10 would output $\int_0^{q(x)} dt = q(x)$ exactly. The analysis below shows that if the error of A is small on average over t, the quantile estimate is accurate.

Quanting Reduction Analysis

The lemma we prove next relates the average regret of the classifiers h_t (how well the classifiers do in comparison to how well they could do) to the regret of the quantile loss incurred by the Quanting algorithm. For each x, the output produced by the quanting algorithm is denoted by $Q(x)$, whereas $q(x)$ is a correct q-quantile. In this analysis, we use the standard one-classifier trick [28]: instead of learning different classifiers, we learn one classifier $h = \{h_t\}$ with an extra feature t used to index classifier h_t.

The quanting reduction induces an importance weighted binary classification problem, which we denote as D'.

Lemma 1.3. (Quanting Regret Transform [27]) *For all distribution D over $X \times \mathbb{R}$, and all classifiers h,*

$$\mathbf{E}_{(x,y) \sim D}[\ell_q(y, Q(x))] - \mathbf{E}_{(x,y) \sim D}[\ell_q(y, q(x))] \le e(D', h) - \min_{h'} e(D', h')$$

where $e(D', h)$ is the expected importance weighted binary loss of h on the induced distribution D'.

Proof. For any function $f = f(x)$, $\mathbf{E}_{(x,y) \sim D}[\ell_q(y, f(x))]$ is given by eqn. (1.6):

$$q\mathbf{E}_{(x,y) \sim D}[(y - f(x))\mathbf{1}(y - f(x) > 0)] + (1 - q)\mathbf{E}_{(x,y) \sim D}[(f(x) - y)\mathbf{1}(f(x) - y > 0)].$$

It is known that $\mathbf{E}[X \cdot \mathbf{1}(X > 0)] = \int_0^{+\infty} \mathbf{Pr}(X \ge t)dt = \int_0^{+\infty} \mathbf{Pr}(X > t)dt$ for any random variable X, so we rewrite

$$\mathbf{E}_{(x,y) \sim D}[\ell_q(y, f(x))] = q\mathbf{E}_x \int_0^\infty D(y - f(x) \ge t_1|x)dt_1 + (1 - q)\mathbf{E}_x \int_0^\infty D(f(x) - y > t_2|x)dt_2$$

$$= q\mathbf{E}_x \int_{f(x)}^1 D(y \ge u|x)\,du + (1 - q)\mathbf{E}_x \int_0^{f(x)} D(y < u|x)\,du.$$

Applying this formula to $f(x) = Q(x)$ and $f(x) = q(x)$ and taking the difference yields

$$\mathbf{E}_{(x,y)\sim D}[\ell_q(y,Q(x)) - \ell_q(y,q(x))]$$

$$= \mathbf{E}_x \int_{Q(x)}^{q(x)} [qD(y \geq u|x) - (1-q)D(y < u|x)]\, du$$

$$= \mathbf{E}_x \int_{Q(x)}^{q(x)} [q - qD(y < u|x) - (1-q)D(y < u|x)]\, du$$

$$= \mathbf{E}_x \int_{Q(x)}^{q(x)} [q - D(y < u|x)]\, du. \tag{1.1}$$

We will show that $e(D',h) - \min_{h'} e(D',h')$ is at least this last expression. The expected importance-weighted error incurred by the classifiers $\{h_t\}$ is

$$e(D',h) = \mathbf{E}_{(x,y)\sim D} \int_0^1 \begin{bmatrix} q\mathbf{1}(y \geq t)(1 - h_t(x)) \\ +(1-q)\mathbf{1}(y < t)h_t(x) \end{bmatrix} dt$$

$$= \mathbf{E}_x \int_0^1 \begin{bmatrix} qD(y \geq t|x) \\ +(D(y < t|x) - q)h_t(x) \end{bmatrix} dt$$

$$= q\mathbf{E}_x[y] + \mathbf{E}_x \int_0^1 [D(y < t|x) - q]h_t(x)\, dt \tag{1.2}$$

$$\geq q\mathbf{E}_x[y] + \mathbf{E}_x \int_0^{Q(x)} [D(y < t|x) - q]\, dt. \tag{1.3}$$

Here only the last line is non-trivial, and it follows from the fact that $D(y < t|x) - q$ is increasing in t. Thus the smallest possible value for the integral in (1.2) is achieved by placing as much "weight" $h_t(x)$ as possible on the smallest t while respecting the constraints $\int_0^1 h_t(x)\, dt = Q(x)$ and $0 \leq h_t(x) \leq 1$. This corresponds precisely to setting $h_t(x) = \mathbf{1}(t \leq Q(x))$, from which (1.3) follows.

Inequality (1.3) is in fact an equality when instead of $\{h_t\}$ we use the (optimal) classifiers

$$\{h_t^*(x) = \mathbf{1}(D(y \leq t|x) \leq q)\}$$

and substitute $q(x)$ for $Q(x)$. Therefore,

$$e(D',h) - e(D',h^*) \geq \quad \mathbf{E}_x \int_{q(x)}^{Q(x)} [D(y < t|x) - q]\, dt$$

$$= \mathbf{E}_{(x,y)\sim D}[\ell_q(y,Q(x)) - \ell_q(y,q(x))],$$

using (1.1). This finishes the proof.   ∎

We now show how to reduce q-quantile estimation to unweighted binary classification using the results in Section 1.3. To apply *rejection sampling*, we feed a binary classifier learner samples of the form $((x,t),\mathbf{1}(y \geq t))$, each of the samples being independently discarded with probability $1 - w(\mathbf{1}(y \geq t))$, where $w(b) = qb + (1-q)(1-b)$ is the example's weight.

Corollary 1.3. (Quanting to Binary Regret [27]) *For any D as above and any binary classifier* $g = \{g_t\}$,

$$\mathbf{E}_{(x,y)\sim D}[\ell_q(y,Q(x))] - \mathbf{E}_{(x,y)\sim D}[\ell_q(y,q(x))] \leq e(\tilde{D},g) - \min_{g'} e(\tilde{D},g'),$$

where $\tilde{D}$ is the distribution produced by rejection sampling.

Proof. Let $h = \{h_t\}$ be the importance-weighted classifier induced by the rejection sampling reduction. Theorem 1.1 implies that

$$e(D,h) - \min_{h'} e(D,h') = e(\tilde{D},h) - \min_{g'} e(\tilde{D},g')$$

and the result follows from Lemma 1.3. ∎

Experimental results: The Quanting reduction compares favorably with two existing direct methods for quantile regression: linear quantile regression [25] and kernel quantile regression [40]. See [27] for details on the performed experiments.

1.7 Ranking

Finally, we consider the problem of ranking a set of instances. In the most basic version, we are given a set of unlabeled instances belonging to two classes, 0 and 1, and the goal is to rank all instances from class 0 before any instance from class 1. A common measure of success for a ranking algorithm is the area under the ROC curve (AUC). The associated loss, $1 - AUC$, measures how many pairs of neighboring instances would have to be swapped to repair the ranking, normalized by the number of 0s times the number of 1s. The loss is zero precisely when all 0s precede all 1s; one when all 1s precede all 0s. It is greater for mistakes at the beginning and the end of an ordering, which satisfies the intuition that an unwanted item placed at the top of a recommendation list should have a higher associated loss than when placed in the middle.

At first, this problem appears very different from binary classification. A misclassified instance in classification incurs the same loss independently of how other instances are classified, while the AUC loss depends on the whole (ranked) sequence of instances. However, it turns out that we don't need different algorithms to optimize these two loss functions: there is a robust mechanism for translating any binary classifier learning algorithm into a ranking algorithm.

Balcan et al. [4] present a simple deterministic reduction with a guarantee that any binary classifier with regret r on the induced problem implies AUC regret at most $2r$, for arbitrary distributions over instances. This is the best possible with any deterministic algorithm. This is also a large improvement over naive approaches such as ordering according to regressed scores.

In a subsequent paper, Ailon and Mohri [1] describe a randomized quick-sort reduction, which guarantees that AUC loss is bounded by binary loss, in expectation over the randomness of the algorithm. When there are more than two labels, the expected generalized AUC loss is bounded by twice the binary loss. The quick-sort algorithm is quick efficient, requiring only $O(n \log n)$ classifier evaluations at test time, which makes it practical in larger settings.

1.8 Conclusion

There are certain key concepts that we want to emphasize for readers interested in studying or building further reductions.

1. Regret vs. Error Reductions. An error reduction simply states that the error rate on an induced problem bounds the error rate on the original problem. While an error reduction might be a good first-pass approach, it has certain undesirable properties which are removed by a regret reduction. For example, all regret reductions are necessarily consistent.
2. Prediction Minimality. Embedded in the logic of reductions is a preference for systems which don't make unnecessary ancillary predictions. If there is a core set of n predictions to make, adding an unnecessary extra prediction always makes the regret bound worse by a factor of $(n+1)/n$.
3. Importance weighting. Many reductions use importance weighting of some sort to carefully control how much they care about one prediction versus another. Mastering the use of importance weighting is essential.
4. Thresholding. When a continuous parameter needs to be predicted as with the Quanting reduction, setting up a continuous family of classification problems appears necessary.
5. Orthogonal Prediction. The PECOC analysis relies deeply on the ability to setup orthogonal prediction problems which happen to cancel out in just the right way to achieve good performance.

This tutorial has covered a number of different methods for reducing general learning problems to core problems, including essentially all supervised learning problems. There are at least three directions of future progress:

1. Extending the scope of learning reductions to new learning problems.
2. Improving existing reductions.
3. Shifting the foundations. Existing reductions theory finds a happy medium between the provable, practical, and useful, but there is no proof that it is canonical. A reexamination of the foundations may yield new directions of research.

Learning reductions are an effective tool for designing automated solutions to learning problems. They also tell us something about the organization of learning problems and have a remarkably clean analysis. Reductions are a basic tool which make a handy component in a tool-chest of solutions.

References

1. N. Ailon and M. Mohri (2007) An Efficient Reduction of Ranking to Classification, *New York University Technical Report*, TR-2007-903.
2. E. Allwein, R. Schapire, and Y. Singer (2000) Reducing multiclass to binary: A unifying approach for margin classifiers, *Journal of Machine Learning Research*, 1:113–141.

3. A. Asuncion, D. Newman (2007) UCI Machine Learning Repository, http://mlearn.ics.uci.edu/MLRepository.html, University of California, Irvine.
4. N. Balcan, N. Bansal, A. Beygelzimer, D. Coppersmith, J. Langford, and G. Sorkin (2007) Robust reductions from ranking to classification, *Proceedings of the 20th Annual Conference on Learning Theory* (COLT), Lecture Notes in Computer Science 4539: 604–619.
5. A. Beygelzimer, V. Dani, T. Hayes, J. Langford, and B. Zadrozny (2005) Error limiting reductions between classification tasks, *Proceedings of the 22nd International Conference on Machine Learning* (ICML), 49–56.
6. A. Beygelzimer, J. Langford, and P. Ravikumar (2008) Filter trees for cost sensitive multiclass classification.
7. A. Beygelzimer, J. Langford, and P. Ravikumar (2008) Error Correcting Tournaments.
8. A. Beygelzimer, J. Langford, B. Zadrozny (2005) Weighted One-Against-All, *Proceedings of the 20th National Conference on Artificial Intelligence* (AAAI), 720–725.
9. E. Bredensteiner and K. Bennett (1999) Multicategory classification by Support Vector Machines, *Computational Optimization and Applications*, 12(1-3): 53–79.
10. L. Breiman (1996) Bagging predictors, *Machine Learning*, 26(2):123–140.
11. K. Crammer and Y. Singer (2001) On the algorithmic implementation of multiclass mernelbased vector machines, *Journal of Machine Learning Research* 2: 265–292.
12. K. Crammer and Y. Singer (2002) On the learnability and design of output codes for multiclass problems, *Machine Learning*, 47, 2-3: 201–233.
13. T. Dietterich and G. Bakiri (1995) Solving multiclass learning problems via error-correcting output codes, *Journal of Artificial Intelligence Research*, 2: 263–286.
14. P. Domingos (1999) MetaCost: A general method for making classifiers cost-sensitive, *Proceedings of the 5th International Conference on Knowledge Discovery and Data Mining* (KDD), 155–164.
15. C. Drummond and R. Holte (2000) Exploiting the cost (in)sensitivity of decision tree splitting criteria, *Proceedings of the 17th International Conference on Machine Learning* (ICML), 239–246.
16. C. Elkan (2001) The foundations of cost-sensitive learning, *Proceedings of the 17th International Joint Conference on Artificial Intelligence* (IJCAI), 973–978.
17. Y. Freund, Y. Mansour and R. Schapire (2004) Generalization bounds for averaged classifiers, *The Annals of Statistics*, 32(4): 1698–1722.
18. Y. Freund and R. Schapire (1997) A decision-theoretic generalization of on-line learning and an application to boosting, *Journal of Computer and System Sciences*, 55(1): 119–139.
19. Y. Guermeur, A. Elisseeff, and H. Paugam-Moisy (2000) A new multi-class SVM based on a uniform convergence result, *Proceedings of the IEEE International Joint Conference on Neural Networks* 4, 183–188.
20. V. Guruswami and A. Sahai (1999) Multiclass learning, boosting, and error-correcting codes, *Proceedings of the 12th Annual Conference on Computational Learning Theory* (COLT), 145–155.
21. T. Hastie and R. Tibshirani (1998) Classification by pairwise coupling, *Advances in Neural Information Processing Systems* (NIPS), 507–513.
22. L. Huang, X. Nguyen, M. Garofalakis, J. Hellerstein, M. Jordan, A. Joseph, and N. Taft (2007) Communication-efficient online detection of network-wide anomalies, *Proceedings of the 26th Annual IEEE Conference on Computer Communications* (INFOCOM), 134–142.
23. A. Kalai and R. Servedio (2003) Boosting in the presence of noise, *Proceedings of the 35th Annual ACM Symposium on the Theory of Computing* (STOC), 195–205.
24. M. Kearns (1998) Efficient noise-tolerant learning from statistical queries, *Journal of the ACM, 45:6*, 983–1006.
25. R. Koenker and K. Hallock (2001) Quantile regression, *Journal of Economic Perspectives*, 15, 143–156.
26. J. Langford and A. Beygelzimer (2005) Sensitive Error Correcting Output Codes, *Proceedings of the 18th Annual Conference on Learning Theory* (COLT), 158–172.

27. J. Langford, R. Oliveira and B. Zadrozny (2006) Predicting conditional quantiles via reduction to classification, *Proceedings of the 22nd Conference in Uncertainty in Artificial Intelligence* (UAI).

28. J. Langford and B. Zadrozny (2005) Estimating class membership probabilities using classifier learners, *Proceedings of the 10th International Workshop on Artificial Intelligence and Statistics*.

29. J. Langford and B. Zadrozny (2005) Relating reinforcement learning performance to classification performance, *Proceedings of the 22nd International Conference on Machine Learning* (ICML), 473–480.

30. Y. Lee, Y. Lin, and G. Wahba (2004) Multicategory support vector machines, theory, and application to the classification of microarray data and satellite radiance data, *Journal of American Statistical Association*, 99: 67–81.

31. C. Hsu and C. Lin (2002) A comparison of methods for multi-class support vector machines, *IEEE Transactions on Neural Networks*, 13, 415–425.

32. D. Margineantu (2002) Class probability estimation and cost-sensitive classification decisions, *Proceedings of the 13th European Conference on Machine Learning*, 270–281.

33. M. Mesnier, M. Wachs, R. Sambasivan, A. Zheng, and G. Ganger (2007) Modeling the relative fitness of storage, *International Conference on Measuremen and Modeling of Computer Systems* (SIGMETRICS), 37–48.

34. J. von Neumann (1951) Various techniques used in connection with random digits, *National Bureau of Standards, Applied Mathematics Series*, *12*: 36–38.

35. J. Platt (1999) Probabilistic outputs for support vector machines and comparisons to regularized likelihood methods. In A. Smola, P. Bartlett, B. Schölkopf, and D. Schuurmans, editors, *Advances in Large Margin Classifiers*, 61–74.

36. J. Platt, N. Cristiani and J. Shawe-Taylor (2000) Large margin DAGs for multiclass classification, *Advances of Neural Information Processing Systems*, 12: 547–553.

37. J. Platt, E. Kiciman and D. Maltz (2008) Fast variational inference for large-scale internet diagnosis, *Advances in Neural Information Processing Systems* 20.

38. R. Rifkin and A. Klautau (2004) In defense of one-vs-all classification, *Journal of Machine Learning Research*, 5: 101–141.

39. I. Rish, M. Brodie and S. Ma (2002) Accuracy versus efficiency in probabilistic diagnosis, *Proceedings of National Conference on Artificial Intelligence* (AAAI), 560–566.

40. I. Takeuchi, Q. Le, T. Sears, and A. Smola (2006) Nonparametric quantile estimation, *The Journal of Machine Learning Research*, 7, 1231–1264.

41. G. Tesauro, R. Das, H. Chan, J. Kephart, D. Levine, F. Rawson, and C. Lefurgy (2008) Managing power consumption and performance of computing systems using reinforcement learning, *Advances in Neural Information Processing Systems* 20.

42. V. Vapnik (1998) *Statistical Learning Theory*, John Wiley and Sons.

43. H. Wang, J. Platt, Y. Chen, R. Zhang, and Y. Wang (2004) Automatic Misconfiguration Troubleshooting with PeerPressure, *Proceedings of the 6th Symposium on Operating Systems Design and Implementation*, (2004). Also in *Proceedings of the International Conference on Measurements and Modeling of Computer Systems*, SIGMETRICS 2004, 398–399.

44. J. Weston and C. Watkins (1998) Multiclass support vector machines, *Proceedings of the 11th European Symposium on Artificial Neural Networks*, 219–224.

45. I. Witten and E. Frank (2000) *Data Mining: Practical machine learning tools with Java implementations*, Morgan Kaufmann, http://www.cs.waikato.ac.nz/ml/weka/.

46. B. Zadrozny and C. Elkan (2001) Learning and making decisions when costs and probabilities are both unknown, *Proceedings of the 7th International Conference on Knowledge Discovery and Data Mining* (KDD), 203–213.

47. B. Zadrozny, J. Langford and N. Abe (2003) Cost-sensitive learning by cost-proportionate example weighting, *Proceedings of the 3rd IEEE International Conference on Data Mining* (ICDM), 435–442.

Chapter 2
Performance Engineering and Management Method — A Holistic Approach to Performance Engineering

Dave Jewell

Abstract Experience has shown that there is no one "silver bullet" for achieving acceptable performance in IT solutions. Early performance models help us ask the right questions but may not be as accurate as we would like in predicting future performance and capacity utilization. Performance testing of the solution once it is built gives us more accurate information, but may occur too late in the life cycle to permit fixing persistent performance problems in a timely manner. The Performance Engineering and Management Method (PEMM), first proposed by IBM in 1998, integrates these and other techniques into the Information Technology (IT) solution development life cycle, yielding a more comprehensive approach to addressing the risks related to IT performance, capacity and scalability. This paper provides an overview of the major themes of PEMM, including examples of its application and potential synergy to be gained by combining PEMM with other disciplines such as Information Technology Infrastructure Library (ITIL®) Capacity Management.

2.1 Background

The Performance Engineering and Management Method (PEMM) was first formally outlined in March 1998, in the form of a reference document for IBM system architects. PEMM was based on the experience of practitioners in IBM's United Kingdom organization. Many of the life cycle principles embodied in PEMM had already been used successfully during the 1980s, with associated technical papers presented at forums such as IBM's Information Management System (IMS) Guide and Computer Measurement Group (CMG), and had been included in client education between 1988 and 1994.

Dave Jewell

Performance Engineering Practice, Systems Engineering, Architecture & Test (SEA&T), IBM Global Business Services, e-mail: jewell@us.ibm.com

The developers of PEMM had come to believe that the best way to address system performance was to proactively manage it throughout the solution development life cycle, from the system's inception through its deployment and maintenance in a production setting. It has been IBM's experience that throughout the last twenty five years; the principles within the PEMM have been long lasting and continue to deliver high value.

In an information technology (IT) context, *performance* generally refers to the speed with which a system[1] accomplishes the tasks it was designed to do, and is commonly expressed using measurements such as response time and throughput. Performance is closely related to and often dependent upon *capacity* (the measured ability of a system to perform work) and *scalability* (the ability of a system to accommodate workload growth). The dilemma faced by the IT industry with respect to performance and capacity is at least two-fold:

1. While systems, the technology on which they are based and the demands placed upon them are leading to increased complexity and therefore greater risk of poor performance, software engineering as a whole has traditionally been focused on ensuring the *functional correctness* of those systems rather than addressing performance, capacity and scalability concerns.
2. Even when so-called best practices for performance are followed during a system's development, it is difficult to grasp the full extent of inherent performance issues until all the components of the system can be integrated and tested to see how they perform together.

This has led to the situation where the industry has been working backwards over time to get a better handle on system performance. Poor performance in production led to the recognition of the value performance testing prior to deployment to identify and address performance issues. This in turn has led to focus on performance best practices, the notion of designing for performance, estimating and modeling in attempt to predict future performance, and creating requirements which unambiguously describe the users performance requirements and clearly link them to the needs of the business. The intent of the PEMM is to organize these activities in a cohesive manner, and to successfully manage performance requirements and mitigate risks throughout the software development life cycle.

---

[1] Throughout this paper, *system* refers to an interrelated group of IT components working together; *solution* refers to the application of IT systems, products, etc., to solve a customers business problem and/or address a customers business opportunity.

2.2 What is Performance Engineering?

Performance Engineering (PE) is a technical discipline which aims to ensure that a development project results in the delivery of a system which meets a prespecified set of performance objectives [2]. This is done by:

- managing the performance risk of a project,
- controlling or coordinating activities in the project that have an impact on performance, and
- applying specialized performance estimation and design skills to the architecture of the system under development.

In order to properly apply PEMM, it is important to understand the reasoning behind this view of performance engineering.

- **Performance objectives should be specified prior to development of the system.** A system that must consistently furnish subsecond response time or support 10,000 concurrent online users may be more expensive and time-consuming to design, build and support than an identical system with less stringent performance objectives. Requirements related to scalability, performance, capacity and scalability should be given the same level of attention given to the system's functional requirements when considering architecture, design and implementation alternatives.
- **Performance risks must be managed rather than eliminated.** It is generally not feasible to eliminate *all* risk of poor performance of a future system. The best we can hope to do is to find a cost-effective balance between performance *risk containment* (i.e. PE) activities and performance *risk acceptance*.
- **Achieving good performance requires coordinated effort.** Since so many groups and individuals are involved in defining, designing, implementing and deploying systems, typically there will not be just one group that makes or breaks performance. Coordinating PE activities throughout the life cycle will help to achieve the best possible results.
- **performance engineering is more than just waiting for performance testing to start.** There are a number of proactive PE techniques which can be applied even before performance testing starts in order to reduce performance risk. Proactive techniques such as performance modeling, performance budgeting, and application profiling can be used to get an idea of what performance will be like before an integrated system is available for performance testing purposes.

---

[2] The term Software Performance Engineering (SPE) is sometimes used in some of the literature pertaining Performance Engineering (PE) [10, 11, 12], although PE as discussed in this paper refers to information technology solutions in general and not just software.

2.3 Overview of PEMM

The central notion of PEMM is that performance engineering activities must be linked to the relevant portions of the system development life cycle. Figure 2.1 shows the conceptual view of PEMM in the context of a "typical" IT solution development project.

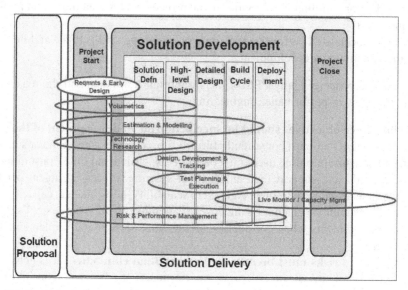

Fig. 2.1 Conceptual View of the Performance Engineering and Management Method (PEMM)

PEMM consists of eight interrelated, overarching "themes" which are active at various stages of the development project. The vertical bars depict stages which could be expected in a typical development project (proposal, project start, definition/requirements, design, build/test, deployment, project close). While the solution development process itself can take place with or without the use of PEMM, the ovals in the diagram above illustrate the relative chronology of the PEMM themes with respect to the solution development stages.

The PEMM themes can be described as follows:

- **Requirements and Early Design** - Performance activities occurring at the start of the development life cycle;
- **Volumetrics** - Quantitative elements of the workload and its data are vital to establishing the basis for the performance of the system;
- **Technology Research** - Gaining understanding of new solution elements (hardware, software, network, etc.) for which limited performance information is available;
- **Estimation and Modeling** - The central core of the predictive work done in Performance Engineering;

- **Design, Development and Tracking** - Helping the designers and developers deliver on the performance objectives;
- **Test Planning and Execution** - Testing to validate that the system will meet its performance and capacity objectives;
- **Risk Management / Performance Management** - Assessing and managing of the performance risks throughout;
- **Live Monitoring and Capacity Management** - Managing system performance and capacity for the rest of its operational life.

Each of these themes will be discussed in more detail in the chapters to follow. By applying the PEMM themes in a holistic manner throughout the development life cycle, the potential exists to

- improve system performance,
- reduce or more effectively manage system capacity and related costs,
- reduce or more effectively manage project and business risks related to performance,
- reduce the cost of addressing performance defects or issues by finding them and fixing them earlier.

2.4 PEMM Theme – Requirements and Early Design

Figure 2.2 illustrates some of the key considerations associated with the "Requirements and Early Design" theme.

Requirements and early design activities may require a certain amount of negotiation and iteration to come to completion. IT architects work with business analysts to document solution requirements. These requirements not only describe the system's desired capabilities, but also the dependencies and constraints (technical, financial, etc.) being imposed on the system. The architecture team will then consider one or more candidate solutions and evaluate whether they can meet requirements. Requirements that cannot be met may be renegotiated before going forward. This process is important not only for establishing a strong *technical baseline* [3] for change control purposes, but also for setting realistic expectations on the part of stakeholders.

While all of this is true for the general case of requirements and early design, there are additional considerations that are worth mentioning in regard to performance.

---

[3] Baseline documents include requirements documents, design documents and other materials defining the current state of the solution under development that have been reviewed and accepted by the projects business and technical stakeholders. Changes to baseline documents are carefully managed to prevent uncontrolled impacts to the project costs, quality and schedule.

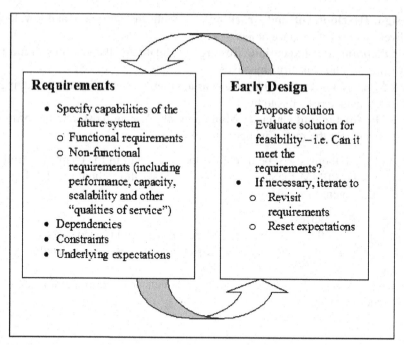

Fig. 2.2 Requirements and Early Design theme considerations.

2.4.1 Requirements and Performance

In engineering circles both inside and outside of IT, it is widely accepted that functional requirements must be understood before design can proceed – in other words, "what" is to be built must be known before "how" to build is addressed. Whether starting with formal written requirements using a waterfall development methodology or elucidating requirements incrementally using incremental development techniques, it is well recognized that systems development must be driven by requirements.

The notion of requirements can also be extended to what are referred to as *nonfunctional requirements*, i.e. assertions about the operational quality of service (QoS) constraints and dependencies which extend beyond application functionality. Menasce et al. [5] lists some typical IT quality of service characteristics which may be included in nonfunctional requirements:

- Response time
- Throughput
- Availability
- Reliability
- Security
- Scalability
- Extensibility

Architects and designers of IT systems attempt to choose the technical solution alternative which best satisfies all of the requirements, which in some cases may mean making trade-offs between requirements that may lead in different directions. For example, certain high availability measures may be more resource-intensive and impact response time or throughput. Behind some solution requirements may be contractual commitments, unstated expectations and other factors. An important first step towards achieving good performance is to ensure that performance requirements are sufficiently well documented and defined for each stage of the development process, and that they are clearly tied to the actual needs of the business. Vague or unrealistic performance requirements will hamper efforts to make the right technical decisions when trade-offs relating to performance must be made.

An important notion here is that in development projects, even the requirements themselves have their own engineering process associated with them. Requirements are to be written so that they are "SMART" (i.e. Specific, Measurable, Achievable, Realistic, Testable), as the architecture, design and build process will eventually decompose the high-level requirements into more granular components (system requirements, performance objectives, performance budgets – see also [9]). Throughout the development process, *requirements traceability* should be maintained so that all subsequent activities are clearly linked to the original requirements. While this is often done for functional requirements, this is sometimes neglected for performance and other nonfunctional requirement areas. PEMM helps ensure that nonfunctional requirements are addressed.

2.4.2 Early Design and Performance

The "Design for Performance" philosophy asserts that system performance cannot necessarily be taken for granted; therefore, when a certain level of performance is required, part of the design effort should be concerned with how the performance requirement will be met. While exact predictions of performance may be impossible to make during the architecture and high-level design stages of a project, to the extent possible, studies of the feasibility of the solution with respect to performance and other factors should be conducted.

Performance or capacity estimates made as part of an early feasibility study may be made with spreadsheets, formal sizing tools or comparisons to previously built systems. While they may not have the accuracy that future estimates would have when more is known about the solution, feasibility estimates provide a means of managing performance risk by evaluating design alternatives in terms of their effect on performance. If an area of performance risk can be flagged early, the requirements and business case can be revisited, and other technical solutions can be considered before going forward. While not all performance risk can be removed this way, feasibility estimates can disclose areas of performance risks that can be revisited in later stages of the development process.

2.5 PEMM Theme – Volumetrics

Figure 2.3 illustrates some of the key considerations associated with the "Volumetrics" theme [4]. As stated before, volumetrics refers to the quantitative elements of the workload and its data that are relevant to the performance and capacity of the system being built. Volumetrics can be considered as being in two categories: Business volumes and Technical volumes.

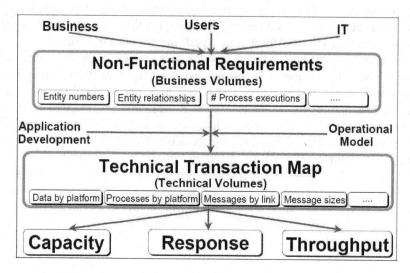

Fig. 2.3 Volumetrics theme considerations.

2.5.1 Business Volumes

Business volumes provide a business view of the quantitative elements that are important for planning system performance and capacity. These may include projections or assumptions for things such as the number of orders per day or week, the number of customers in the database and so on. At this level, the volumes are stated in terms that are relevant to the business, and may require someone with access to authoritative projections for business growth, etc., to be rendered accurately. Busi-

---

[4] Figure 3 includes a reference to an IBM architectural deliverable known as an Operational Model. The Operational Model (OM) defines and documents the distribution of an IT system's components onto geographically distributed nodes, together with the connections necessary to support the required component interactions, in order to achieve the IT system's functional and nonfunctional requirements within the constraints of technology, skills and budget.

ness, user and IT personnel may all be involved in developing the business volumes portion of the nonfunctional requirements.

Business volumes are often included with the nonfunctional requirements because they provide a critical context to the architects and designers of the system. For example, two systems with identical functionality may both have a mean response time requirement of 5 seconds, but if one of the systems only needs to support 300 concurrent online users while the other must support 30,000 concurrent online users, the design and capacity attributes of those two systems may need to be substantially different from each other. Similarly, the number of a key entity such as customer affects the amount of data to be processed or searched, ultimately affecting the responsiveness and resource intensiveness of data processing operations.

When developing business volume assumptions, the requirements team should take into account factors such as:

- whether a given volume element is likely to be static (not changing) or dynamic (changing over time)
- patterns of change in a dynamic volume element
- whether peak, average or point-in-time volumes are the most meaningful way to express a given volumetric's performance requirements
- the relationship between volumes and requirements for scalability (i.e. the ability to accommodate additional workload or data over time, given assumptions relative to resource capacity growth)

Business volumes are notoriously unstable, due to a number of factors. Business projections which support the volumetrics may be at best well-informed "guesses" as to the behavior of an unpredictable business climate. Projections may be overly optimistic or inflated to justify projects that would not otherwise have a viable business case. On the other hand, they may be overly low in an effort to contain costs. For critical volumes, it may be wise to come up with a low-to-high range of estimates so that options for "scaling up" or "scaling down" the solution can be considered. Corresponding assumptions should be well documented.

2.5.2 Technical Volumes

Technical volumes provide an IT solution view of the quantitative elements that are important for planning system performance and capacity. While technical volumes are based on the business volumes, they also take into account knowledge about the structure and behavior of the proposed solution gleaned from working with system architects, designers and developers.

Technical volumes are often captured in spreadsheet form using what is sometimes referred to as a technical transaction map. As a simplified example, assume that the business volumes reveal that there will be 10,000 orders per peak hour submitted on the order processing system. If the system interaction diagram reveals that each order produces:

- 1 order submit message from the client to the web server,
- 1 order submit message from the web server to the application server,
- 3 database request messages from the application server to the database server,
- 25 message database response messages from the database server to the application server,
- 1 order confirmation message from the application server to the web server,
- 1 order confirmation message from the web server to the client,

it can then be concluded that in a peak hour, order submit activity alone will generate:

- 20,000 incoming messages to the web server,
- 260,000 incoming messages to the application server,
- 250,000 incoming database requests to the database server,
- 10,000 outgoing message from the web server to clients.

In this example, it is clear that from the standpoint of the number of messages which must be handled for order submission traffic, the greatest message processing workload will fall to the application and database servers. Depending on the needs of the project, the technical transaction map can be expanded to include the volumes of data transferred and processed, message sizes and any other information that may prove relevant to estimating or modeling future performance and capacity.

2.6 PEMM Theme – Estimation and Modeling

Figure 2.4 illustrates a typical approach to the "Estimation and Modeling" theme. Estimation and modeling techniques are used to attempt to predict the performance and capacity behaviors of potential future systems, or of existing systems using potential future scenarios. The ideal means of estimating system performance is obviously to observe and measure the performance of a live system. When this cannot be done it may be necessary to develop a performance model (an abstract representation of the performance behavior of the future system) for this purpose.

Volumetrics, which have already been discussed, obviously constitute a key input to the performance estimation process. In addition, performance estimation must take into account other factors, such as:

- **Parametric costs** - The amount of a given system resource (CPU seconds, I/O operations, etc.) consumed per transaction, message or other estimating unit of work processed
- **Resource model** ? The computing hardware and other infrastructure elements which affect overall system performance, with capacity and processing power assumptions stated
- **Queuing model** - The means of predicting wait time (i.e. how long transactions are likely to wait for busy system resources to free up)

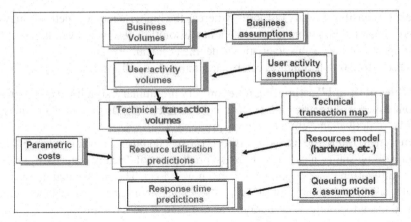

Fig. 2.4 Typical Estimation theme approach.

2.6.1 Performance Estimating Techniques

One of the more important aspects of performance engineering is the selection of the appropriate estimating technique for the situation at hand. Figure 2.5 shows some of the common estimating techniques and the corresponding cost vs. accuracy trade-offs. From a technical perspective, the difference in the techniques comes from the manner in which volumetrics, parametric costs, the resource model and the queuing model are represented and used to estimate performance.

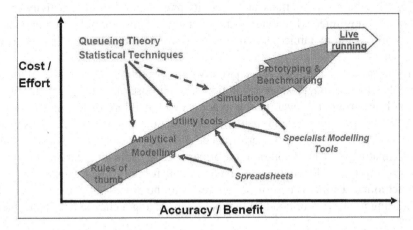

Fig. 2.5 Cost/Effort and Accuracy/Benefit trade-offs between performance estimation techniques
.

Typically, more than one of these estimation techniques should be used during the life of the project. Low-cost, low-effort methods are commonly used early in the project for feasibility study purposes, whereas the higher-accuracy methods may be employed later, when more is known about the solution design and validation of the solutions performance characteristics is deemed critical.

These estimating techniques can be summarized as follows.

- **"Rules of thumb" estimating** relies on very preliminary, simplified assumptions concerning volumetrics, parametric costs, system resources and wait times in order to deliver an estimate relatively quickly.
- **Analytical modeling** uses spreadsheets (or special purpose tools [5] in some cases) performing static calculations to make predictions of "steady state" performance and utilization of a system under a given workload. The static calculations typically take into account some amount of queuing theory and statistical techniques, in addition to volumetrics, parametric costs and system resources.
- **Utility tools** utilize data gathered from multiple performance benchmark results to facilitate the capacity sizing of systems based on reference workload types [6]. While such tools do not enable the creation of custom performance models for specific future systems, they do allow for limited specifications of volumetrics and system resources, and the parametric costs are gleaned from benchmark data tied to the reference workloads, allowing the sizing to be based on a similar workload to that of the target solution.
- **Simulation modeling** typically utilizes what is known as a discrete event simulation tool [7] to mimic the transaction processing behavior of the live system from a resource utilization and timing perspective. With these kinds of tools, the modeler must spend a considerable amount of time populating the model with the resource model, the parametric costs and transaction processing behavior (e.g. flows between the application tiers). Once this is done, the modeling tool simulates both the incoming transaction activity and the queuing/flow activity of the system being modeled, including the interaction between system components. This allows the dynamic performance behavior of the system over time to be examined.
- **Prototypes** can be thought of as partially built or preliminary versions of a contemplated invention, product or solution. The purpose of building any prototype is to learn from and leverage the experience of building or testing the prototype before making a commitment to the production version of whatever is being produced. For IT solutions, performance prototyping can serve as a means of investigating aspects of solution performance (e.g. estimating parametric costs) before a fully developed live system is available for performance testing.
- **Benchmark testing** as described here refers to the process of performance testing using a known workload before and after making a change or enhancement

---

[5] Accretive Technologies [1] is one vendor that offers analytical modeling tools.

[6] Examples of utility tools from IBM include the OPERA and SONOMA tools [2].

[7] A number of vendors (including HyPerformix and OpNet) and academic sources (e.g. Ptolemy II from Berkeley) offer discrete event modeling tools [3, 7, 8]. IBM Research has also developed an experimental performance modeling tool called AMBIENCE, which includes both analytical and simulation modeling capabilities. AMBIENCE also uses an inferencing engine to populate the initial model with starting parametric costs based on performance test results [4].

to the system, in order to determine whether the system's performance has been impacted by the change.

2.6.2 Selection of Performance Estimating Methods

Figure 2.5 has already introduced the general notion that increased accuracy in performance estimation comes only with increased cost and effort. We should not automatically reject the most accurate methods because of their expense or the least expensive methods because of their potential for inaccuracy. Performance estimation techniques, as is the case with most other performance engineering techniques, are intended to help us manage risks related to performance and capacity, so we must find ways to effectively balance the cost of accepting risk with the cost of containing those risks. The following recommendations are offered to help in making this selection.

1. **Consider how quickly an estimate is needed.** If an estimate is needed sooner rather than later, rough estimates and other low-effort techniques may be acceptable. This is particularly true in the early stages of a project, where the initial concern is to evaluate overall solution feasibility.
2. **Consider when the information needed for an estimate will become available.** If a certain estimating technique requires information that is not yet available, that technique may need to wait until later.
3. **Estimating techniques are not necessarily mutually exclusive.** While it may be tempting to use performance modeling in lieu of performance testing to reduce expense, the abstract nature of any performance model means that its accuracy has limitations. Rather, use performance modeling to help highlight the areas of risk that performance testing should focus on, and harvest the performance testing results as a means of calibrating the performance model for future use and achieving greater accuracy.
4. **Consider the return on investment.** Simulation modeling and performance testing often require significant investment in tools, training and development to be beneficial. Additionally, performance testing requires investment in a "production-like" hosting environment and test hardware. For these techniques in particular, there generally needs to be a return on investment in the form of reuse of the modeling and/or testing assets over time in order to justify the investments. Estimation efforts that will result in one-time, "throw-away" work may be better off using less expensive estimation methods.
5. **Consider the risk and criticality of performance for a given project.** Where poor performance has serious implication or the risk of poor performance is high, additional investment in performance estimating may be justified. Consider using performance estimation approaches which highlight likely risk areas, targeting those for additional estimation, testing and measurement.

2.7 PEMM Theme – Technology Research

A great deal of performance engineering requires dealing with uncertainty. This is certainly true of the "Technology Research" theme. Technology research is used here to describe techniques for gaining understanding of new solution elements (hardware, software, network, etc.) for which limited performance information is available. Frequently, the process of finding the data needed to populate a performance model (e.g. with volumetrics, parametric costs, etc.) ends up driving much of the technology research which takes place.

Typical approaches to technology research include the following.

- **Compare the future system with similar systems that already exist.** This is potentially one of the best sources of data available, particularly if the existing system is comparable in terms of the execution platform, volumetrics and so on.
- **Use published benchmarks to get an idea of the relative performance of solution alternatives.** Publicly available benchmarks are published by independent standards organizations such as TPC or SPEC, or in some cases by vendors, as a means of assessing solution alternatives using a common standard (e.g. to compare the relative processing power of two different server models). A benchmark usually involves a reference workload to be executed and a set of measurements to be gathered. Benchmarks may be executed either by vendors or independent test organizations that have an interest in evaluating or publicizing benchmark results for competitive evaluation purposes. The key thing to keep in mind is that benchmark results are only useful to the extent that the benchmark workload is representative of the projected system workload being modeled.
- **Consider using information from other reliable sources.** These may include published books, consulting reports, manufacturer specifications, Internet sources, or people with relevant experience.
- **Consider technical prototypes when needed information is difficult to get by other means.** As discussed earlier, performance prototyping involves building a partial solution to estimate performance attributes of the future solution.
- **Gather measurements from the system under development.** While this information will not be available at project planning time, information gleaned by development may prove very useful for refining existing performance models.

2.8 PEMM Theme – Design, Development and Tracking

Even if performance requirements have been well constructed, the solution is well architected and performance estimates show that the performance goals are attainable, ensuring that all of this comes together at implementation time is the responsibility of the development team. Performance considerations should be taken into account during detailed design and coding, and progress against performance goals should be validated as components become available for development testing.

From a process perspective, development activities are often carried out by someone other than the performance engineer or architect who helped to establish the original solution requirements, solution architecture and performance goals. Ensuring that continued progress is made towards meeting these goals requires close cooperation between all concerned. Fortunately, there are a number of approaches which can be successfully applied to address performance at implementation time.

2.8.1 Recognizing Performance Patterns and Anti-Patterns

Connie Smith and Lloyd Williams [9] described the notion of *performance principles, performance patterns* and *performance anti-patterns*. Table 2.8.1 illustrates each of these concepts in greater detail.

Concept	Description	Example
Principle for good performance	A general rule for creating designs that help achieve performance objectives	The principle of locality states that actions, functions and results should be located close to the computer resources, in order to reduce processing overhead.
Performance pattern	A frequently used design approach that tends to yield good performance results because it successfully exploits one or more principles of good performance	The alternate paths pattern helps improve the performance of data networks by providing multiple ways to send TCP/IP traffic from point A to point B, thus relieving network congestion.
Performance anti-pattern	A frequently used design approach that tends to yield poor performance results because it is inappropriately applied, or because it violates one or more principles of good performance	The one-lane bridge might be an acceptable solution for crossing a creek on a secluded country road, but would be an anti-pattern for a major highway crossing a river, or by analogy, for a low-bandwidth connection used where a high-bandwidth connection is needed.

Table 2.1 Performance Principles, Performance Patterns and Performance Anti-Patterns explained.

Smith and Williams list several principles, patterns and anti-patterns relating to performance, and quite likely more instances of each could be listed. The point is that a key to designing IT solutions that perform well is the understanding of design patterns that either do or do not work well from a performance perspective, and why that may be the case. Ultimately, performance is only one of several considerations that IT architects and designers must take into account as they create solution designs. However, an understanding of performance patterns and anti-patterns will help in making the inevitable trade-offs between performance goals and other solution requirements.

2.8.2 Designing for Performance

Software engineering practitioners have long recognized the need to design for functionality, and accordingly, software quality techniques and best practices have been instantiated again and again, taking the forms of waterfall development, structured programming, iterative development, object-oriented development, agile development methods and so on. The means of designing for performance, however, have arguably been less conspicuous as part of software engineering practice.

The "Design for Performance" philosophy is one that takes a goal-oriented approach to developing IT solutions that perform well, rather than taking it for granted that everything will somehow get worked out in the end. This involves more than just having programmers keep a handy checklist of Java and SQL performance "dos and don'ts". "Design for Performance" essentially means that performance goals or targets are consciously set, and design and implementation decisions are made and validated with respect to their effects on performance, in such a way that performance does not become a "nasty surprise" at the end of the project.

As much as possible, this means that design decisions creating good performance reduce the need to make "tuning" changes to the implemented solution after the fact. Applying the correct performance patterns, avoiding the correct performance anti-patterns, leveraging the advanced performance capabilities of the implementation platforms and then validating performance throughout the development process will go a long way towards making our performance engineering activities more proactive and less reactive.

2.8.3 Performance Budgeting

As with functional requirements, initial performance requirements are typically defined at a high level for business and end-user audiences. However, in order to be useful for tracking at the development level, they must eventually be decomposed into more granular components as the solution design takes shape. These more granular, component-level goals for performance are often assembled into what are known as performance budgets. A performance budget allocates time or system resources (not money!) required to complete a task for planning and estimation purposes. Figure 6 shows an example of a response time performance budget.

Initially, a response time budget such as this one might be based on estimates of the time spent processing a transaction at each layer of the infrastructure. Eventually,

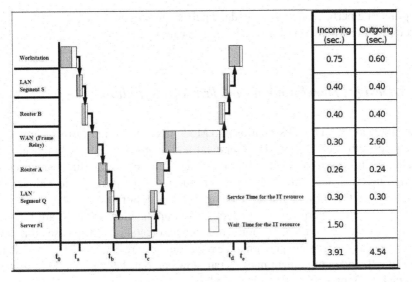

	Incoming (sec.)	Outgoing (sec.)
Workstation	0.75	0.60
LAN Segment S	0.40	0.40
Router B	0.40	0.40
WAN (Frame Relay)	0.30	2.60
Router A	0.26	0.24
LAN Segment Q	0.30	0.30
Server #1	1.50	
	3.91	4.54

Fig. 2.6 Example of a simple response time budget.

through the use of some kind of tracing or instrumentation, actual times for each of these components can be gathered and compared to the original budget. At that time, the process for staying in budget is similar to one that would be used on a monetary budget; developers would look for opportunities to reduce or eliminate unnecessary processing and/or make modifications to the budget that reflect the current reality. If this meant that a critical response time target was not being met after applying potential tuning changes, either the solution design or the performance requirement would need to be revisited.

2.8.4 Performance Debugging and Profiling

Developers often have available to them debugging and profiling tools that can help isolate performance problems. While the term debugging has long been associated with isolating and removing functional defects from application code, many debugging tools and techniques can help improve performance as well. For example, thread contention and memory leaks are examples of functional defects which can be found using debugging tools and techniques which also serve to improve performance.

Profiling tools and techniques, on the other hand, are generally involved with measuring application and/or subsystem performance. In particular, profiling tools and techniques are especially helpful for

- locating and resolving performance inefficiencies,
- isolating problems in a vertically large multi-tiered architecture,

- optimizing performance at the code, database or network level,
- determining whether performance budgets can be met.

2.8.5 *Design, Development and Tracking Guidance*

As was the case with the "Estimation and Modeling" theme, the various approaches associated with the "Design, Development and Tracking" theme should be used judiciously. Just as it is not feasible to exhaustively test an application system of any significant size, it is not generally feasible to apply all of the techniques discussed here to the entire application being developed. For example, labor-intensive techniques such as performance budgeting and application profiling are typically reserved for areas of the application which are associated with use cases for which performance is critical and performance requirements are challenging. The balance between risk and containment may dictate how each of the "Design, Development and Tracking" approaches should be used.

2.9 PEMM Theme – Test Planning and Execution

Performance testing is concerned with ensuring that nonfunctional requirements having to do with performance, capacity and scalability can be met by the solution as implemented. The job of the performance tester is made much easier if there are clear performance requirements and a proactive "Design for Performance" philosophy has been followed in architecting, designing and implementing the solution. Starting with an understanding of the designed solution and its performance requirements, the performance tester must design, implement and execute performance testing scenarios which validate the ability of the solution to meet the performance requirements.

To understand performance testing, it is helpful to understand the distinctions between functional testing and performance testing as shown in Table 2.9.

As with other kinds of testing, performance testing requires the use of effective test management practices (e.g. planning, entrance and exit criteria, designing test cases that are traceable to requirements, test execution tracking, defect management). However, the focus on performance rather than function means that different tools, skills, methods and approaches must be brought to bear. Moreover, traditional test progress metrics such as percentage of test cases complete, defect counts and defect severity may not convey the seriousness of underlying performance problems which the performance testing is starting to reveal.

Table 2.9 illustrates a number of typical activities, deliverables and work products associated with performance testing.

Performance testing of this kind is not a novel industry concept, nor is it unique to PEMM. However, with PEMM we no longer depend exclusively on performance

Functional Testing	Performance Testing
Concerned with coverage and correctness of function	Concerned with responsiveness, throughput and behavior under heavy workload with limited resources
Validates behavior in response to executing individual test cases	Validates behavior in the operational environment in response to a representative "mix" of activity
Defects note incorrect behavior.	Performance deficiencies may be a matter of degree.
Test tools and skills are oriented towards the single-user perspective.	Test tools and skills are oriented towards multi-user, system perspective.

Table 2.2 Differences between Functional Testing and Performance Testing.

testing to manage risks related to performance. Applying the preceding PEMM themes in a proactive manner can go a long way towards averting performance issues before testing or deployment. Furthermore, by applying PEMM, the performance tester can

- benefit from having performance requirements to use in developing test scenarios,
- leverage the findings of earlier estimation and modeling work to help prioritize testing efforts, and
- share test results with the modeling team to help refine the predictive models for future use.

2.10 PEMM Theme – Live Monitoring and Capacity Planning

The "Live Monitoring and Capacity Management" theme is concerned with activities needing to take place to ensure that the solution performs well in the live production environment.

The "needs of the business" should dictate the business requirements for the system, including those nonfunctional requirements related to performance, capacity and scalability. While these requirements place certain demands on the teams responsible for building the solution, they also place demands on the teams responsible for deploying, hosting and operating the solution in its production environment. For example, capacity plans must be developed and validated to ensure that the infrastructure is ready to handle the workload. Tools and procedures (preferably auto-

Test Process Stage	Activity	Deliverables and work products
Test Planning	Analyze requirements	• Nonfunctional requirements • Volumetrics
	Determine test strategy	• Selected use cases / business functions • Infrastructure scope • Application components • Monitoring tools • Test process, including phases and scenarios
	Create test plan	• Test plan
Test Preparation	Develop workload	• Workload design • Workload scripts • Workload procedures, execution plan
	Develop measurement procedures	• Measurement procedures
	Set up environment	• Prepared test environment, agreement for operations support
Test Execution	Run tests	• Test run output, measurement data • Test progress reporting
	Analyze results	• Interim results reports
	Follow-up	• Defect documentation • Problem resolution correspondence
Test Reporting	Prepare results report	• Results reports by test phase
	Publish and review results	• Review minutes
	Decision checkpoint with stakeholder	• Sign-off by phase • Deployment recommendation and decision

Table 2.3 Performance testing stages, activities, deliverables and work products.

mated) must be put in place to respond to poorly performing applications and transactions. Furthermore, there may be service level agreements between the provider (operations) and consumer (users) of IT services, in order to set expectations concerning the projected workload and resulting performance of the live production system.

2.10.1 Relating PEMM to Performance and Capacity Management

Performance management has to do with ensuring that the deployed production system performs as required, and taking corrective action when it does not. Closely related to this is *capacity management*, which has to do with planning for, deploying and monitoring physical computing resources and infrastructure to ensure that the system has sufficient resources to do its job.

Performance Management and Capacity Management of live, operational production systems are not new concepts. For years, data center operations professionals have understood that these and other systems management disciplines (problem management, change management, etc.) as being essential to running things smoothly in the production environment. In more recent years, these disciplines have become part of what is now known in the industry as *IT Service Management*, with frameworks such as the *IT Infrastructure Library (ITIL®*) beginning to codify the industry consensus on the leading practices in this area [6].

Figure 2.7 illustrates the key IT service management processes encompassed by ITIL Version 2 [8]. Note that in ITIL terminology, both performance management and capacity management are addressed by the ITIL Capacity Management process.

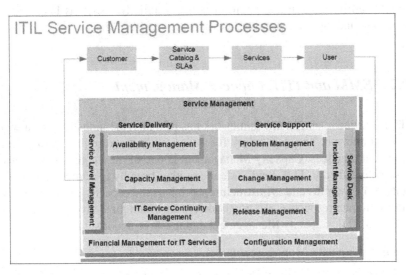

Fig. 2.7 Overview of ITIL Service Management processes.

While PEMM is not overly prescriptive about how performance and capacity management ought to be done, the chief PEMM recommendation in this area is that the potential for synergy between Performance Engineering efforts and performance / capacity management (PCM) efforts should be leveraged. This is not

---

[8] As of this writing, the latest version of ITIL is Version 3. However, the comments concerning the key ITIL service management processes still apply.

always as easy is it would seem to be. In many IT organizations, the differing skills, responsibilities and locations of the development and operations shops prevent the respective groups from working together, and what interfaces there are take the form of required meetings and paperwork hurdles needed to get final approvals for deployment. However, looking at the PEMM themes from a life cycle perspective, it is not hard to see potentials for achieving synergy with and improving hand-offs to the PCM team. For example:

- The "Requirements and Early Design" theme can contribute to the definition of candidate *service level requirements* (SLRs), which may become the basis for later service level agreements and for some of the development performance targets.
- The "Estimation and Modeling" theme can and should contribute to capacity planning efforts.
- The "Test Planning and Execution" theme can include exercising the performance monitoring tools and procedures that will be used in production, and providing final guidance with respect to performance and capacity expectations prior to deployment.

Achieving these kinds of synergies may become a requirement for organizations seeking to fulfill the spirit and intent of industry initiatives such as ITIL Capacity Management and the full solution life cycle scope of PEMM.

2.10.2 PEMM and ITIL Capacity Management

The ITIL service management framework has provided the industry with a widely accepted framework and vocabulary for understanding and implementing service management practices. Capacity Management is one of the major service delivery processes described in ITIL, and is defined rather broadly to address not only the capacity of IT systems and infrastructure, both also the capacity of other resources (facilities, human resources, electrical power) on which the delivery of IT services may depend. ITIL Capacity Management defines three major subprocesses:

- **Business Capacity Management**

  - Manage Service Level Agreements (SLAs) and future Service level Requirements (SLRs)
  - Study Business Plans & Create resultant Capacity Plans
  - Perform Modeling & Application Sizing for Business Services

- **Service Capacity Management**

  - Translate Business SLAs & SLRs into IT SLAs & SLRs
  - Measure Throughput & Performance for System, Network & Service
  - Perform Monitoring, Measuring, Analysis, Tuning & Demand Management

- **Resource Capacity Management**
  - Optimize & Configure Current Technology
  - Research Future Technology and other alternatives
  - Guarantee System and Service Resilience

There is a sequential flow inherent to this arrangement of the subprocesses.

1. **Business capacity** – How much business work must the solution perform?
2. **Service capacity** – How much work must the IT services do to meet the business capacity requirements?
3. **Resource capacity** – What physical resources, etc., are needed to address service capacity requirements?

Moreover, most (if not all) of the activities supporting the ITIL Capacity Management subprocesses are essentially performance engineering activities as described in PEMM. Because PEMM and ITIL Capacity Management originate from different perspectives (development vs. operational), they are actually complementary in many respects, and can be used effectively together.

2.11 PEMM Theme – Performance and Risk Management

Figure 2.8 illustrates some of the key considerations associated with the "Performance and Risk Management" theme. This theme is concerned with activities needing to effectively manage performance-related risk throughout the life of the project.

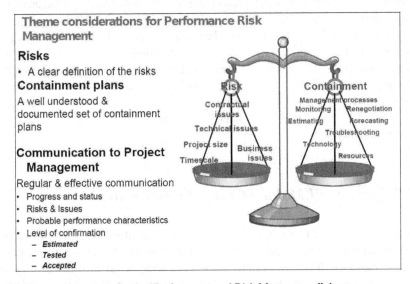

Fig. 2.8 Key considerations for the "Performance and Risk Management" theme.

Managing performance-related risks is one of the chief overall objectives of PEMM. Nearly every one of the other more "technical" PEMM themes is intended to help reduce risks related to the potential for poor performance. Just as a project manager is responsible for the management of risks to the overall project, the performance engineer must be concerned with identifying and mitigating technical risks related to performance, capacity and scalability, by engaging the right resources and/or management attention when significant performance issues or risks arise. This is done with the recognition that since it is not feasible to eliminate all sources of performance-related risks, *finding an effective balance between risk containment and risk acceptance* should be the goal.

From a project perspective, there are other things that can also be done to facilitate the management of performance risk.

2.11.1 Assignment of Dedicated Performance Engineering Resources

For complex systems with critical performance requirements, it is important to establish accountability for the management and coordination of activities needed to achieve the project's IT performance goals. The terms *performance architect* or *performance engineer* are sometimes used to describe the role of those who assume this responsibility for a given project. Depending on the project, there may be a team of performance engineers sharing this responsibility.

While the size of the performance engineering team may vary depending on the complexity and the level of performance risk associated with the project, it is not unusual to see 1% to 5% of an IT projects total cost invested in performance engineering activities, or more for complex projects [9, 10, 11, 12]. While performance engineers are typically most involved in the earlier themes of PEMM, there is a great deal to be gained if there is active PE involvement throughout the solution life cycle. The Performance Engineer may not own direct responsibility for activities such as development, testing and post-deployment performance and capacity management; however, the PE must nevertheless find ways to maintain the influence and accountability needed to help the project meet its performance, capacity, and scalability requirements.

2.11.2 Applying PEMM to IT Project Governance

The need of the performance engineer to influence activities and decisions not under his or her direct control begs the question of how PEMM relates to overall IT project governance. Most IT organizations have some level of methodology and process documentation which describes how activities such as architecture, design, development testing, deployment and live operations are to be handled, along with a governance structure which monitors and enforces adherence to these methodologies and processes. A prudent means of applying PEMM is not necessarily to replace existing processes, but rather to ensure time and resources are allotted to integrate PE activities into the existing plans, and to identify touch points between PEMM and the local process/methodologies to ensure that adequate progress is being made towards meeting the performance goals.

2.11.3 Applying PEMM to Complex Projects

Inevitably, projects will be encountered where it is not possibly to exhaustively apply PEMM techniques to all aspects of the solution. In such cases, one must be selective about the scope and focus of performance engineering efforts. Some considerations for managing this complexity from a PEMM perspective are listed below.

- **Divide and conquer** – Rather than trying to estimate or model all the aspect of a large system or group of systems in their entirety, it may make more sense to split them into more manageable subsystems for separate consideration.
- **Prioritize** – As was stated earlier, be selective about which parts of the system warrant detailed PE studies. Concentrate on those areas where the risk and/or potential impact of performance issues is most significant. Special consideration should be given in the following cases.
- **Special cases** – The following classes of solutions often have specific performance challenges requiring special attention.
  - **Multi-channel solutions** – If a central system is being accessed by multiple channels (direct web users, telephone VRU, call center users, etc.), be aware that each channel will have different effects on and requirements pertaining to system performance.
  - **Distributed solutions** – If a common solution is replicated at multiple data centers, keep in mind that there could be site-specific performance and capacity considerations depending on how the worldwide workload is distributed.
  - **Commercial Off-The-Shelf (COTS) Packages** – It is increasingly common for customers to use vendor-provided packaged solutions or frameworks to meet their specific business needs. Ensuring that a vendor solution continues to meet performance requirements after being configured, tailored or extended to meet the customers needs is often challenging.
  - **Large programs** – Some organizations may have major conversion or transformation initiatives that take months or years to implement. These situations may have governance and technical considerations that make PE challenging in those cases.
  - **Unpredictable workloads** – The advent of the web era has shown that web-enabled workloads originating from the Internet can be difficult to predict.

Making contingency plans for additional capacity and scalability is especially important in those situations.
- **Complex interactions** – Solutions that are based on SOA and other highly modular architectures can pose workload balancing issues and other performance challenges in their own right.

2.12 Summary

The Performance Engineering and Management Method is a collection of IBM's leading practices with respect to performance engineering and performance management of IT systems. PEMM is organized as a framework consisting of eight overarching and interrelated "themes" which operate in concert with whatever locally used IT solution life cycle is in place. While the themes themselves are not necessarily unique to IBM or to PEMM, the overall framework provided by PEMM helps to conceptualize the performance engineering activities that are appropriate for each stage of the solution life cycle.

Even when users of PEMM have not had the opportunity to apply all of PEMM to a given project, having an understanding of the PEMM themes still helps to understand what things should have been done previously and should be done now to manage performance-related risks during the project life cycle. Within IBM, acquainting architects, developers, testers, and operations personnel with the concepts of PEMM have raised awareness of both the potential for applying PE in a proactive manner and the potential for achieving synergies across the themes by working together.

Implementing PEMM is not without its challenges. Managers seeking to reduce costs and shorten schedules may need convincing before they are willing to dedicate resources to performance engineering activities, and even then the scope of PE activities may be limited due to the current state of the project. Performance estimating and modeling methods are arguably immature, and commercially available performance modeling and testing tools are sometimes prohibitively expensive. Even within IBM, the process of institutionalizing PEMM has been a gradual one, relying on educational offerings, methodology enhancements, project experience and an active internal PE advocacy community to encourage PEMM adoption over time.

Nevertheless, progress continues to be made. New training has been introduced to train IBM practitioners in applying PEMM to SOA projects. PEMM concepts have been applied by IBM in both internal and commercial projects for years, and now customer demand has led to the development of commercially offered PEMM training. Moreover, the continued acceptance of process maturity frameworks such as ITIL is leading to increased awareness among IT organizations that system performance must be treated as a business imperative, and not left to chance. Given this, PEMM and similar holistic approaches to PE will fulfill a vital need in the IT industry for years to come.

Acknowledgements The author thanks Martin Jowett, Damian Towler, Chris Winter, Ann Dowling, Zhen Liu and Cathy Xia for their review of and contributions to this paper.

References

1. Accretive Technologies home page. http://www.acrtek.com/acc_home.swf.
2. E. Hung, Q. He, and J. Zhu. Sonoma: Web service for estimating capacity and performance of Service-Oriented Architecture (SOA) workloads, 2006.
   ftp://ftp.software.ibm.com/software/dw/wes/hipods/SONOMA_wp9Oct_final.pdf.
3. HyPerformix home page. http://www.hyperformix.com.
4. Z. Liu, L. Wynter, C. Xia, and F. Zhang. Parameter inference of queueing models for it systems using end-to-end measurements. *Performance Evaluation*, 63:36–60, 2006.
5. D. A. Menasce and Others. *Performance by Design: Computer Capacity Planning by Example*. Prentice Hall, Upper Saddle River, NY, 2004.
6. Official ITIL® web site home page. http://www.itil-officialsite.com/home/home.asp.
7. OpNet home page. http://www.opnet.com.
8. Ptolemy II home page. http://ptolemy.berkeley.edu/ptolemyII.
9. S. C. U. and L. G. Williams. *Performance Solutions: A Practical Guide to Creating Responsive, Scalable Software*. Prentice Hall, Upper Saddle River, NY, 2002.
10. SPE Experience: An Economic Analysis. http://www.perfeng.com/papers/hesselg2.pdf.
11. The Economics of SPE Panel. http://www.perfeng.com/papers/jennings.pdf.
12. What Does Software Performance Engineering Cost?
    http://www.cs.ucl.ac.uk/staff/ucacwxe/lectures/3C05-01-02/aswe13.pdf.

Chapter 3
Economic Models of Communication Networks

Jean Walrand

Abstract
Standard performance evaluations of communication networks focus on the *technology layer* where protocols define precise rules of operations. Those studies assume a model of network utilization and of network characteristics and derive performance measures. However, performance affects how users utilize the network. Also, investments by network providers affect performance and consequently network utilization. We call the actions of users and network providers the *"economic layer"* of the network because their decisions depend largely on economic incentives. The economic and technology layers interact in a complex way and they should be studied together. This tutorial explores economic models of networks that combine the economic and technology layers.

3.1 Introduction

Why were QoS mechanisms for end users not implemented in the Internet? Should users have a choice of grade of service for different applications? Why is security of the Internet so poor? Should Internet service providers be allowed to charge content providers for transporting their traffic? Should cell phones be unlocked to work with multiple operators? Should municipalities deploy free Wi-Fi networks? How should different services of a WiMAX network be priced?

These questions that affect the future of communication networks go beyond technology. However, their answers certainly depend on technological features. Different protocols enable or prevent choices of users and influence the revenue of operators and, consequently, their investment incentives. The engineers who define network protocols typically focus on their performance characteristics but are largely unaware of the market consequences of their designs.

Jean Walrand
Department of EECS, University of California at Berkeley, e-mail: wlr@eecs.berkeley.edu

This tutorial explains some combined models of user and provider incentives and performance of the network. The objective is not to present a comprehensive survey of research in this area. Rather, it is to illustrate some key aspects of these studies.

3.1.1 General Issues

This tutorial is not concerned with the strategic behavior of users who manipulate protocols, such as cheating the backoff algorithm of a multiple access protocol or the window adjustment rules of TCP. For a review of the game-theoretic formulation of such behavior, see [3]. Instead, this tutorial explores the behavior of more typical users and providers that do not modify the basic hardware and software of the communication devices. The questions concern investments, pricing, and usage patterns. Users of a communication network decide to use services based on their utility for the services. The utility of a service for a given user depends on how much the user values the service and on its price. Services include access to content, to applications, and communication services. Users also add content through their web sites, possibly through a social network, or by making files available in a peer-to-peer network. The valuation of a service depends on the richness of the content, the quality of the transport service (bandwidth and delay), and the third parties with whom the user can communicate. Network operators choose their investments, prices, and the services they offer to maximize their profit or some other objective that depends on profits. Figure 3.1 illustrates the interactions among users and providers through the network. Thus, through the network, a user affects other users and providers and a provider affects other providers and users.

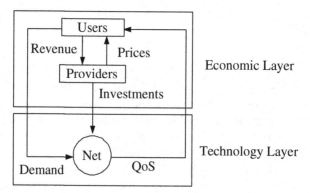

Fig. 3.1 Users and providers respond to economic incentives and affect the network.

When you drive on a congested highway, you increase the travel time of other vehicles and the air pollution. That is, your utilization of the highway has a negative impact on the welfare of other people. Similarly, in a network, the actions of users, content providers (such as Google and Yahoo!), and transport providers (such as AT&T and Comcast) affect the other users and providers. Economists call *externality* the impact on others of some action when prices do not reflect that impact. Externalities are present in most systems and they play a crucial role in the actual outcomes that economic agents face. We explain that networks exhibit positive and negative externalities, as summarized in Figure 3.2. The table also identifies the sections of the paper where we analyze the corresponding effects.

	Users	Content	Transport
Users	+ Contacts - Congestion 1.2, 2 + Security 3.3	+ Interest 3.2	+ Access 1, 2, 3
Content	+ Revenue 3.2	+ Appeal - Competition	+ Access 3.2
Transport	+ Revenue 1, 2, 3	+ Traffic 3.2	+ Access - Competition 2.4

Fig. 3.2 Externalities of an agent in a column on the agents in the rows.

The first column of the table shows the externalities of users on other users and on content and transport providers. The presence of users on the network has a positive externality on other users by adding one person they can contact through the network or by adding content in a peer-to-peer network, on a web site, or on a social network. However, the usage of the network by a user has a negative externality because it may increase congestion in the network and reduce the value of other services by slowing them down. The security investments of a user have a positive externality on other users because they reduce the chances of denial of service attacks, leak of confidential information, or the likelihood of virus infection of the computers of other users. The usage of the network by users increases the revenue of transport and content providers, a positive externality.

The second column shows that if a content provider invests more, it increases the interest that users have in the network and increases the utility they derive from the network, a positive externality. The column also shows that an increased investment in content by a provider may increase the revenue of other content providers indirectly by increasing the general appeal of the network and, consequently, the usage of the network. However, if a content provider is much more attractive, it may reduce the traffic of its competitors, a negative externality typical of competition. Improving content servers increases the traffic and the demand for transport provider services, a positive externality.

The third column shows that an increase in investment by a transport provider improves the access to content and other users, which improve the experience of users, a positive externality. Moreover, such an investment increase may generate more traffic on the content provider servers. Finally, if a transport provider improves its network, this may increase the traffic on the network of other transport providers, but it may decrease that of some competitors.

The standard view is that economic agents are selfish in the sense that they choose actions that maximize their own utility without regard for that of other agents. Because of externalities, it is generally the case that the selfish behavior of agents results in a less-than-maximum *social welfare*, defined as the total utility of all the agents minus the cost of providing the services. As an example, the negative externality of congestion results in a selfish demand by users that is larger than socially optimal. This effect is called the *tragedy of the commons* [16] as we discuss in Section 3.2.1. Also, the positive externality of investments typically results in selfish investments that are lower than socially optimal, an effect called *free-riding* [48] that we review in Section 3.3.1.

Another important effect in economic systems is the role of information in the efficiency of markets. If you suspect that a used car might be a lemon, you are not willing to pay much for it. For instance, if the dealer asks $10,000 for the car, you expect that he probably paid $5,000 for it, so that you might be willing to pay $6,000 for it, but not the asking price. However, the dealer may have a car that he paid $9,000 for that he would be willing to sell for $10,000 and that you might want to buy for that price. Consequently, the lack of information results in good used cars not being sold even though some buyers would be willing to purchase them at a price agreeable to the dealer, an effect called *missing market* by economists [2]. One could argue that the inability to select the quality of Internet connections results in missing markets. Users might be willing to pay more for dependable high-quality connections. See [43] for an interesting discussion of the importance of economic aspects of the Internet and [49] for a broader presentation of the economic aspects of the information technology.

Summing up, important issues in economic models of networks are the effects of externality of activity and of investments and the quality of information available to agents and when that information is available.

3.1.2 Paris Metro Pricing

This section illustrates the interdependence of the economic and technology layers on a simple example due to A. Odlyzko [39]. Imagine a metro whose otherwise identical cars are divided into expensive first class cars and inexpensive second class cars. The first class cars are less crowded because they are more expensive, which justifies their higher price. The general effect behind this example is that quality of service affects utilization (the number of users of the service) and utilization affects quality of service. Consequently, the closed-loop behavior of the system is more subtle than might be anticipated. We consider two models of this situation. The first model assumes that the utility of a network for each user depends on its utilization. The second model is more radical and considers applications that are incompatible.

Model 1: Utility Depends on Utilization

Imagine a network whose delays are acceptable for voice-over-IP as long as the utilization (number of users) is less than 200 and acceptable for web-browsing if the utilization is less than 800. Assume that the demand (potential utilization) for voice-over-IP is 100 as long as the price does not exceed 20 and that the demand for web-browsing is 400 as long as the price does not exceed 5 and that these demands vanish if the prices exceed those values, because users switch to a competitor's network. How much should the operator charge for the service?

If the operator charges 20, the web-browsing users do not connect. All the voice-over-IP users connect because their total demand (100) is small enough for the network delays to be acceptable for that application. The revenue of the operator is then the utilization (100) multiplied by the price (20), or 2,000. On the other hand, if the operator charges 5, then all the web-browsing users connect, the voice-over-IP users do not because the utilization is too large and the delays are not acceptable for them. The resulting revenue is now the utilization (400) multiplied by the price (5), or again 2,000.

Now consider the following strategy of the operator. He divides the network into two subnetworks, each with half of the capacity of the original network. The actual technology (e.g., time-division multiplexing or deficit-round-robin) used for this splitting of the network does not really matter. In each network, the delays are acceptable for voice-over-IP if the utilization is less than 100 (half of the previous acceptable utilization). Also, the delays are acceptable for web-browsing if the utilization is less than 400. The operator charges 20 for one network and 5 for the other. The voice-over-IP users connect to the first network and the web-browsing users connect to the second. The operator revenue is now 100×20 for the first network and 400×5 for the second, or a total of 4,000. The situation is illustrated in Figure 3.3 that shows that the quality of service (QoS) of the first network is automatically better than that of the second because it is more expensive.

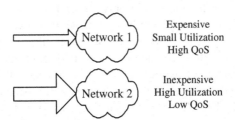

Fig. 3.3 Two identical networks with different prices have different QoS.

Obviously the example was designed specifically for the service differentiation to increase the revenue substantially. What happens in a more general situation? If the demand for voice-over-IP is of the form $A \times 1\{x \le x_1, p \le a\}$ and the demand for web browsing is $B \times 1\{x \le x_2, p \le b\}$ when the utilization is x and the price is p, then one can show that the revenue of the Paris Metro pricing cannot be more than twice the revenue of a single network.

As this example shows, even though the two networks are identical, the higher price of the first network results in a lower utilization and, consequently, a higher quality that justifies the higher price. Note that the ability to differentiate the service doubles the revenue of the operator by eliminating the negative congestion externality of the users of one class on the users of the other class. This differentiation requires the users to signal their service preference and the operator to charge differently for the two services.

Model 2: Incompatible Applications

The devices in a Wi-Fi network use a multiple access protocol to share one radio channel. The protocol specifies that a node must wait a random time after the channel is silent before it starts transmitting. If the transmission of one device happens to collide with another one, as the device notices because it does not get an acknowledgment of its transmission, the device increases the interval from which it picks a random waiting time before the next attempt. This protocol has the advantage of sharing the channel fairly among the different devices and also of stabilizing the network by avoiding many repeated collisions. However, because of this random waiting time, it may happen that the delay before transmission is occasionally quite long, especially if some packets are large and require a long transmission time. As a consequence, voice-over-IP and web browsing do not mix well in a Wi-Fi network. Experiments show that the delays become excessive for voice-over-IP as soon as more than four or five web browsing connections are active in the network [18].

Some technological solutions were developed to try to mitigate this problem. However, they tend to be complicated and incompatible with the widely available technology. A Paris Metro pricing approach would be to run two networks, on non-overlapping radio channels and with different prices. One network would be too expensive for web browsing and would only be used by voice-over-IP users. The other network would be used by web browsers. Wi-Fi networks have a few non-overlapping channels. Typically, the network manager allocates the channels to the access points to limit interference, using some spatial reuse that cannot be perfect. In a Paris metro scheme, one would have a set of access points on one channel with an expensive connection fee, and other access points using the remaining non-overlapping channels. This scheme would support voice-over-IP with a good quality because that application generates little traffic, so that the lack of spatial reuse would not matter. The other applications would suffer somewhat because their network has been deprived of one channel.

A similar situation arises for other applications. For instance, imagine an application that tolerates only very short delays but that does not generate a lot of traffic. One such application could be a class of quick-reflex networked games. Another could be some remote control applications. Such highly delay-sensitive applications are not compatible with web-browsing or with most other applications. A

Paris metro scheme would divide the network into two parallel networks, one being expensive per byte and having a relatively small capacity; the other being cheap and having most of the capacity of the original network. Because of the negligible amount of traffic that these delay-sensitive applications generate, they have essentially no impact on the other applications. Accordingly, this scheme generates additional revenues from the new applications with no loss of revenue from the others. The increase in revenue depends on the demand for the new applications.

Conclusions

The Paris metro pricing scheme provides quality of service by selecting the prices so that the applications automatically find a network with a utilization that results in suitable performance measures. A more expensive network has a lower utilization and, accordingly, lower delays and more throughput for each of its connections. It may be possible to adjust prices to guarantee that the performance measures remain adequate for the applications even if the demand increases. The advantage of the approach is that the technologies of the two parallel networks are identical. The users choose which network to use and the routers and switches do not differentiate packets. This approach contrasts with the a standard implementations of quality of service where routers and switches use different scheduling rules for different classes of packets.

A variation of the implementation of this scheme is to have users mark packets as type 1 or type 2 and charge them differently for the two types. In this variation, the routers can serve the packets of type 1 with high priority and those of type 2 with low priority. The technology for such differentiated service is deployed in the routers (it is called DiffServ). However, this technology is typically not used for end-users.

Why is a Paris metro scheme not implemented today? We have seen that it has the potential to increase operator revenues and to enable new applications for which there is probably a demand. One possible reason is that the implementation of such a scheme requires agreements between network operators about the meaning and pricing of the service types. Moreover, transport providers must agree on how to share the revenue. Finally, there is uncertainty about the additional revenue that the new service would generate.

3.2 Pricing of Services

WiMAX is a wireless cellular broadband access technology that enables the operator to define multiple services, from guaranteed bit rate to best effort. How much more should the operator charge for a guaranteed 1Mbps service than for a best effort service? In this section, we explain that pricing of services is complicated but has a substantial impact on user satisfaction and on operator revenue.

The interaction of a few effects make network pricing different and more complicated than pricing other goods and services:

(1) Customers vary in their valuation of services and providers may want to offer multiple services to capture that diversity;
(2) Congestion changes the quality of services as more people use them;
(3) Heterogeneity in valuations makes congestion externalities asymmetric;
(4) Service providers compete for customers.

Other products or services have some of the above effects, but networks have all of them interacting. For instance, there is a considerable literature on effect (1) that studies how to create versions of a product to ensure that high-end consumers buy the deluxe version and low-end consumers buy the basic version. We explore effect (2) in Section 3.2.1 where we demonstrate that, because of the negative externality of congestion, selfish users tend to over-consume. In Section 3.2.2 we show that congestion pricing can *internalize* the externality. That is, congestion pricing can make the selfish agent pay for the cost his usage imposes on other agents and force him to behave in a way that is socially optimal. Section 3.2.3 illustrates that effect when users can choose when they use the network. In Section 3.2.4 we explore the pricing of different services. When effects (1)-(2)-(3) are combined, the quality of the different services changes as a function of consumer choices, which also depend on the quality of the services. We explore that combination in our discussion of the Paris metro pricing scheme. We show that when effect (4) is included, the resulting pricing game may not have a pure-strategy Nash Equilibrium (a concept that we review in that section). Finally, in Section 3.2.5 we study bandwidth auctions where users compete for acquiring transmission capacity. The text [10] offers a comprehensive discussion of pricing of network services. See also [41] for a nice presentation of related recent results on pricing and competition of transport providers.

3.2.1 Tragedy of the Commons

We expect that agents who are not sensitive to the negative impact of their consumption on the utility of other agents tend to over-consume. We use a simple mathematical model to illustrate that effect called the *tragedy of the commons*.

The tragedy of the commons refers to the unfortunate inevitable result of people sharing a common good. Following Hardin [16], picture a pasture shared by many herdsmen that keep cattle in it. Each herdsman observes that he benefits more than he loses by adding one head of cattle. Indeed, he then gets to raise and sell one more animal whereas his herd suffers only a fraction of the loss due to the additional overgrazing. The inevitable outcome is then that the herdsmen add an excessive number of animals in the pasture. This story is another example of externality. Each herdsman imposes a total externality on the others that exceeds his own benefit increment.

Model

To cast the tragedy of the commons in a simple model, imagine that N identical users share a network and designate by $x_n \geq 0$ the level of activity of user n ($n = 1,\ldots,N$). Assume that user n derives a utility $U(x_n)$ from using the network but also faces a disutility $x_1 + \cdots + x_N$ due to the congestion in the network. (We could use more complicated model of the congestion disutility as a function of the total activity level, but this simple model suffices for our purpose.) That is, for $n \in \{1,\ldots,N\}$, user n has a net utility

$$U(x_n) - (x_1 + \cdots + x_N).$$

We assume that $U(\cdot)$ is an increasing and strictly concave function.

Say that user n chooses his activity level x_n to maximize his net utility. In that case, he chooses $x_n = \tilde{x}$ where $\tilde{x}$ is such that $U'(\tilde{x}) = 1$, as shown in Figure 3.4.

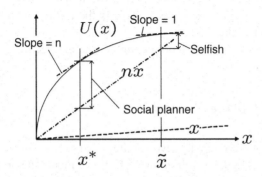

Fig. 3.4 Selfish users choose $\tilde{x}$ whereas the socially optimal choice is x^*.

The net utility of each user is then $R_A := U(\tilde{x}) - N\tilde{x}$.

Since all the users are symmetric, one expects the social optimal activity levels to be identical. If all the users agree to choose the same activity level x^* that maximizes $U(x) - Nx$, then $U'(x^*) = N$ and each user's net utility is $R_S := U(x^*) - Nx^*$ (see Figure 3.4). We see that *selfish users over-consume* because they are not penalized fully for the externality of their consumption.

The *price of anarchy* (a concept introduced in [24]; see also [45], [22] and [1]), defined as the ratio of the maximum social welfare over that achieved by selfish users, is

$$\pi = \frac{R_S}{R_A} = \frac{U(x^*) - Nx^*}{U(\tilde{x}) - N\tilde{x}}.$$

The price of anarchy is unbounded in this model. For a given N one can find a function U so that π is as large as one wants.

3.2.2 Congestion Pricing

Selfish users overconsume because they do not fully pay the cost that their consumption imposes on other users. To correct the situation, imagine that each user has to pay an explicit cost equal to $p = (N-1)x$ when his activity level is x.

The net utility of user n is now

$$U(x_n) - (x_1 + \cdots + x_N) - (N-1)x_n.$$

To maximize the net utility, user n selects an activity level $x_n = x^*$, which is socially optimal. The cost $(N-1)x_n$ is the congestion cost that user n imposes on the others by choosing an activity level x_n. Indeed, each of the $N-1$ other users sees an additional congestion cost equal to x_n because of the activity of user n. This congestion price *internalizes* the externality.

Note that the choice $x_n = x^*$ is socially optimal in that it maximizes the net utility $U(x_n) - (x_1 + \cdots + x_N)$ of each user n. This is the utility without subtracting the price p that every user pays.

For a discussion of congestion pricing in the Internet, see [23].

3.2.3 When to Use the Network?

Instead of choosing their activity level, assume that users may choose when to use the network, say during the day. Following [30], we model the problem as follows. There is a large population of users who can choose when to use the network among $T+1$ periods $\{0,1,\ldots,T\}$ where period 0 means not using the network at all. The users belong to N different classes characterized by their dislike for time slots. The quantity g_t^n measures the disutility of slot t for users of class n. In particular, g_0^n is the disutility for a user of class n of not using the network.

Designate by x_t^n the number of users of class n that use the network during time slot t. The utility to some user of class n who uses the network in period t is

$$u = u_0 - [g_t^n + d(N_t)1\{t > 0\} + p_t], t = 0,1,\ldots,T$$

where u_0 is the maximum utility for using the network, $N_t = \sum_n x_t^n$, $d(N_t)$ is a congestion delay of period t, and p_t is the price that users are charged for using period t. In this expression, $d(.)$ is a given increasing strictly convex differentiable function. Note that there is no congestion cost for time slot 0 as the term $1\{t > 0\}$ is equal to zero when $t = 0$ and to 1 when $t > 0$. By convention, $p_0 = 0$. We then have the following result.

Theorem 3.1. *Assume that each user is a negligible fraction of the population of users in each time slot that is used. Assume also that*

$$p_t = N_t d'(N_t), t = 1,\ldots,T.$$

Then selfish users choose the socially optimal time slots, i.e., the time slots that maximizes the total utility $Nu_0 - V(\mathbf{x})$ where

$$V(\mathbf{x}) := \sum_{t=0}^{T}[\sum_{n=1}^{N} x_t^n g_t^n + N_t d(N_t) 1\{t > 0\}].$$

Note that the price p_t is the incremental total disutility per increase of one user in time slot t since each of the N_t users faces an increase in disutility equal to $d'(N_t)$. This price does not depend on the preferences g_t^n, which is fortunate for otherwise the scheme would not be implementable.

Proof. Selfish users choose the time slots that offer the smallest disutility. Thus, at equilibrium, the disutility of all the slots is the same for a user of class n, thus reaching what is called a Wardrop equilibrium [52]. Designate by λ_n that disutility. Accordingly, we have

$$g_t^n + d(N_t) 1\{t > 0\} + p_t = \lambda_n \text{ for } t \in \{0, \ldots, T\} \text{ and } n \in \{1, \ldots, N\}. \quad (3.1)$$

The social optimization problem is as follows:

$$\text{Minimize } V(\mathbf{x})$$
$$\text{Subject to } \sum_{t=0}^{T} x_t^n = x^n \text{ for } n = 1, \ldots, N$$

where x^n is the total population of class n.

The problem is convex, so that the following KKT conditions characterize the solution. There are some constants λ_n such that the partial derivative with respect to x_t^n of

$$L(\mathbf{x}, \lambda) := V(\mathbf{x}) - \sum_{n=1}^{N} \lambda_n [\sum_{t=0}^{T} x_t^n - x^n]\}$$

is equal to zero for all n and t.

That condition states that the Lagrangian is stationary. To understand why the condition is necessary, note that, if the derivative of $V(\mathbf{x})$ with respect to x_t^n is smaller than that with respect to x_s^n, then one could decrease $V(\mathbf{x})$ by slightly increasing x_t^n and decreasing x_s^n by the same amount. Consequently, if x^n is optimal, the derivatives of $V(\mathbf{x})$ with respect to x_t^n must have the same value, say λ_n, for all t. It follows that the derivative of $L(\mathbf{x}_t, \lambda)$ must be equal to zero for some λ_n. The sufficiency of the conditions results from the convexity that implies the uniqueness of the optimal $\mathbf{x}$. (See e.g., [7] or [8] for a presentation of the theory of convex optimization.)

Now observe that the conditions (3.1) that characterize the selfish choices of the users imply that the KKT conditions are satisfied. To see this, note that

$$\frac{d}{dx_t^n} L(\mathbf{x}_t, \lambda) = g_t^n + d(N_t) + \sum_{n=1}^{N} x_t^n d'(N_t) - \lambda_n = g_t^n + d(N_t) + p_t - \lambda_n = 0,$$

by (3.1).

This result shows once again that *internalizing the externality* of each user's choice leads selfish users to make socially optimal choices.

For a study of pricing with asymmetric information between user and provider, see [35].

Congestion Game

In our example, users choose which network to use and the utility of a network depends on how many users also select it. This situation is a particular case of a *congestion game* [44]. In a congestion game, there is a set A of resources and a number N of users. Each user i selects a set $A_i \subset A$ of resources so that there are $n_j = \sum_{i=1}^{N} 1\{j \in A_i\}$ users of resource j, for $j \in A$. The utility of user i is then

$$u_i = \sum_{j \in A_i} g_j(n_j).$$

That is, user i derives some additive utility for each of the resources he uses and the utility of a resource is a function of the number of users of the resource. We assume that each $g_j(n)$ is positive, strictly convex and decreasing in n.

We explain that these games have a nice structural property: as each user tries to increase his utility, he increases a global function of the allocation. That function is called the *potential* of the game; it is concave in this case. Thus, as users act selfishly, they increase the potential that then converges to its maximum which corresponds to the unique Nash equilibrium for the game. By definition, a set of strategies for the users is a *Nash equilibrium* when no user benefits from changing his strategy unilaterally (see e.g., [14]).

Assume that user i changes his selection from A_i to A_i' and that the other users do not change their selection. Designate by u_i' the new utility of user i and by n_j' the number of users of resource j under the new selection. Let $B_i = A_i \setminus A_i'$ and $C_i = A_i' \setminus A_i$. Observe that $n_j = n_j' - 1$ for $j \in C_i$ and $n_j' = n_j - 1$ for $j \in B_i$. Also, $n_j = n_j'$ for $j \notin B_i \cup C_i$. Finally, let

$$\phi := \sum_j f_j(n_j) \text{ with } f_j(n) := \sum_{k=0}^{n} g_j(k)$$

and let ϕ' be the value that corresponds to the new selection. Then we find that

$$f_j(n_j) - f_j(n_j') = \begin{cases} g_j(n_j), & \text{for } j \in B_i \\ -g_j(n_j'), & \text{for } j \in C_i \\ 0, & \text{for } j \notin B_i \cup C_i. \end{cases}$$

Consequently,

$$u_i - u_i' = \sum_{j \in A_i} g_j(n_j) - \sum_{j \in A_i'} g_j(n_j') = \sum_{j \in B_i} g_j(n_j) - \sum_{j \in C_i} g_j(n_j')$$
$$= \sum_j [f_j(n_j) - f_j(n_j')] = \phi - \phi'.$$

This calculation shows that if user i changes his selection to increase its utility u_i, he also increases the value of ϕ. Thus, a congestion game is a potential game in that it has a potential. The converse is also true: potential games are congestion games [34].

Thus, as the users selfishly modify their selection to increase their utility, the value of ϕ increases to its maximum. Once the selections A_i achieve the maximum value of ϕ, no change in selection by a user would increase his utility. Consequently, the *natural dynamics* of the game converge to the Nash equilibrium (which may not be the social optimum).

3.2.4 Service Differentiation

Coming back to the Paris metro model, assume that you have to choose between first and second class before you get to the metro and that you cannot change when you get there. This assumption is certainly contrived for a metro since you see the occupancy of the different classes when you get to the train. However, the assumption might be reasonable for selecting a service class in a communication network. Thinking that the second class might be very crowded, you are tempted to buy a first class ticket. However, if the price difference is small, it might be that most users buy a first class ticket and end up worse off than in second class. On a future trip, you learn from that mistake and buy a second class ticket. If all users behave like you, you are out of luck again. This is frustrating for the users and probably not in the interest of the provider. We examine this situation in this section. See [17] for a related study and a discussion of revenue sharing among network providers.

One Network

Consider a communication system with a large population of N users each characterized by a type θ that is an independent random variable uniformly distributed in $[0,1]$. A user of type θ finds the network connection acceptable if the number of users X using the network and the price p are such that

$$\frac{X}{2N} \leq 1 - \theta \text{ and } p \leq \theta.$$

In this expression, $2N$ is the capacity of the network. We use $2N$ because we will later divide the network into two networks, each with capacity N. The interpretation is that a user with a large value of θ is willing to pay quite a lot for the connection but he expects a low utilization for a high quality of service. Conversely, a user with a small value of θ does not want to pay much for his connection but is willing to tolerate high delays. For instance, we can think of users with a large θ as users of VoIP and those with a small θ as web browsers.

We solve the provider revenue maximization problem. That is, we find the price p that maximizes the product of the number of users of the network times the price p. Because the utility depends on the utilization and the utilization depends on the utility, we have to solve a fixed point problem to find the utilization that corresponds to a price p.

Assume that the network connection price is $p \in (0,1)$. If the number of users in the network is X, then a user of type θ connects if the inequalities above are satisfied, i.e., if $\theta \in [p, 1 - X/(2N)]$. Since θ is uniformly distributed in $[0,1]$, the probability that a random user connects is $(1 - X/(2N) - p)^+$. Accordingly, the number X of users that connect is binomial with mean $N \times (1 - X/(2N) - p)^+$, so that

$$\frac{X}{N} \approx (1 - \frac{X}{2N} - p)^+$$

by the law of large numbers, since N is large. Solving this expression we find that $x := X/N = (2 - 2p)/3$. The operator can maximize his revenues by choosing the value of p that maximizes $px = p(2 - 2p)/3$. The maximizing price is $p = 1/2$ and the corresponding value of px is $1/6$, which measures the revenue divided by N.

Paris Metro

Consider now a Paris metro situation, as discussed in the Introduction, where the operator divides the network into two subnetworks, each with half the capacity of the original network. That is, there are two networks: network 1 with price p_1 and capacity N and network 2 with price p_2 and capacity N. We expect the users to select one of the two networks, based on the prices and utilizations.

To be consistent with the previous model, each of the two networks is acceptable for a user of type θ if the utilization X of the network is such that $X/N \le 1 - \theta$ and if the price p is such that $p \le \theta$. Indeed, the capacity of each network is N, so that the ratio of the number of users to the capacity is X/N instead of $X/(2N)$ in the previous model. This ratio determines the quality of service in the network. A user joins an acceptable network if any. Moreover, he chooses the cheapest network if both are acceptable. Finally, if both are acceptable and have the same price, a user joins the one with the smallest utilization because it offers a marginally better quality of service.

We determine the prices p_1 and p_2 that maximize the revenue of the operator. We then compare the maximum revenue to the revenue in a single network. Our analysis shows that the Paris metro scheme increases the revenue of the operator by 35%. To perform the analysis, we consider separately the cases $p_2 < p_1$ and $p_1 = p_2$.

First assume that $p_2 < p_1$. If the numbers of users in the two networks are X_1 and X_2, respectively, then a user of type θ chooses network 2 if $X_2/N \le 1 - \theta$ and $p_2 \le$

θ. The probability that θ falls between p_2 and $1 - X_2/N$ is then $(1 - X_2/N - p_2)^+$. Arguing as in the case of a single network in the previous section, we conclude that $x_2 := X_2/N$ is given by

$$x_2 = \frac{1}{2}(1 - p_2). \qquad (3.2)$$

A user of type θ selects network 1 if $X_1/N \leq 1 - \theta, p_1 \leq \theta$, and $X_2/N > 1 - \theta$. Arguing as before, we find that $x_1 := X_1/N$ is such that

$$x_1 = (1 - x_1 - \max\{p_1, 1 - x_2\})^+.$$

Substituting the value of x_2 and solving for x_1, we find

$$x_1 = \min\{\frac{1 - p_1}{2}, \frac{1 - p_2}{4}\}. \qquad (3.3)$$

The revenue $R \times N$ of the operator is then such that

$$R = x_1 p_1 + x_2 p_2 = p_1 \min\{\frac{1 - p_1}{2}, \frac{1 - p_2}{4}\} + p_2 \frac{1}{2}(1 - p_2)$$

when $p_2 < p_1$.

Second, assume that $p_2 = p_1$, then a user of type θ with $\theta \geq p_1$ and $X_1/N \leq 1 - \theta, X_2/N \leq 1 - \theta$ selects the network with the smallest number of users. In that case, $x_1 = x_2 = x$ and we find that half of the users with $\theta \in [p_1, 1 - x]$ join network 1. Consequently, the number X_1 of users that join network 1 is such that

$$\frac{X_1}{N} = \frac{1}{2}(1 - \frac{X_1}{N} - p_1)^+,$$

and similarly for X_2. Consequently, $x_1 = (1 - x_1 - p_1)^+/2$ and one finds

$$x_1 = x_2 = \frac{1 - p_1}{3}. \qquad (3.4)$$

The revenue $R \times N$ is then such that

$$R = 2p_1 \frac{1 - p_1}{3}$$

when $p_2 = p_1$.

Maximizing R over p_1 and p_2, we find that the maximum occurs for $p_1 = 7/10$ and $p_2 = 4/10$ and that the maximum is equal to $9/40$.

The example shows that the service differentiation with Paris metro pricing increases the revenue from $1/6$ to $9/40$, or by 35%.

Competition

Our previous example shows that two networks with the same capacity and different prices generate more revenue than a single network with twice the capacity. Now assume that the two networks belong to two competing operators. Will one operator settle on a network with high price to attract users of high-quality services and the other on a network with low price to attract users of lower-quality services? We know that this strategy would yield the maximum total revenue. However, this maximum revenue corresponds to the revenue $R_i := x_i p_i$ for network $i = 1, 2$ with $R_1 = 21/200$ and $R_2 = 12/100$. That is, the low-price network generates more revenue than the high-price network. We then suspect that both operators would compete to have the low-price network, which might lead to a price war. However, if the prices become too low, the operators might prefer to raise the price to serve the users of high-quality services. We explore this situation in more detail. In our model, we find that the operators try to segment the market but that there may not be prices that they find satisfactory (no pure Nash equilibrium).

To avoid technical complications that are not essential, assume that the prices p_1 and p_2 are restricted to multiples of $\varepsilon := 1/N$ for some large N. This makes the game finite and guarantees the existence of a best response.

Assume that p_2 is fixed. If $p_1 > p_2$, then using (3.3) we find that

$$R_1 = p_1 x_1 = p_1 \min\{\frac{1-p_1}{2}, \frac{1-p_2}{4}\}. \tag{3.5}$$

Also, if $p_1 = p_2$, from (3.4) we obtain

$$R_1 = p_1 \frac{1-p_1}{3}. \tag{3.6}$$

Finally, if $p_1 < p_2$, then

$$R_1 = p_1 \frac{1-p_1}{2}. \tag{3.7}$$

These expressions show that there is no pure-strategy Nash equilibrium. That is, there is no pair (p_1, p_2) from which no operator can deviate without decreasing its revenue. To see this, assume that (p_1, p_2) is a Nash equilibrium. We claim that $p_1 \neq p_2$. Indeed, if $p_1 = p_2$, then comparing (3.6) and (3.7) shows that operator 1 can increase R_1 by replacing p_1 by $p_2 - \varepsilon$. This is the price war that we anticipated. Assume now that $p_1 \neq p_2$. Comparing (3.5) and (3.7), together with some simple algebra, shows that the maximizing value of R_1 is $p_1 \approx (1+p_2)/2$ if $p_2 \leq 1/3$. (More precisely, p_1 is the multiple of ε closest to $(1+p_2)/2$.) If $p_2 > 1/2$, then R_1 is maximized by $p_1 \approx 1/2$. Finally, if $1/3 < p_2 \leq 1/2$, then the value of R_1 is maximized as $p_1 = p_2 - \varepsilon$.

Figure 3.5 illustrates the best response function $p_1(p_2)$ and the symmetric best response function $p_2(p_1)$ and shows that they do not intersect.

By trying to use the best response to a price of the competitor, an operator realizes that his price should be between $1/3$ and $1/2$. However, there is not pair of prices

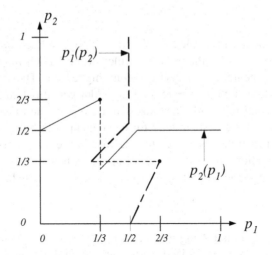

Fig. 3.5 The figure shows the best responses of the two providers: $p_2(p_1)$ and $p_1(p_2)$. Since the best responses do not intersect, the game has no pure-strategy Nash equilibrium.

from which the selfish operators have no incentive to deviate. See e.g. [14], [15], [40], [42], or [37] for an introduction to game theory.

The lesson of this example is that the pricing of services by competing operators can be quite complex and may not have a satisfactory solution. The situation would be simpler if the operators could collude and agree to split the total revenue they get by charging 4/10 and 7/10. The users would also be better served by such an arrangement.

See [1] and [24] for related results on the price of anarchy in pricing of competitive services.

3.2.5 Auctions

Auctions are an effective technique for eliciting the willingness to pay of potential buyers. Instead of having a set price for an item and hoping that one buyer will purchase the item at that price, the auction makes the potential buyers compete against one another. We review some standard results on auctions and then apply them to networks. For a presentation of the theory of auctions, see [25] and [38]. For related models, see [11], [31] and [32].

Vickrey Auction

Assume there is one item for sale and N potential buyers. Each buyer $i = 1, \ldots, N$ has a private valuation v_i for the item. The rules of the *Vickrey auction* are that the highest bidder gets the item and pays the second-highest bid. These rules are similar to those of ascending auctions where the last bidder gets the item and pays essentially what the second-highest bidder was willing to pay. The remarkable property of this auction is that the best strategy for each agent is to bid his true valuation, independently of the strategies of the other agents. To see this, consider the net utility $u_i(x_i, x_{-i})$ (valuation minus payment) of agent i when he bids x_i and the other agents' bids are represented by the vector $x_{-i} = \{x_j, j \neq i\}$. One has

$$u_i(x_i, x_{-i}) = [v_i - w_{-i}] 1\{x_i > w_{-i}\}$$

where $w_{-i} := \max_{j \neq i} x_j$ is the highest bid of the other agents. Note that this function is maximized by $x_i = v_i$. Indeed, if $v_i > w_{-i}$, then the value for $x_i = v_i$ is the maximum $v_i - w_{-i}$. Also, if $v_i \leq w_{-i}$, then the maximum value is 0 and it is also achieved by $x_i = v_i$. We say that this auction is *incentive-compatible* because it is in the best interest of each agent to bid truthfully. Note that if the agents bid their true valuation, then the item goes to the agent who values it the most. In that case, the allocation of the item maximizes the social welfare, defined as the sum of the utilities that the agents derive by getting the item. Only one agent gets the item, so the social welfare is the valuation of the item by that agent. See [50].

Generalized Vickrey Auction

Consider the following generalization of the Vickrey auction [33]. There is a set A of items and N agents. Each agent i has a private valuation $v_i(S)$ for each subset S of A. For $i = 1, \ldots, N$, agent i announces a valuation $b_i(S)$ for every subset S of A. The auctioneer then allocates disjoint subsets A_i of A to the agents $i = 1, \ldots, N$ to maximize the sum $\sum_i b_i(A_i)$ of the declared valuations, over all possible choices of such disjoint subsets. Agent i has to pay a price p_i for his subset A_i. The price p_i is the reduction in the declared valuation of the other agents caused by agent i's participation in the auction. That is, if agent i did not bid, then agent j would receive a subset B_j^i and the total valuation of the agents other than i would be $\sum_{j \neq i} b_j(B_j^i)$ instead of $\sum_{j \neq i} b_j(A_j)$. The reduction in valuation is then

$$p_i := \sum_{j \neq i} b_j(B_j^i) - \sum_{j \neq i} b_j(A_j).$$

Thus, p_i is the externality of agent i on the other agents.

The claim is that each agent should bid his true valuations for the subsets. More precisely, that strategy dominates all other strategies, no matter what the other agents bid. To see this, first note that if agent i bids $v_i(.)$ his net payoff is

$$\alpha = v_i(A_i) - \sum_{j \neq i} [b_j(B^i_j) - b_j(A_j)].$$

Also, if agent i bids $b_i(.)$ the allocations are $\{A'_j\}$ and agent i's net payoff is

$$\beta = v_i(A'_i) - \sum_{j \neq i} [b_j(B^i_j) - b_j(A'_j)].$$

(Note that the B^i_j are the same in both cases since they do not involve i's bid.) The difference is

$$\alpha - \beta = [v_i(A_i) + \sum_{j \neq i} b_j(A_j)] - [v_i(A'_i) + \sum_{j \neq i} b_j(A'_j)] \geq 0$$

since the A_j's maximize the first sum.

Thus, this auction mechanism is incentive-compatible. Each user should bid truthfully. Consequently, the allocation maximizes the social welfare. The number of partitions of a set with M elements into $N < M$ subsets is exponential in M. Accordingly, the calculation of the optimal allocation and of the prices is generally numerically complex. However, if the problem has some additional structure, then the solution may in fact be quite tractable, as the next section illustrates.

Bidding for QoS

The mechanism we describe here is described in [47]. Consider a network that offers C classes of service characterized by a different bit rate, as could be implemented in WiMAX, for instance. Say that class c can accept n_c connections and offers a bit rate $r(c)$ with $r(1) > r(2) > \cdots > r(C) \geq 0$. There are N users that compete for access using an auction mechanism. Each user i has a valuation $v_i(r)$ for rate $r \in \{r(1), \ldots, r(C)\}$, where $v_i(r)$ is strictly increasing in r. User i declares a valuation $b_i(r)$ for the possible rates r. The network operator allocates the service classes to the users so as to maximize the sum of the declared valuations. This sum is

$$V := \sum_{i=1}^{N} b_i(c(i))$$

where $c(i)$ is the class of service of user i. If user i were not present, then user j would receive the service class $c^i(j)$ instead of $c(j)$. The price that user i has to pay is

$$p_i := \sum_{j \neq i} b_j(c^i(j)) - \sum_{j \neq i} b_j(c(j)).$$

In this level of generality, the problem is numerically hard. Let us assume that $v_i(r) = v_i f(r)$ and $b_i(r) = b_i f(r)$ where $f(r)$ is an increasing function. User i declares a coefficient value b_i that may not be correct. In this case the allocation that maximizes V is as follows. Assume without loss of generality that $b_1 \geq b_2 \geq \cdots \geq$

b_N. The operator allocates the first class to the first n_1 users, the second class to the next n_2 users, and so on. To see why this allocation maximizes V, consider an allocation where two users i and j with $i < j$ are such that $c(j) < c(i)$. Modify the allocation by interchanging the classes of the two users. Letting $f_i := f(r(c(i)))$, we see that the sum V then increases by $b_i f_j + b_j f_i - b_i f_i - b_j f_j \geq 0$. Note that if user i were not bidding, then some user j_1 would move from class $c(i) + 1 =: d + 1$ to class $c(i) = d$ and see his declared utility increase by $b_{j_1} f_d - b_{j_1} f_{d+1}$. Also, some user j_2 would move from class $d + 2$ to class $d + 1$, and so on. Consequently, the externality of user i is

$$p_i = \sum_{k \geq 1} b_{j_k} [f_{d+k-1} - f_{d+k}].$$

Bandwidth Auction

We describe a mechanism introduced in [54] that the authors call a *VCG-Kelly Mechanism.* See also [22], [31], [32] and [46] for related ideas. An operator has a link with capacity C that she wants to divide up among a set of N users. The goal of the operator is to maximize the sum of the utilities of the users. For instance, the link could be owned by a city that wants to use it to improve the welfare of its citizens. The difficulty is that the operator does not know the utility of the users and that they may declare incorrect utilities to try to bias the capacity allocation in their favor.

Each user i has utility $u_i(x_i)$ when he gets allocated the rate x_i. Here, $u_i(\cdot)$ is an increasing strictly convex function. Thus, the goal of the operator is to find the allocations x_i that solve the following social welfare maximization problem:

$$\text{Maximize} \sum_i u_i(x_i)$$
$$\text{over } x_1, \ldots, x_N \tag{3.8}$$
$$\text{subject to } x_1 + \cdots + x_N \leq C.$$

The auction rules are as follows. Each user i bids $b_i > 0$. The operator then implements a Vickrey mechanism assuming that the utility of user i is $b_i \log(x_i)$. The claim is that the unique Nash equilibrium solves problem (3.8). Thus, remarkably, the users do not have to reveal their actual utility function to the operator.

More precisely, the operator selects the allocations $x_i = x_i^*$ that solve the following problem:

$$\text{maximize} \sum_{i=1}^N b_i \log(x_i)$$
$$\text{over } x_1, \ldots, x_N$$
$$\text{subject to } x_1 + \cdots + x_N \leq C.$$

The problem being convex, we know that x^* is the solution of the first order KKT conditions:

$$b_i \frac{1}{x_i^*} = \lambda, i = 1, \ldots, N,$$

for some $\lambda > 0$. Consequently, since $\sum_i x_i^* = C$, one finds

$$x_i^* = C \frac{b_i}{B},$$

with $B = b_1 + \cdots + b_N$, so that the users get a rate proportional to their bid.

To calculate the price p_i, the operator performs the same optimization problem, assuming that i does not bid. Designate by $\{x_j^i, j \neq i\}$ the solution of that problem. Then the price p_i is given by

$$p_i = \sum_{j \neq i} b_j \log(x_j^i) - \sum_{j \neq i} b_j \log(x_j^*).$$

When user i is not bidding, the allocations are

$$x_j^i = C \frac{b_j}{B - b_i}.$$

Consequently, we find

$$p_i = \sum_{j \neq i} b_j [\log(\frac{Cb_j}{B - b_i}) - \log(\frac{Cb_j}{B})] = \sum_{j \neq i} b_j \log(\frac{B}{B - b_i})$$

$$= (B - b_i) \log(\frac{B}{B - b_i}).$$

Thus, the net utility of user i is

$$u_i(x_i^*) - p_i = u_i(\frac{Cb_i}{B}) - (B - b_i) \log(\frac{B}{B - b_i})$$

$$= u_i(\frac{Cb_i}{B_i + b_i}) - B_i \log(\frac{B_i + b_i}{B_i})$$

where $B_i := B - b_i$ does not depend on b_i. Accordingly, to maximize his net utility, user i chooses b_i so that the derivative of the expression above with respect to b_i is zero. That is,

$$u_i'(\frac{Cb_i}{B})[\frac{C}{B} - \frac{Cb_i}{B^2}] - \frac{B - b_i}{B} = 0,$$

i.e.,

$$u_i'(\frac{Cb_i}{B}) = \frac{B}{C} =: \lambda.$$

This shows that the bids b_i and the resulting allocations $x_i^* = Cb_i/B$ satisfy the KKT conditions of problem (3.8).

For other mechanisms of bandwidth auction, see [27], [28], [26], [19], [20], and [21].

3.3 Investment Incentives

As we explained in the introduction, if investments of agents have a positive externality on the revenue of the other agents, then one may expect some *free-riding*. That is, each agent ends up investing less than socially optimal because he relies on the investments of the other agents. We explain that effect on simple models in section 3.3.1. We then illustrate the effect in a model of network neutrality in section 3.3.2. We conclude the section with a discussion of free-riding in security investment.

3.3.1 Free Riding

If your neighbor paints his house, your house value typically goes up as the neighborhood becomes generally more attractive. This effect may reduce your incentive to paint your own house. This situation is an example of free-riding. We start with a simple model borrowed from [48] that illustrates the free-riding effect. We then explore a model of joint investments by content and transport providers.

Illustrative Example

Assume that two agents jointly invest in a production. Agent 1 invests x and agent 2 invests y; the resulting revenue is $g(ax + by)$ for each of the agent where $g(\cdot)$ is a strictly concave increasing function and $0 < a < b$. The profits of agents 1 and 2 are

$$g(ax + by) - x \text{ and } g(ax + by) - y,$$

respectively. Acting selfishly, each agent tries to maximize his profit. Thus, given y, agent 1 chooses x so that the derivative of his profit with respect to x is equal to zero if that occurs for some $x > 0$ and chooses $x = 0$ otherwise. That is, agent 1 chooses x such that

$$ag'(ax + by) = 1,$$

or $ax + by = A$ where $g'(A) = 1/a$, if that x is positive. Thus, $x = [A/a - (b/a)y]^+$. Similarly, we find that, given x, agent 2 chooses $y = [B/b - (a/b)x]^+$ where $g'(B) = 1/b$. Figure 3.6 shows these best response functions. As the figure shows, the unique intersection of the best response functions is $x_N = 0, y_N = B/b$, which is then the unique pure-strategy Nash equilibrium. Note that this value of y maximizes

$$g(by) - y.$$

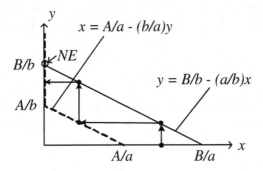

Fig. 3.6 The best response functions intersect at the unique pure-strategy Nash equilibrium $(0, B/b)$.

In this example, agent 1 free-rides on the investment of agent 2 by not investing at all and yet collecting a profit. As you probably suspect, these choices of the agents are not socially optimal. We explore that aspect of the game next.

Consider the sum of the profits of the two agents, the *social welfare* of this model. This sum is

$$W = 2g(ax + by) - x - y.$$

Imagine a *social optimizer* who chooses $x = x^*$ and $y = y^*$ to maximize W. To maximize $ax + by$ for a given value of $x + y$, one must choose $x = 0$ because $a < b$. Accordingly, the social optimizer must find the value of y that maximizes

$$2g(by) - y.$$

Thus, whereas the Nash equilibrium is the value of y that maximizes $g(by) - y$, the social optimal maximizes $2g(by) - y$. That is, in the social optimization, agent 2 knows that his investment contributes to the utility of agent 1 whereas in the Nash equilibrium agent 2 ignores that effect. Figure 3.7 illustrates the results. As the figure

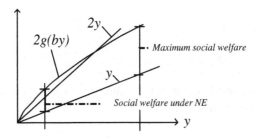

Fig. 3.7 The social welfare under the Nash equilibrium and its maximum value.

suggests, one can find a function $g(\cdot)$ for which the ratio between the maximum social welfare and that achieved by a Nash equilibrium is as large as one wishes.

Cobb-Douglas Example

Assume a content provider C invests c and a transport provider T invests t. As a result of these investments, there is demand for the network services and that demand generates revenues for C and T. Assume that

$$R_C = c^v t^w - c \text{ and } R_T = c^v t^w - t.$$

In these expressions, $v, w > 0$ and $v + w < 1$. The traffic in the network is proportional to $c^v t^w$, a function that is increasing and concave in the investments. That expression, called a Cobb-Douglas function, is commonly used to model the joint production by labor and capital investments [9]. In R_C, the first term is the revenue generated by the traffic on the web site and the term c is the *opportunity cost* that C loses by investing in the network instead of in some other productive activity. The term R_T admits an interpretation similar to that of R_C. One could make the model more general, but this would only complicate notation.

Being selfish, C chooses c to maximize R_C and T chooses t to maximize R_T. That is, for a given t, C chooses c so that the derivative of R_C with respect to c is equal to zero. This gives

$$v c^{v-1} t^w = 1, \text{ or } c = (v t^w)^{1/(1-v)}.$$

Similarly,

$$t = (w c^v)^{1/(1-w)}.$$

The Nash equilibrium is the intersection of these two best response functions. One finds

$$c = v^{(1-w)/\Delta} w^{w/\Delta} \text{ and } t = w^{(1-v)/\Delta} v^{v/\Delta}$$

where $\Delta = 1 - v - w$. The resulting revenues R_C and R_T are

$$R_C = (1-v) v^{v/\Delta} w^{w/\Delta} \text{ and } R_T = (1-w) w^{w/\Delta} v^{v/\Delta}.$$

In particular, the sum of the revenues is

$$R_C + R_T = [2 - v - w] v^{v/\Delta} w^{w/\Delta}.$$

Now assume that C and T are in fact the same operator that can choose c and t to maximize $R_T + R_C$, i.e., to maximize

$$2 c^v t^w - c - t.$$

Setting the derivatives with respect to c and t equal to zero, we find

$$2 v c^{v-1} t^w = 1 \text{ and } 2 c^v w t^{w-1} = 1.$$

Solving these equations we get

$$c^* = 2^{1/\Delta} v^{(1-w)/\Delta} w^{w/\Delta} \text{ and } t^* = 2^{1/\Delta} w^{(1-v)/\Delta} v^{v/\Delta},$$

with

$$\Delta := 1 - v - w,$$

which corresponds to the sum of revenues

$$R_C^* + R_T^* = 2^{1/\Delta} \Delta v^{v/\Delta} w^{w/\Delta}.$$

Consequently, the price of anarchy of free-riding π is given by

$$\pi = \frac{R_C^* + R_T^*}{R_C + R_T} = \frac{2^{1/\Delta} \Delta}{[1+\Delta]}.$$

For instance, π is equal to 7.7 for $\Delta = 0.3$ and to 1.32 for $\Delta = 0.8$. We can also compare the investments of C and T under the socially optimal and the Nash equilibrium.

$$\frac{c^*}{c} = \frac{t^*}{t} = 2^{1/\Delta}.$$

For instance, this ratio is equal to 10 for $\Delta = 0.3$ and to 2.4 for $\Delta = 0.8$.

As we expected, free-riding reduces the investments and the social welfare.

3.3.2 Network Neutrality

In today's Internet, a user or content provider pays the transport provider to which he is directly attached. For instance, if a content provider C is attached to transport provider S, then C pays S a cost that depends on the rate of the traffic that C sends to S. However, to reach the end users of C's content, the traffic from C has to go through the Internet Service Provider (ISP) of those users. Should ISPs be allowed to charge C for transporting that traffic? The ISPs argue that they need to invest in their network to improve the delivery of the content and that C would benefit from those improvements. On the other hand, C argues that the additional charges would reduce his incentive to invest in new content, which would hurt the transport providers' revenue. Thus, the question is whether a *neutral network* where such charges are not allowed increases or reduces the revenue of content and transport providers and the demand for network services.

The question is important as neutrality regulation would have a substantial impact on investment incentives and on the future of Internet. Obviously, the answers depend on the assumptions made implicitly or explicitly in the model. It is certainly irresponsible to claim definite conclusions about such an important question based on cavalier models. That is not our pretention here. Rather, we want only to give a sense of how one can approach the question. We discuss a study developed in [36]. For a background on network neutrality, see [12], [13] and [55].

Model

Our model focuses on the impact on investments and revenues of additional charges paid by content providers to ISPs. Accordingly, the model, illustrated in Figure 3.8 includes a content provider C – that gets revenue from advertisers A – and users U attached to ISP T. The payments in the model are normalized per click on spon-

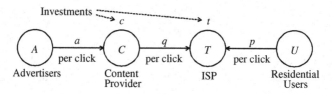

Fig. 3.8 Model to study the impact of neutrality.

sored advertisement. Advertisers pay a per click to the content provider. The content provider pays q and users pay p to the ISP, also per click on sponsored advertisement. Of course, C pays T based on the traffic rate, but that rate is roughly proportional to that of clicks on ads. Also, T gets revenue roughly in proportion to the number of users interested in content, and therefore roughly in proportion to the rate of clicks on ads.

In our model, C invests c and T invests t. The demand for network services increases with the richness of content and the ability of the network to transport it. Thus, the rate of clicks on sponsored ads increases with c and t and it decreases with p as fewer users are willing to pay a higher connection fee that corresponds to a higher value of the price p normalized per click on sponsored ads. We model the rate as

$$B = c^v t^w e^{-p}$$

where, as in the last example of section 3.3.1, $v, w > 0$ with $v + w < 1$. Accordingly, the revenue R_C of C ad the revenue R_T of T are given as follows:

$$R_C = (a - q)B - \alpha c \text{ and } R_T = (q + p)B - \beta t.$$

In these expressions, α and β are positive numbers that model the opportunity costs of the providers.

We consider that, because of different time scales of investment, T first selects (t, p, q) and C then chooses c. Moreover, in a neutral network $q = 0$ whereas in a non-neutral network, q can take any value. A positive value of q is a payment from C

to T. However, we allow q to be negative, which corresponds to a transfer of revenue from T to C.

The analysis then proceeds as follows. In the non-neutral network, assume that (t,p,q) are fixed by T. Then C finds the value $c(t,p,q)$ that maximizes R_C. Anticipating this best response by C, ISP T replaces c by $c(t,p,q)$ in the expression for R_T and then optimizes over (t,p,q). Designate by $(c_1,t_1,p_1,q_1,R_{C1},R_{T1},B_1)$ the resulting values for the non-neutral network. In the neutral network, the approach is identical, except that $q = 0$. Designate by $(c_0,t_0,p_0,q_0,R_{C0},R_{T0},B_0)$ the resulting values for the neutral network.

After some algebra, one finds the following results:

$$p_0 = p_1 + q_1 = a(1-v)$$
$$q_1 = a - v$$
$$\frac{R_{C0}}{R_{C1}} = \frac{c_0}{c_1} = \left(\frac{a}{v}\right)^{(1-w)/(1-v-w)} e^{(v-a)/(1-v-w)}$$
$$\frac{R_{T0}}{R_{T1}} = \frac{t_0}{t_1} = \frac{B_0}{B_1} = \left(\frac{a}{v}\right)^{v/(1-v-w)} e^{(v-a)/(1-v-w)}.$$

Figure 3.9 illustrates those ratios when $v = 0.5$ and $w = 0.3$, as a function of a. As

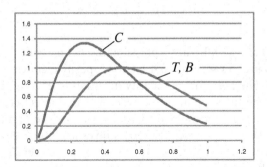

Fig. 3.9 Ratios of investments, revenues, and user demand (neutral/non-neutral) as a function of a.

this example shows, the neutral regime is never favorable for the ISP and it is favorable for the content provider only when the amount a that it can charge to the advertisers is neither large nor small. When a is small, the non-neutral regime is better for the content provider because it enables the ISP to pay him for generating content. Specifically, $q_1 = a - v < 0$ when $a < v$. When a is large, the non-neutral regime is preferable to C because he can provide revenues to T that uses them to improve the network. The results are similar when there are multiple content providers and ISPs [36].

3.3.3 Economics of Security

Many researchers agree that the main bottleneck to a secure Internet is not the absence of cryptographic tools or key distribution mechanisms. Rather, they point to the lack of proper incentives for users. For instance, most denial of service attacks come from many computers that were not properly patched to prevent intrusion. The users of those computers do not see the external cost of their lack of security and, accordingly, they do not bother to install the appropriate security software. Another example is the lack of encryption of private information in laptops or hard drives that can be easily stolen. The users of those devices do not understand the potential cost of their lack of basic precaution. See [5] for a survey of these issues. In this section, we explain one study of security investment and show that free-riding explains the sub-optimal investments. The discussion is borrowed from [29].

Model

Consider a set of N users of computers attached to the network. Designate by x_i the investment in security by user i. We model the utility of user i by $u_0 - u_i(\mathbf{x})$ where

$$u_i(\mathbf{x}) = g_i(\sum_j \alpha_{ji} x_j) + x_i$$

is the *security cost* of user i. In this expression, $\alpha_{ji} \geq 0$ measures the impact of user j's investment on user i's security and $g_i(\cdot)$ is a positive convex decreasing function. Thus, as user i invests more in security measures, such as purchasing software and configuring it on his system, he faces an increased direct cost but he reduces his probability of being vulnerable to an attack and also the probability that other users will be attacked. The impact of user j's investment on user i depends on the likelihood that a virus would go from user j's computer to user i's of the likelihood that user i's confidential information can be stolen from user j's computer.

Given the positive externality, one expects a free-riding effect. We study that effect. Designate by $\mathbf{x}^*$ the vector of efforts that minimizes the social cost $\sum_i u_i(\mathbf{x})$. Let also $\bar{\mathbf{x}}$ be a Nash equilibrium where each user minimizes his individual security cost. We are interested in characterizing the ratio ρ where

$$\rho := \frac{\sum_i u_i(\bar{\mathbf{x}})}{\sum_i u_i(\mathbf{x}^*)}.$$

This ratio quantifies the price of anarchy , which is the factor by which the cost to society increases because of the selfish behavior of users. (Note that this ratio differs from that of the utilities, which we designated previously by π.) One has the following result [29].

Theorem 3.2. *The ratio ρ satisfies*

$$\rho \le \max_j \{1 + \sum_{i \ne j} \frac{\alpha_{ji}}{\alpha_{ii}}\}.$$

Moreover, the bound is tight.

As a first illustration, assume that $\alpha_{ij} = 1$ for all i, j. Assume also that $g_i(z) = [1 - (1 - \varepsilon)z]^+$ for all i where $0 < \varepsilon \ll 1$. In this case, we find that $u_i(\mathbf{x}) = [1 - (1 - \varepsilon)(x_1 + \ldots + x_N)]^+ + x_i$, for all i. For any choice of $\{x_j, j \ne i\}$, the function $u_i(\mathbf{x})$ is increasing in x_i. Consequently, the unique Nash equilibrium is $\mathbf{x} = \mathbf{0}$, which is an extreme form of free-riding. The total security cost under that Nash equilibrium is $u_1(\mathbf{0}) + \cdots + n_N(\mathbf{0}) = N$. By symmetry, the value $\mathbf{x}^*$ of $\mathbf{x}$ that minimizes $u_1(\mathbf{x}) + \cdots + n_N(\mathbf{x})$ is such that $x_i^* = v/N$ where v minimizes $N[1 - (1 - \varepsilon)v]^+ + v$. That value of v is $v = 1$ and it corresponds to the total security cost approximately equal to 1. The price of anarchy in this example is $N/1 = N$ which is the value of the upper bound for ρ in the theorem.

As a second illustration, consider a network with $N + 1$ identical nodes with N even and $g_i(v) = \delta e^{-\lambda v}$ for all i. We assume $\lambda \delta > 1$ to avoid cases where the optimal investment is zero. To simplify the algebra, picture the $N + 1$ nodes arranged consecutively and regularly on a large circle and let $\alpha_{ij} = \beta^{d(i,j)}$ where $d(i, j)$ is the minimum number of hops between i and j. Then $\sum_{i \ne j} \alpha_{ji} = 2(\beta + \beta^2 + \cdots + \beta^{N/2}) = 2(\beta - \beta^{N/2+1})/(1 - \beta)$. Assuming that $\beta^{N/2} \ll 1$, one finds that the upper bound is $\rho \le (1 + \beta)/(1 - \beta) =: \gamma$. At the social optimal, by symmetry, one has $x_i^* = z$ where z minimizes

$$N\delta \exp\{-\lambda z(1 + 2\beta + 2\beta^2 + \cdots + 2\beta^{N/2})\} + Nz \approx N\delta \exp\{-\lambda \gamma z\} + Nz.$$

Hence, $z = (1/(\lambda \gamma)) \log(\lambda \gamma \delta)$. The resulting total security cost is

$$N(\lambda \gamma)^{-1}(1 + \log(\lambda \gamma \delta)).$$

On the other hand, at the Nash equilibrium, each user selects x_i to minimize

$$\delta \exp\{-\lambda x_i - \lambda \sum_{j \ne i} \alpha_{ji} x_j\} + x_i.$$

Consequently, $\bar{x}_i = u$ where $-\lambda \delta \exp\{-\lambda \gamma u\} + 1 = 0$. Hence, $\bar{x}_i = (1/(\lambda \gamma)) \log(\lambda \delta)$. This result shows that free-riding reduces the investment in security from the socially optimal value. At the Nash equilibrium, the total security cost is

$$N\delta e^{-\lambda \gamma u} + Nu = \frac{N}{\lambda} + \frac{N}{\lambda \gamma} \log(\lambda \delta).$$

The ratio of the costs in this example is

$$\rho = \frac{\gamma + \log(\lambda \delta)}{1 + \log(\gamma) + \log(\lambda \delta)}.$$

For numerical values, say that $\lambda\delta \approx 1$. Then Figure 3.10 illustrates the price of anarchy as a function of β. As the graph confirms, the price of anarchy increases

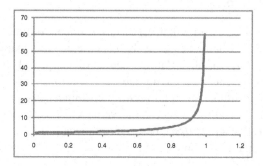

Fig. 3.10 The price of anarchy in security investments as a function of β.

with β because users have more impact on each other.

3.4 Conclusions

The main point of this tutorial is that the economic and technology layers of a communication network interact in a complex way. Accordingly, to understand their combined behavior, we must study these two layers jointly. The design of protocols affects not only the technology layer that determines the performance of the network under given operating conditions. It also affects the operating conditions by impacting the economic layer: the incentives for providers to invest in that technology and for users to use the network and the choices they make.

Our focus is the activity of users and the investments of providers. We stayed away from situations where users cheat with the rules of protocols to gain some strategic advantage. A recurrent theme is the externalities of actions of users and providers. These externalities result in selfish behavior that is not socially optimal. We characterized the social cost of selfish behavior (the price of anarchy) because of excessive usage or insufficient investments. We explored a number of schemes to entice selfish agents to align their behavior with the interest of society. For instance, we discussed congestion pricing and Vickrey auctions. In our analysis, we used simple ideas from game theory and convex optimization. More importantly, we were inspired by concepts from economics.

We used the Paris metro scheme to illustrate the inter-dependency of utilization and performance. In the introduction, we considered an example where the provider can double his revenue by using such a scheme. Remarkably, the Paris metro scheme does not require any QoS mechanism; only splitting the network into two identical networks, each with half the capacity of the original network and both with different prices. We discussed other situations where such a scheme could be employed, when applications are not compatible.

In Section 2, we explored the pricing of services. Our starting observation is that the price should reflect the congestion externality. Otherwise, all users tend to over-consume and they suffer from excessive congestion. We illustrated that point on a model where users select when to use the network. We observed that the pricing does not depend on the preferences of users for when to use the network; that pricing depends only on the congestion. We then revisited the Paris metro scheme using a more general model of user diversity. We examined whether two providers would end up splitting the market by having one choose a high price and the other a low price. That example illustrated the possibility of the absence of a pure-strategy Nash equilibrium. We concluded that section by a discussion of auctions applied to service differentiation.

Section 3 was devoted to investment incentives. After a discussion of the free-riding problem where positive externality leads to under-investments, we explored the delicate question of network neutrality. The conclusion of our simple example is that a good scheme should enable the sharing of revenue that results in the best investment incentives. If content providers are able to generate more revenue than ISPs, it might be beneficial for the content providers to share some of their revenue with the ISPs, and conversely. We concluded the section with a study of incentives for investments in network security. The model focused on externality and the resulting price of anarchy.

We hope that this brief tutorial will motivate you to explore the economic aspects of networks further. We believe that we all will benefit if future network designers have a deeper appreciation of these issues. These questions are the subject of an increasing number of papers in the traditional networking journals. Multiple sessions and special workshops are organized frequently to explore the economics of networks.

Acknowledgements The author thanks his collaborators Venkat Anantharam, Antonis Dimakis, Mark Felegyhazi, Assane Gueye, Linhai He, Rahul Jain, Libin Jiang, Jiwoong Lee, John Musacchio, Shyam Parekh, Galina Schwartz, Nikhil Shetty and Pravin Varaiya for multiple conversations and joint work on the topics of this tutorial and for comments about this material. He also thanks the National Science Foundation for supporting his work under Grant NeTS-FIND 0627161. Finally, the author is grateful to Zhen Liu, Cathy Xia and Sigmetrics for inviting him to present this tutorial and for arranging for its publication.

References

1. D. ACEMOGLU AND A. OZDAGLAR, "Competition and Efficiency in Congested Markets," *Mathematics of Operations Research*, vol. 32, no. 1, pp. 1-31, February 2007.
2. G. AKERLOF, "The Market for 'Lemons': Quality Uncertainty and the Market Mechanism," *Quarterly Journal of Economics*, 84 (3): 488–500, 1970.
3. E. ALTMAN, T. BOULOGNE, R. EL AZOUZI AND T. JIMENEZ, "A survey on networking games in telecommunications," *Computers & Operations Research*, 33, 286–311, 2006.

4. V. ANANTHARAM, "On the Nash dynamics of congestion games with player-specific utility," *Proc. 2004 43rd IEEE Conf. on Decision and Control*, 2004.
5. R. ANDERSON AND T. MOORE, "The Economics of Information Security: A Survey and Open Questions," *Fourth bi-annual Conference on the Economics of the Software and Internet Industries*, Toulouse, 1/2007; http://www.cl.cam.ac.uk/ rja14/Papers/toulouse-summary.pdf
6. T. BASAR AND G.J. OLSDER, *Dynamic Noncooperative Game Theory*, Second edition, SIAM, 1999.
7. D. BERTSEKAS, A. NEDIC AND A. OZDAGLAR, *Convex Analysis and Optimization*, Athena Scientific, Cambridge, Massachusetts, 2003.
8. S. BOYD AND L. VANDENBERGHE, *Convex Optimization*, Cambridge University Press, 2004.
9. C.W. COBB AND P.H. DOUGLAS "A Theory of Production," *American Economic Review*, 18 (Supplement), 139–165, 1928.
10. C. COURCOUBETIS AND R. WEBER, *The Pricing of Communications Services*, J. Wiley, 2002.
11. C. COURCOUBETIS, M.P. DRAMITINOS AND G.D. STAMOULIS, "An auction mechanism for bandwidth allocation over paths," *ITC-17*, Salvador da Bahia, Brazil, 2001.
12. D. FARBER AND M. KATZ. "Hold Off On Net Neutrality," Washington Post, 1/22/2007; http://www.washingtonpost.com/wp-dyn/content/article/2007/01/18/AR2007011801508.html
13. E. FELTEN, "The Nuts and Bolts of Network Neutrality," *Princeton*, 2006; http://itpolicy.princeton.edu/pub/neutrality.pdf.
14. D. FUDENBERG AND J. TIROLE, *Game Theory*, MIT Press, 1991.
15. R. GIBBONS, *Game Theory for Applied Economists*, Princeton University Press, 1992.
16. G. HARDIN, "The Tragedy of the Commons," *Science*, 162: 1243-1248, 1968.
17. L. HE AND J. WALRAND, Pricing and Revenue Sharing Strategies for Internet Service Providers, *IEEE JSAC*, May 2006.
18. N. HEDGE, A. PROUTIERE, AND J. ROBERTS, "Evaluating the voice capacity of 802.11 WLAN under distributed control," *Proc. LANMAN*, 2005.
19. R. JAIN, "An Efficient Nash-Implementation Mechanism for Allocating Arbitrary Bundles of Divisible Resources," *IEEE JSAC*, 2007.
20. R. JAIN AND P. VARAIYA, "Combinatorial Exchange Mechanisms for Efficient Bandwidth Allocation," *Communications in Information and Systems*, 3, no. 4, 305–324, 2004.
21. R. JAIN, A. DIMAKIS AND J. WALRAND, "Mechanisms for efficient allocation in divisible capacity networks," *Proc. Control and Decision Conference (CDC)*, December 2006.
22. R. JOHARI AND J. N. TSITSIKLIS, "Efficiency loss in a resource allocation game," *Mathematics of Operations Research*, 29(3): 407-435, 2004.
23. F.P.KELLY, "Charging and rate control for elastic traffic," *European Trans. on Telecommunications*, 8(1): 33-37, 1996.
24. E. KOUTSOUPIAS AND C. PAPADIMITRIOU, "Worst-case equilibria," *Proc. Symp. on Theoretical Aspects of Computer Science*, 16: 404-413, 1999.
25. V.KRISHNA, *Auction Theory*, Academic Press, 2002.
26. R.J.LA AND V.ANANTHARAM, "Network pricing using a game theoretic approach," *Proc. Conf. on Decision and Control*, 1999.
27. A. LAZAR AND N. SEMRET, "The progressive second price auction mechanism for network resource sharing," *Proc. Int. Symp. on Dynamic Games and Applications*, 1997.
28. A. LAZAR AND N. SEMRET, "Design and analysis of the progressive second price auction for network bandwidth sharing," *Telecommunication Systems - Special issue on Network Economics*, 1999.
29. L. JIANG, V. ANANTHARAM, AND J. WALRAND, "Efficiency of selfish investment in network security," *preprint*, 2008; http://robotics.eecs.berkeley.edu/~wlr/Papers/libin-security.pdf
30. L. JIANG AND J. WALRAND, "Congestion Pricing of Network Access," *preprint*, 2008; http://robotics.eecs.berkeley.edu/~wlr/Papers/libin-pricing.pdf

31. R.MAHESWARAN AND T.BASAR, "Nash equilibrium and decentralized negotiation in auctioning divisible resources," *J. Group Decision and Negotiation* 12:361-395, 2003.
32. R.MAHESWARAN AND T.BASAR, "Social Welfare of Selfish Agents: Motivating Efficiency for Divisible Resources," *CDC*, 2004.
33. J. K. MACKIE-MASON AND H. R. VARIAN, "Generalized Vickrey Auctions," 1994; citeseer.ist.psu.edu/mackie-mason94generalized.html
34. D. MONDERER AND L.S. SHAPLEY, "Potential Games," *Games and Economic Behavior*, 14, 124143, 1996.
35. J. MUSACCHIO AND J. WALRAND, WiFi Access Point Pricing as a Dynamic Game, *IEEE/ACM Transactions on Networking*, vol.14, no.2, April 2006, pp. 289-301.
36. J. MUSACCHIO, G. SCHWARTZ, AND J. WALRAND, "A Two-Sided Market Analysis of Provider Investment Incentives with an Application to the Net-Neutrality Issue: Long Version," September 2007; http://robotics.eecs.berkeley.edu/~wlr/Papers/MSW-Long.pdf
37. R.B. MYERSON, *Game Theory: Analysis of Conflict*, Harvard University Press, 1997.
38. R. B. MYERSON AND M. A. SATTERTHWAITE, "Efficient mechanisms for bilateral trading," *J. of Economic Theory* 28: 265-281, 1983.
39. A. ODLYZKO, "Paris Metro Pricing for the Internet," *ACM Conference on Electronic Commerce*, 1998.
40. M.J. OSBOURNE AND A. RUBINSTEIN, *A course in game theory*, MIT Press, 1994.
41. A. OZDAGLAR AND R. SRIKANT, Incentives and Pricing in Communication Networks, chapter in *Algorithmic Game Theory*, Noam Nisan, Tim Roughgarden, Eva Tardos, and Vijay Vazirani (Editors), Cambridge University Press, 2007.
42. G. OWEN, *Game Theory*, Third edition, Academic Press, 1995.
43. C.H.PAPADIMITRIOU, "Algorithms, games, and the internet," *Proc. STOCS*, 2001.
44. R. W. ROSENTHAL, "A class of games possessing pure-strategy Nash equilibria," *International Journal of Game Theory*, 2, 6567, 1973.
45. T. ROUGHRADEN AND E. TARDOS, "How bad is selfish routing?" *Proceedings of the 41st Annual Symposium on Foundations of Computer Science*, 2000.
46. S.SANGHAVI AND B.HAJEK, "A new mechanism for the free-rider problem," *IEEE Transactions on Automatic Control*, to appear March 2008.
47. J. SHU AND P. VARAIYA, "Smart pay access control via incentive alignment," *IEEE JSAC*, 24(5): 1051-1060, May 2006.
48. H. VARIAN, "System Reliability and Free Riding," *Proceedings of ICEC 2003*, 355-366, ACM Press 2003.
49. H. VARIAN, J. FARRELL AND C. SHAPIRO, *The Economics of Information Technology: An Introduction*, Cambridge University Press, 2004.
50. W. VICKREY, "Counterspeculation, Auctions, and Competitive Sealed Tenders," *Journal of Finance*, XVI, 8-37, 1961.
51. J. VON NEUMANN AND O. MORGENSTERN, *Theory of Games and Economic Behavior*, Princeton University Press, 1953.
52. J. G. WARDROP, "Some theoretical aspects of road traffic research," *Proceedings of the Institute of Civil Engineers*, vol. 1, pp. 325-378, 1952.
53. H.YAICHE, R.R.MAZUMDAR AND C.ROSENBERG, "A game theoretic framework for bandwidth allocation and pricing in broadband networks," *IEEE/ACM Trans. on Networking* 8(5): 667-678, 2000.
54. S. YANG AND B. HAJEK, "VCG-Kelly mechanisms for allocation of divisible goods: Adapting VCG mechanisms to one-dimensional signals," *IEEE JSAC (Issue on noncooperative behavior in networks)*, vol. 25, pp. 1237-1243, 2007.
55. C.S. YOO, "Network Neutrality and the Economics of Congestion," *Georgetown Law Journal*, Vol. 94, June 2006.

Chapter 4
Algorithmic Methods for Sponsored Search Advertising

Jon Feldman and S. Muthukrishnan

Abstract Modern commercial Internet search engines display advertisements along side the search results in response to user queries. Such sponsored search relies on market mechanisms to elicit prices for these advertisements, making use of an auction among advertisers who bid in order to have their ads shown for specific keywords. We present an overview of the current systems for such auctions and also describe the underlying game-theoretic aspects. The game involves three parties—advertisers, the search engine, and search users—and we present example research directions that emphasize the role of each. The algorithms for bidding and pricing in these games use techniques from three mathematical areas: mechanism design, optimization, and statistical estimation. Finally, we present some challenges in sponsored search advertising.

4.1 Introduction

Targeted advertisements on search queries is an increasingly important advertising medium, attracting large numbers of advertisers and users. When a user poses a query, the search engine returns search results together with advertisements that are placed into positions, usually arranged linearly down the page, top to bottom. On most major search engines, the assignment of ads to positions is determined by an auction among all advertisers who placed a bid on a keyword that matches the query. The user might click on one or more of the ads, in which case (in the pay-per-click model) the advertiser receiving the click pays the search engine a price determined by the auction.

Jon Feldman
Google, Inc., 76 9th Avenue, 4th Floor, New York, NY, 10011. e-mail: jonfeld@google.com

S. Muthukrishnan
Google, Inc., 76 9th Avenue, 4th Floor, New York, NY, 10011. e-mail: muthu@google.com

In the past few years, the sponsored search model has been highly successful commercially, and the research community is attempting to understand the underlying dynamics, explain the behavior of the market and improve the auction algorithms. This survey will provide an overview of the algorithmic issues in sponsored search.

The basic view we emphasize is the role of the *three parties*.

- The first party is the *advertisers* who have multiple objectives in seeking to place advertisements. Some advertisers want to develop their brand, some seek to make sales, and yet others advertise for defensive purposes on specific keywords central to their business. Some have budget constraints, while others are willing to spend as much as it takes to achieve their goal. Some seek to obtain many clicks and eyeballs, yet others attempt to optimize their return on investment. So, in general, advertisers are of varied types.
- The second party is the *auctioneer*, in this case, the search engine. The search engines have to balance many needs. They must maintain useful search results and have advertisements enhance, rather than interfere with, the search experience. They need to make sure the advertisers get their needs fulfilled, and at the same time ensure that the market the advertisers participate in is efficient and conducive to business.
- The third party is perhaps the most important in the game: these are *search users*. Users come to search engines for information and pointers. In addition, they also come to discover shopping opportunities, good deals, and new products. There are millions of users with different goals and behavior patterns with respect to advertisements.

These three parties induce a fairly sophisticated dynamics. While economic and game theory provide a well-developed framework for understanding the auction game between the advertisers and the auctioneer, the community has had to generalize such methods and apply them carefully to understand the currently popular Internet auctions. Likewise, while there has been recent work on understanding models of user behavior for posing search queries and their click behavior for search responses, little is known about user behavior on advertisements, and crucially, these affect the value of the slots and thus the very goods that are sold in auction.

In this survey, we will show examples of research themes in algorithmic, optimization and game-theoretic issues in sponsored search. In particular, we present three examples each emphasizing the perspective of one of the three different parties involved in sponsored search: the advertisers (who act as the bidders), the search engine (who acts as the auctioneer), and the search engine user (who determines the commodity). More specifically,

- We present results for how an advertiser should choose their bids given the currently used auction mechanism and implicit user behavior models. This result appears as [17]. It shows that a very simple bidding strategy is very effective for the advertiser.
- We study a new mechanism for the auctioneer to allocate advertisements to slots in order to optimize efficiency, and analyze the game-theoretic aspects of this

mechanism. This result appears in [18]. It shows that a simple price-setting mechanism is suitable for determining the outcome of several auctions simultaneously for the auctioneer.

- We present a novel Markovian model of user behavior when shown advertisements, and for this model, develop mechanisms and game theory. This result appears in [4]. It shows that under a model of user behavior more general than the one that is implicit in existing auctions, entirely different allocation and pricing will be optimal. Hence, user models have significant impact.

The results above are joint work with Gagan Aggarwal, Evdokia Nikolova, Martin Pál and Cliff Stein, and represent work done at Google Research.

In the rest of the document, we will first describe the foundations behind the existing auctions. Then we will describe the three results above. After that, we will be able to point to open issues and provide concluding remarks more generally on Internet advertising and auctions.

4.2 Existing Auctions

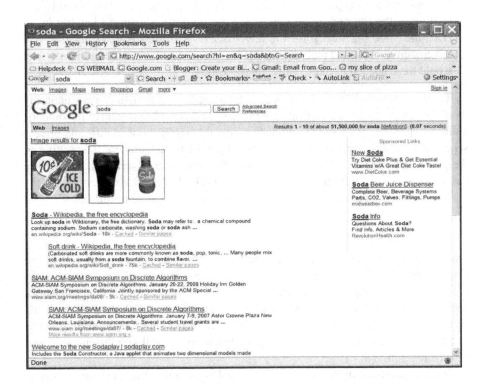

Fig. 4.1 Screen shot of a user query with the search results on the left, and the ads on the right.

The basic auction behind sponsored search occurs when a user submits a query to the search engine. The screen shot in Figure 4.1 shows an example user query "soda" and search results page returned from the search engine. This page includes web search results on the left, and independently, a set of three text ads on the right, arranged linearly top to bottom, clearly marked "Sponsored links." Each advertiser i has previously submitted a bid b_i stating their value for a click, tying their bid to a specific *keyword*. The auction is held in real-time among advertisers whose keywords match that user's query. The result of the auction is the list of advertisements on the right. So, after selecting the set of eligible (matching) ads, running the auction involves the search engine determining (a) the ordering of bidders and (b) pricing.

- **Ordering:** The most natural ordering is to sort by decreasing bid, but that does not take into account the quality of ads and their suitability to users. Thus, it is common practice to place the bidders in descending order of $b_i\alpha_i$, where α_i is what is called the *click-through-rate* (ctr) of advertiser i, i.e., the probability that a user will click on the ad, given that the user looks at it. (The ctr is usually measured by the search engine.) This is the ordering currently in use by search engines like Yahoo! and Google.
- **Pricing:** The natural method is to make bidders pay what they bid, but that leads to well-known race conditions [13]. Instead, the most common method is to use a "generalized second price" (GSP) auction. Say the positions are numbered $1, 2, \ldots$ starting at the top and going down, and the bidder at position i has bid b_i. In GSP, the price for a click for the advertiser in position i is determined by the advertisement below it and is given by $b_{i+1}\alpha_{i+1}/\alpha_i$, which is the minimum they would have needed to bid to attain their position.

The first academic treatments of the sponsored search auction were naturally from the perspective of auction and game theory. Fixing this ordering of the bidders, authors in [13, 41, 5] focused on understanding the implications of different pricing schemes, assuming strategic behavior on the part of the advertisers. The setting of the game that is modeled in this work is as follows: each advertiser has a *private value* v_i for a click from this user, and wants to set a bid that maximizes her *utility* u_i. The natural economic utility model in this context would be profit: i.e.,

$$u_i = (v_i - p_i)c_i,$$

where p_i is the price per click, and c_i is the probability of a click occurring. Of course c_i is determined by the *user*, and may depend on any number of factors. One common model is to assume that the click probability is *separable* [5]: if ad i is placed into position j, then $c_i = \alpha_i\beta_j$ where α_i is the ad-specific "click-through rate" and β_j is a position-specific visibility factor. (We will later explore other utility models in Sections 4.3 and 4.4 when we incorporate budgets, as well as non-separable user models in Section 4.5.)

Natural questions in this context include asking whether there is a *pure-strategy Nash equilibrium* of this game, and analyzing the economic efficiency and revenue of such equilibria. By *economic efficiency* we mean the total advertiser value generated by the assignment. This is also commonly referred to as the *social welfare*. In the context of sponsored search, the efficiency is the sum of the individual advertisers' values; i.e., $\sum_i c_i v_i$, where c_i is the probability that i will receive a click under this assignment and v_i is i's private value for a click. By a *pure-strategy Nash equilibrium* we mean a set of bids such that no single bidder can change her bid and increase her utility.

Among the most desirable properties of a mechanism is to be *truthful*, which is also referred to as being *incentive compatible*. This property says that each bidder's best strategy, regardless of the actions of other bidders, is simply to report her true value; i.e., submit v_i as her bid. Truthfulness immediately implies the existence of a pure-strategy Nash equilibrium (where every bidder reports v_i). Furthermore, it is simple to compute economic efficiency, since the assignment (and thus the efficiency) is simply a function of the values v_i. Unfortunately, it turns out that the GSP auction is *not* truthful. However, there is a pricing scheme that is truthful, which is based on an application of the famous Vickrey-Clarke-Groves (VCG) mechanism [42, 10, 23]. Furthermore, the GSP auction, while not truthful, still has a well-understood pure-strategy Nash equilibrium:

Theorem 4.1 ([13, 41, 5]). *Suppose we have a set of bidders participating in a particular sponsored search auction. Assume each bidder has a private value and a profit-maximizing utility function. Suppose further that the click probabilities are separable. Then, the GSP auction is not truthful, but it does have a pure-strategy Nash equilibrium whose outcome (in terms of assignment and prices) is equivalent to an application of the truthful VCG auction.*

For a more detailed discussion of this line of research, we refer the reader to [29]. Authors in [5] also show that under a more general click probability model, there is a pricing method that is truthful. (This pricing method reduces to the VCG pricing method when the click-through rates are separable.) Furthermore, they show that in this more general setting the GSP has a Nash equilibrium that has the same outcome as their mechanism.

4.2.1 Practical Aspects

The results described above regard GSP as an isolated auction, abstracting away the context of the larger system of which it is a part. While this is useful from a modeling perspective, there are many other elements that make sponsored search a more complex environment. Here we list some of those complicating factors, and mention examples of work done to address them.

- **Multiple queries, multiple keywords.** Each sponsored auction is conducted for a particular search engine user with a potentially unique query. There are perhaps millions of such queries every day. Advertisers must submit bids on *keywords*, and cannot adjust those bids on a per-query basis. The degree to which the keyword matches a particular query determines not only whether the advertiser will participate in the auction (and also who her competitors will be), but also can factor into the click-through rate α_i that is used for ranking. Theorem 4.1 only applies to the case where the same auction—with the same set of advertisers, and the same click-through rates—is repeated, and the bids qualify only for that set of auctions. A lot of the work mentioned below takes on this complication in various ways; we give two such examples in Sections 4.3 and 4.4.

- **Budgets.** In the private-value model each advertiser has a value v_i per click, but is willing to spend an arbitrary amount to maximize her profit. In reality, many advertisers have operating budgets or spending targets, and simply want to maximize their value given the constraints of that budget. This budget can be reported to the search engine, who can then employ techniques to use the budget efficiently. Analysis of incentives becomes more difficult in the presence of budgets. This has been addressed in e.g., [8, 33, 32, 34, 32, 2, 35, 39, 17, 4], and we discuss two examples in much more detail in Sections 4.3 and 4.4.

- **Reserve prices.** The major search engines enforce *reserve prices*, dictating the minimum price that an advertiser can pay for a click. Sometimes these reserve prices will even be specific to a particular bidder. Reserve prices are useful for controlling quality on the search results page, and also have implications for revenue. The effect of reserve prices on the game theory of sponsored search is discussed in detail in [15].

- **Interdependent click probabilities.** The "separable" assumption implies that an advertiser's click probability depends only on the properties and position of her own ad. This ignores the other ads on the search results page, which certainly affect the user experience, and therefore the click probability of this advertiser. We discuss this further in Section 4.5.

- **Branding.** The private click-value model assumes that a click is what the advertiser is ultimately interested in. However a *branding* advertiser could be interested in her ad appearing in a high position, but not really care whether or not it gets a click (other than due to the fact that they only pay if it does). (Indeed, a recent empirical study by the Interactive Advertising Bureau and Nielsen//NetRatings concluded that higher ad positions in paid search have a significant brand awareness effect [38].) Thus we might be interested in an auction where an advertiser can express the lowest position she is willing to tolerate for her ad. This is the approach taken in [3], where Theorem 4.1 is generalized to this setting.

- **Conversions.** The private click-value model also assumes that each click is worth the same to an advertiser, which is not always the case in practice. Indeed many advertisers track whether or not a click leads to a *conversion*, which is some sort of event on the linked page (e.g., a sale, a sign-up, etc.) Given this data, the advertiser can learn which keywords lead to conversions and therefore which clicks are worth more to them.

- **Estimating various parameters.** Most work in the context of the game theory of sponsored search has assumed that the parameters like click-through rate and position visibility are known. However, estimating these parameters is a difficult task (e.g., [36, 31]). Indeed, there is an inherent tradeoff between learning these parameters and applying them; one cannot learn that an ad has a bad ctr unless it is exposed to the user, but then it was a bad idea to show it in the first place. This "exploration/exploitation" tradeoff turns out to be related to the "multi-armed bandit" problem (see e.g. [21, 44, 16]).

• **Incomplete Knowledge.** Both the advertisers and the search engine have incomplete knowledge of the "inventory" available to them, since they do not know which queries will arrive. In addition the bidders do not know the other bids or click-through rates. This makes the advertiser's optimization problem much more difficult (see e.g., [28, 7, 9, 17, 43, 30, 45, 40, 39]). From the search engine's point of view, we can model incomplete knowledge of the future as an *online algorithm*; see e.g. [34, 39, 35, 44, 32, 33, 1, 21, 19, 20].

4.3 The Advertiser's Point of View: Budget Optimization

The perspective in this section is the advertisers. The challenge from an advertiser's point of view is to understand and interact with the auction mechanism. The advertiser determines a set of keywords of their interest[1] and then must create ads, set the bids for each keyword, and provide a total (often daily) budget.

While the effect of an ad campaign in any medium is a sophisticated phenomenon that is difficult to quantify, one commonly accepted (and easily quantified) notion in search-based advertising on the Internet is to *maximize the number of clicks*. The Internet search companies are supportive towards advertisers and provide statistics about the history of click volumes and prediction about the future performance of various keywords. Still, this is a sophisticated problem for the following reasons (among others):

• Individual keywords have significantly different characteristics from each other; e.g., while "fishing" is a broad keyword that matches many user queries and has many competing advertisers, "humane fishing bait" is a niche keyword that matches only a few queries, but might have less competition.
• There are complex *interactions* between keywords because a user query may match two or more keywords, since the advertiser is trying to cover all the possible keywords in some domain. In effect the advertiser ends up competing with herself.

As a result, the advertisers face a challenging optimization problem. The focus of the work in [17] is to solve this optimization problem.

Problem Formulation. We present a short discussion and formulation of the optimization problem faced by advertisers; a more detailed description is in Section 4.3.1.

---

[1] The choice of keywords is related to the domain-knowledge of the advertiser, user behavior and strategic considerations. Internet search companies provide the advertisers with summaries of the query traffic which is useful for them to optimize their keyword choices interactively. We do not directly address the choice of keywords in this section, which is addressed elsewhere [39].

A given advertiser sees the state of the auctions for search-based advertising as follows. There is a set K of keywords of interest; in practice, even small advertisers typically have a large set K. There is a set Q of queries posed by the users. For each query $q \in Q$, there are functions giving the $\text{clicks}_q(b)$ and $\text{cost}_q(b)$ that result from bidding a particular amount b in the auction for that query, which we will see a more formal model of in the next section. There is a bipartite graph G on the two vertex sets representing K and Q. For any query $q \in Q$, the neighbors of q in K are the keywords that are said to "match" the query q.[2]

The *budget optimization problem* is as follows. Given graph G together with the functions $\text{clicks}_q(\cdot)$ and $\text{cost}_q(\cdot)$ on the queries, as well as a budget U, determine the bids b_k for each keyword $k \in K$ such that $\sum_q \text{clicks}_q(b_q)$ is maximized subject to $\sum_q \text{cost}_q(b_q) \le U$, where the "effective bid" b_q on a query is some function of the keyword bids in the neighborhood of q.

While we can cast this problem as a traditional optimization problem, there are different challenges in practice depending on the advertiser's access to the query and graph information, and indeed the reliability of this information (e.g., it could be based on unstable historical data). Thus it is important to find solutions to this problem that not only get many clicks, but are also simple, robust and less reliant on the information. The notion of a "uniform" strategy is defined in [17] which is essentially a strategy that bids uniformly on all keywords. Since this type of strategy obviates the need to know anything about the particulars of the graph, and effectively aggregates the click and cost functions on the queries, it is quite robust, and thus desirable in practice. What is surprising is that uniform strategy actually performs well, which is proved in [17].

Main Results and Technical Overview. Some positive and negative results are given in [17] for the budget optimization problem:

- Nearly all formulations of the problem are NP-Hard. In cases slightly more general than the formulation above, where the clicks have weights, the problem is inapproximable better than a factor of $1 - \frac{1}{e}$, unless P=NP.
- There is a $(1 - 1/e)$-approximation algorithm for the budget optimization problem. The strategy found by the algorithm is a *two-bid uniform strategy*, which means that it randomizes between bidding some value b_1 on all keywords, and bidding some other value b_2 on all keywords until the budget is exhausted[3]. This approximation ratio is tight for uniform strategies. There is also a $(1/2)$-approximation algorithm that offers a *single-bid uniform strategy*, only using one value b_1. (This is tight for single-bid uniform strategies.) These strategies can be computed in time nearly linear in $|Q| + |K|$, the input size.

Uniform strategies may appear to be naive in first consideration because the keywords vary significantly in their click and cost functions, and there may be complex

---

[2] The particulars of the matching rule are determined by the Internet search company; here we treat the function as arbitrary.

[3] This type of strategy can also be interpreted as bidding one value (on all keywords) for part of the day, and a different value for the rest of the day.

interaction between them when multiple keywords are relevant to a query. After all, the optimum can configure arbitrary bids on each of the keywords. Even for the simple case when the graph is a *matching*, the optimal algorithm involves placing different bids on different keywords via a knapsack-like packing (Section 4.3.1). So, it might be surprising that a simple two-bid uniform strategy is 63% or more effective compared to the optimum. In fact, our proof is stronger, showing that this strategy is 63% effective against a strictly more powerful adversary who can bid independently on the *individual queries*, i.e., not be constrained by the interaction imposed by the graph G.

We will also look at the simulations conducted in [17] using real auction data from Google. The results of these simulations suggest that uniform bidding strategies could be useful in practice. However, important questions remain about (among other things) alternate bidding goals, on-line or stochastic bidding models [35], and game-theoretic concerns [8], which we briefly discuss in Section 4.3.4.

4.3.1 Modeling a Keyword Auction

We begin by considering the case of a *single* keyword that matches a *single* user query. In this section we define the notion of a "query landscape" that describes the relationship between the advertiser's bid and what will happen on this query as a result of this bid [27]. This definition will be central to the discussion as we continue to more general cases.

The search results page for a query contains p possible positions in which our ad can appear. We denote the highest (most favorable) position by 1 and lowest by p. Assuming a separable user model, associated with each position i is a value $\beta[i]$ that denotes the click probability if the ad appears in position i.[4] We assume throughout this section that that $\beta[i] \leq \beta[j]$ if $j < i$, that is, higher positions receive at least as many clicks as lower positions.

In order to place an ad on this page, we must enter the *GSP auction* that is carried out among all advertisers that have submitted a bid on a keyword that matches the user's query. We will refer to such an auction as a *query auction*, to emphasize that there is an auction for each query rather than for each keyword. In GSP, the advertisers are ranked in decreasing order of bid, and each advertiser is assigned a price equal to the amount bid by the advertiser below them in the ranking. Let $(b[1],\ldots,b[p])$ denote the bids of the top p advertisers in this query auction. For notational convenience, we assume that $b[0] = \infty$ and $b[p] = \beta[p] = 0$. Since the auction is a generalized second price auction, higher bids win higher positions; i.e. $b[i] \geq b[i+1]$. Suppose that we bid b on some keyword that matches the user's query, then our position is defined by the largest $b[i]$ that is at most b, that is,

---

[4] We leave out the ad-specific factor α_i from this section for clarity, but all the results in [17] generalize to this case as well.

$$\text{pos}(b) = \arg\max_i (b[i] : b[i] \leq b). \tag{4.1}$$

Since we only pay if the user clicks (and that happens with probability $\beta[i]$), our expected *cost* for winning position i would be $\text{cost}[i] = \beta[i] \cdot b[i]$, where $i = \text{pos}(b)$. We use $\text{cost}_q(b)$ and $\text{clicks}_q(b)$ to denote the expected cost and clicks that result from having a bid b that qualifies for a query auction q, and thus

$$\text{cost}_q(b) = \beta[i] \cdot b[i] \quad \text{where } i = \text{pos}(b), \tag{4.2}$$

$$\text{clicks}_q(b) = \beta[i] \quad \text{where } i = \text{pos}(b). \tag{4.3}$$

When the context is clear, we drop the subscript q. The following observations about cost and clicks follow immediately from the definitions and equations (4.1), (4.2) and (4.3). We use $\mathbb{R}_+$ to denote the nonnegative reals.

Proposition 4.1. *For $b \in \mathbb{R}_+$,*

1. *The tuple $(\text{cost}_q(b), \text{clicks}_q(b))$ can only take on one of a finite set of values $V_q = \{(\text{cost}[1], \beta[1]), \ldots, (\text{cost}[p], \beta[p])\}$.*
2. *Both $\text{cost}_q(b)$ and $\text{clicks}_q(b)$ are non-decreasing functions of b.*
3. *Cost-per-click (cpc) $\text{cost}_q(b)/\text{clicks}_q(b)$ is non-decreasing in b, and is always at most the bid; i.e., $\text{cost}_q(b)/\text{clicks}_q(b) \leq b$.*

Query Landscapes We can summarize the data contained in the functions $\text{cost}(b)$ and $\text{clicks}(b)$ as a collection of points in a plot of cost vs. clicks, which we refer to as a *landscape*. For example, for a query with four slots, a landscape might look like Table 4.1.

bid range	cost per click	cost	clicks
[$2.60, ∞)	$2.60	$1.30	.5
[$2.00, $2.60)	$2.00	$0.90	.45
[$1.60, $2.00)	$1.60	$0.40	.25
[$0.50, $1.60)	$0.50	$0.10	.2
[$0, $0.50)	$0	$0	0

Table 4.1 A *landscape* for a query

It is convenient to represent this data graphically as in Figure 4.2 (ignore the dashed line for now). Here we graph clicks as a function of cost. Observe that in this graph, the cpc $(\text{cost}(b)/\text{clicks}(b))$ of each point is the reciprocal of the slope of the line from the origin to the point. Since $\text{cost}(b)$, $\text{clicks}(b)$ and $\text{cost}(b)/\text{clicks}(b)$ are non-decreasing, the slope of the line from the origin to successive points on the plot decreases. This condition is slightly weaker than concavity.

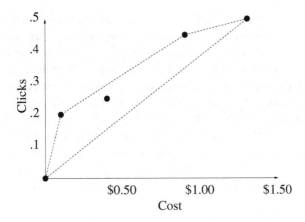

Fig. 4.2 A bid landscape.

Suppose we would like to solve the budget optimization problem for a single query landscape.[5] As we increase our bid from zero, our cost increases and our expected number of clicks increases, and so we simply submit the highest bid such that we remain within our budget.

One problem we see right away is that since there are only a finite set of points in this landscape, we may not be able to target arbitrary budgets efficiently. Suppose in the example from Table 4.1 and Figure 4.2 that we had a budget of $1.00. Bidding between $2.00 and $2.60 uses only $0.90, and so we are under-spending. Bidding more than $2.60 is not an option, since we would then incur a cost of $1.30 and overspend our budget.

Randomized strategies To rectify this problem and better utilize our available budget, we allow *randomized bidding strategies*. Let $\mathscr{B}$ be a distribution on bids $b \in \mathbb{R}_+$. Now we define $cost(\mathscr{B}) = E_{b \sim \mathscr{B}}[cost(b)]$ and $clicks(\mathscr{B}) = E_{b \sim \mathscr{B}}[clicks(b)]$. Graphically, the possible values of $(cost(\mathscr{B}), clicks(\mathscr{B}))$ lie in the convex hull of the landscape points. This is represented in Figure 4.2 by the dashed line.

To find a bid distribution $\mathscr{B}$ that maximizes clicks subject to a budget, we simply draw a vertical line on the plot where the cost is equal to the budget, and find the highest point on this line in the convex hull. This point will always be the convex combination of at most *two* original landscape points which themselves lie *on* the convex hull. Thus, given the point on the convex hull, it is easy to compute a distribution on two bids which led to this point. Summarizing,

Lemma 4.1. [17] If an advertiser is bidding on one query, subject to a budget U, then the optimal strategy is to pick a convex combination of (at most) two bids which are at the endpoints of the line on the convex hull at the highest point for cost U.

---

[5] Of course it is a bit unrealistic to imagine that an advertiser would have to worry about a budget if only one user query was being considered; however one could imagine multiple instances of the same query and the problem scales.

There is one subtlety in this formulation. Given any bidding strategy, randomized or otherwise, the resulting cost is itself a random variable representing the expected cost. Thus if our budget constraint is a hard budget, we have to deal with the difficulties that arise if our strategy would be over budget. Therefore, we think of our budget constraint as *soft*, that is, we only require that our expected cost be less than the budget. In practice, the budget is often an average daily budget, and thus we don't worry if we exceed it one day, as long as we are meeting the budget in expectation. Further, either the advertiser or the search engine (possibly both), monitor the cost incurred over the day; hence, the advertiser's bid can be changed to zero for part of the day, so that the budget is not overspent.[6] Thus in the remainder of this section, we will formulate a budget constraint that only needs to be respected in expectation.

Multiple Queries: a Knapsack Problem As a warm-up, we will consider next the case when we have a set of queries, each with its own landscape. We want to bid on each query independently subject to our budget: the resulting optimization problem is a small generalization of the *fractional knapsack* problem, and was solved in [27].

The first step of the algorithm is to take the convex hull of each landscape, as in Figure 4.2, and remove any landscape points not on the convex hull. Each piecewise linear section of the curve represents the incremental number of clicks and cost incurred by moving one's bid from one particular value to another. We regard these "pieces" as *items* in an instance of fractional knapsack with *value* equal to the incremental number of clicks and *size* equal to the incremental cost. More precisely, for each piece connecting two consecutive bids b' and b'' on the convex hull, we create a knapsack item with value $[\text{clicks}(b'') - \text{clicks}(b')]$ and size $[\text{cost}(b'') - \text{cost}(b')]$. We then emulate the greedy algorithm for knapsack, sorting by value/size (cost-per-click), and choosing greedily until the budget is exhausted.

In this reduction to knapsack we have ignored the fact that some of the pieces come from the same landscape and cannot be treated independently. However, since each curve is concave, the pieces that come from a particular query curve are in increasing order of cost-per-click; thus from each landscape we have chosen for our "knapsack" a set of pieces that form a prefix of the curve.

4.3.1.1 Keyword Interaction

In reality, search advertisers can bid on a large set of keywords, each of them qualifying for a different (possibly overlapping) set of queries, but most search engines do not allow an advertiser to appear twice in the same search results page.[7] Thus, if an advertiser has a bid on two different keywords that match the same query, this conflict must be resolved somehow. For example, if an advertiser has a bid out on the keywords "shoes" and "high-heel," then if a user issues the query "high-heel shoes," it will match on two different keywords. The search engine specifies, in advance, a

---

[6] See https://adwords.google.com/support/bin/answer.py?answer=22183, for example.

[7] See https://adwords.google.com/support/bin/answer.py?answer=14179, for example.

rule for resolution based on the query the keyword and the bid. A natural rule is to take the keyword with the highest bid, which we adopt here, but our results apply to other resolution rules.

We model the keyword interaction problem using an undirected bipartite graph $G = (K \cup Q, E)$ where K is a set of keywords and Q is a set of queries. Each $q \in Q$ has an associated landscape, as defined by $\text{cost}_q(b)$ and $\text{clicks}_q(b)$. An edge $(k,q) \in E$ means that keyword k matches query q.

The advertiser can control their individual *keyword bid vector* $\mathbf{a} \in \mathbb{R}_+^{|K|}$ specifying a bid $\mathbf{a}_k$ for each keyword $k \in K$. (For now, we do not consider randomized bids, but we will introduce that shortly.) Given a particular bid vector $\mathbf{a}$ on the keywords, we use the resolution rule of taking the maximum to define the "effective bid" on query q as

$$b_q(\mathbf{a}) = \max_{k:(k,q)\in E} \mathbf{a}_k.$$

By submitting a bid vector $\mathbf{a}$, the advertiser receives some number of clicks and pays some cost on each keyword. We use the term *spend* to denote the total cost; similarly, we use the term *traffic* to denote the total number of clicks:

$$\text{spend}(\mathbf{a}) = \sum_{q \in Q} \text{cost}_q(b_q(\mathbf{a})); \quad \text{traffic}(\mathbf{a}) = \sum_{q \in Q} \text{clicks}_q(b_q(\mathbf{a}))$$

We also allow randomized strategies, where an advertiser gives a distribution $\mathscr{A}$ over bid vectors $\mathbf{a} \in \mathbb{R}_+^{|K|}$. The resulting spend and traffic are given by

$$\text{spend}(\mathscr{A}) = E_{\mathbf{a} \sim \mathscr{A}}[\text{spend}(\mathbf{a})]; \quad \text{traffic}(\mathscr{A}) = E_{\mathbf{a} \sim \mathscr{A}}[\text{traffic}(\mathbf{a})]$$

We can now state the problem in its full generality:

BUDGET OPTIMIZATION
Input: a budget U, a keyword-query graph $G = (K \cup Q, E)$, and landscapes $(\text{cost}_q(\cdot), \text{clicks}_q(\cdot))$ for each $q \in Q$.
Find: a distribution $\mathscr{A}$ over bid vectors $\mathbf{a} \in \mathbb{R}_+^{|K|}$ such that $\text{spend}(\mathscr{A}) \leq U$ and $\text{traffic}(\mathscr{A})$ is maximized.

We conclude this section with a small example to illustrate some feature of the budget optimization problem. Suppose you have two keywords $K = \{u, v\}$ and two queries $Q = \{x, y\}$ and edges $E = \{(u,x), (u,y), (v,y)\}$. Suppose query x has one position with ctr $\beta^x[1] = 1.0$, and there is one bid $b_1^x = \$1$. Query y has two positions with ctrs $\beta^y[1] = \beta^y[2] = 1.0$, and bids $b_1^y = \$\varepsilon$ and $b_2^y = \$1$ To get any clicks from x, an advertiser must bid at least $\$1$ on u. However, because of the structure of the graph, if the advertiser sets b_u to $\$1$, then his effective bid is $\$1$ on both x *and* y.

Thus he must trade-off between getting the clicks from x and getting the bargain of a click for $\$\varepsilon$ that would be possible otherwise.

4.3.2 Uniform Bidding Strategies

As shown in [17], solving the BUDGET OPTIMIZATION problem in its full generality is difficult. In addition, it may be difficult to reason about strategies that involve arbitrary distributions over arbitrary bid vectors. Advertisers generally prefer strategies that are easy to understand, evaluate and use within their larger goals. With this motivation, we look at restricted classes of strategies that we can easily compute, explain and analyze.

We define a *uniform bidding strategy* to be a distribution $\mathscr{A}$ over bid vectors $\mathbf{a} \in \mathbb{R}_{+}^{|K|}$ where each bid vector in the distribution is of the form $(b, b, \ldots, b)$ for some real-valued bid b. In other words, each vector in the distribution bids the same value on every keyword.

Uniform strategies have several advantages. First, they do not depend on the edges of the interaction graph, since all effective bids on queries are the same. Thus, they are effective in the face of limited or noisy information about the keyword interaction graph. Second, uniform strategies are also independent of the priority rule being used. Third, any algorithm that gives an approximation guarantee will then be valid for *any* interaction graph over those keywords and queries.

Define a *two-bid strategy* to be a uniform strategy which puts non-zero weight on at most two bid vectors. Given the landscapes for all the queries, we can compute the best uniform strategy in linear time; the proof also directly implies that there is always an optimal two-bid strategy:

Lemma 4.2. [17] Given an instance of BUDGET OPTIMIZATION in which there are a total of N points in all the landscapes, we can find the best uniform strategy in $O(N \log N)$ time. Furthermore, this strategy will always be a two-bid strategy.

The authors in [17] also consider *single-bid* strategies, which are uniform strategies that put non-zero weight on at most one *non-zero* vector, i.e. advertiser randomizes between bidding a certain amount b^* on all keywords, and not bidding at all. A single-bid strategy is even easier to implement in practice than a two-bid strategy. For example, the search engines often allow advertisers to set a maximum daily budget. In this case, the advertiser would simply bid b^* until her budget runs out, and the ad serving system would remove her from all subsequent auctions until the end of the day. One could also use an "ad scheduling" tool offered by some search companies[8] to implement this strategy. The best single-bid strategy can also be computed easily from the aggregate landscape. The optimal strategy for a budget U will either be the point x s.t. $\mathrm{cost}(x)$ is as large as possible without exceeding U, or a convex combination of zero and the point y, where $\mathrm{cost}(y)$ is as small as possible while larger than U.

---

[8] See https://adwords.google.com/support/bin/answer.py?answer=33227, for example.

Approximation Guarantees of Uniform Strategies. In fact, not only are uniform strategies easy to optimize over, they are also guaranteed to have good performance compared to the optimal solution. In the case of single-bid strategies, we have the following:

Theorem 4.2. [17] There always exists a uniform single-bid strategy that is $\frac{1}{2}$-optimal. Furthermore, for any $\varepsilon > 0$ there exists an instance for which all single-bid strategies are at most $(\frac{1}{2} + \varepsilon)$-optimal.

For general uniform strategies—where a two-bid strategy is always optimal—[17] proves a tighter approximation ratio:

Theorem 4.3. [17] There always exists a uniform bidding strategy that is $(1 - \frac{1}{e})$-optimal. Furthermore, for any $\varepsilon > 0$, there exists an instance for which all uniform strategies are at most $(1 - \frac{1}{e} + \varepsilon)$-optimal.

Thus if given full information about the landscapes, a bidder has an efficient strategy to get a large fraction of the available clicks at her budget. But perhaps more importantly, these theorems show that the simple uniform bidding heuristic can perform well.

4.3.3 Experimental Results

The authors in [17] ran simulations using the data available at Google which we briefly summarize here. They took a large advertising campaign, and, using the set of keywords in the campaign, computed three different curves (see Figure 4.3) for three different bidding strategies. The x-axis is the budget (units removed), and the y-axis is the number of clicks obtained (again without units) by the optimal bid(s) under each respective strategy. "Query bidding" represents the (unachievable) upper bound Ω, bidding on each query independently. The "uniform bidding" curves represent the results of applying the algorithm: "deterministic" uses a single bid level, while "randomized" uses a distribution. For reference, we include the lower bound of a $(e-1)/e$ fraction of the top curve.

The data clearly demonstrate that the best single uniform bid obtains almost all the possible clicks in practice. Of course in a more realistic environment without full knowledge, it is not always possible to find the best such bid, so further investigation is required to make this approach useful. However, just knowing that there is such a bid available should make the on-line versions of the problem simpler.

4.3.4 Extensions

The algorithmic result presented here gives an intriguing heuristic in practice: bid a single value b on all keywords; at the end of the day, if the budget is under-spent,

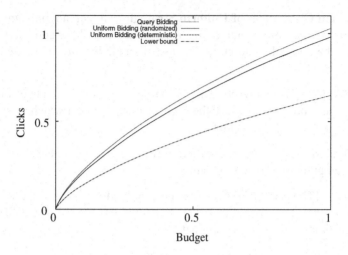

Fig. 4.3 An example with real data.

adjust b to be higher; if budget is overspent, adjust b to be lower; else, maintain b. If the scenario does not change from day to day, this simple strategy will have the same theoretical properties as the one-bid strategy, and in practice, is likely to be much better. Of course the scenario does change, however, and so coming up with a "stochastic" bidding strategy remains an important open direction, explored somewhat by [35, 39].

Another interesting generalization is to consider weights on the clicks, which is a way to model *conversions*. (A conversion corresponds to an action on the part of the user who clicked through to the advertiser site; e.g., a sale or an account sign-up.) Finally, we have looked at this system as a black box returning clicks as a function of bid, whereas in reality it is a complex repeated game involving multiple advertisers. In [8], it was shown that when a set of advertisers use a strategy similar to the one suggested in [17], under a slightly modified first-price auction, the prices approach a well-understood market equilibrium.

4.4 The Search Engine's Point of View: Offline Slot Scheduling

In the previous section we saw that when we take the GSP auction as given, and view the world through the lens of the bidder, the practical problem becomes more complex than what the individual auction was designed for. But we could take the question back to the search engine and ask if there is a more general mechanism that regards the entire day's worth of queries as part of a single overall game. This question is addressed in [18], where the *Offline Ad Slot Scheduling* problem is defined: given a set of bidders with bids (per click) and budgets (per day), and a set of slots over the entire day where we know the expected number of clicks in each slot, find a schedule that places bidders into slots. The schedule must not place a bidder into two different slots at the same time. In addition, we must find a price for each bidder that does not exceed the bidder's budget constraint, nor their per-click bid. (See below for a formal statement of the problem.)

A good algorithm for this problem will have high revenue. Also, we would like the algorithm to be *truthful*; i.e., each bidder will be incented to report her true bid and budget. In order to prove something like this, we need a *utility function* for the bidder that captures the degree to which she is happy with her allocation. Natural models in this context (with clicks, bids and budgets) are *click-maximization*—where she wishes to maximize her number of clicks subject to her personal bid and budget constraints, or *profit-maximization*—where she wishes to maximize her profit (clicks × profit per click). The work in [18] is focused on click-maximization.[9]

We present the efficient mechanism of [18] for *Offline Ad Slot Scheduling*, which is truthful under click-maximization. Also, the revenue-optimal mechanism for *Offline Ad Slot Scheduling* is not truthful, but has a Nash equilibrium (under the same utility model) whose outcome is equivalent to the [18] mechanism; this result is strong evidence that the mechanism has desirable revenue properties.

Problem Definition. The *Offline Ad Slot Scheduling* problem [18] is defined as follows. We have $n > 1$ bidders interested in clicks. Each bidder i has a budget B_i and a maximum cost-per-click (max-cpc) m_i. Given a number of clicks c_i, and a price per click p, the utility u_i of bidder i is c_i if both the true max-cpc and the true budget are satisfied, and $-\infty$ otherwise. In other words, $u_i = c_i$ if $p \leq m_i$ and $c_i p \leq B_i$; and $u_i = -\infty$ otherwise. We have n' advertising slots where slot i receives D_i clicks during the time interval $[0, 1]$. We assume $D_1 > \cdots > D_{n'}$.

In a *schedule*, each bidder is assigned to a set of (slot, time interval) pairs $(j, [\sigma, \tau))$, where $j \leq n'$ and $0 \leq \sigma < \tau \leq 1$. A *feasible schedule* is one where no more than one bidder is assigned to a slot at any given time, and no bidder is assigned to more than one slot at any given time. (In other words, the intervals for a particular slot do not overlap, and the intervals for a particular bidder do not overlap.) A feasible schedule can be applied as follows: when a user query comes at some time $\sigma \in [0, 1]$, the schedule for that time instant is used to populate the ad slots. If we assume that clicks come at a constant rate throughout the interval $[0, 1]$, the number of clicks a bidder is expected to receive from a schedule is the sum of $(\tau - \sigma)D_j$ over all pairs $(j, [\sigma, \tau))$ in her schedule.[10]

---

[9] This choice is in part motivated by the presence of budgets, which have a natural interpretation in this application: if an overall advertising campaign allocates a fixed portion of its budget to online media, then the agent responsible for that budget is incented to spend the entire budget to maximize exposure. In contrast, under the profit-maximizing utility, a weak motivation for budgets is a limit on liquidity. Also, this choice of utility function is out of analytical necessity: Borgs et al. [8] show that under some reasonable assumptions, truthful mechanisms are impossible under a profit-maximizing utility.

[10] All the results of [18] generalize to the setting where each bidder i has a bidder-specific factor α_i in the click-through rate and thus receives $(\tau - \sigma)\alpha_i D_j$ clicks (see Section 4.4.3). We leave this out for clarity.

A *mechanism* for *Offline Ad Slot Scheduling* takes as input a declared budget B_i and declared max-cpc (the "bid") b_i, and returns a feasible schedule, as well as a price per click $p_i \leq b_i$ for each bidder. The schedule gives some number c_i of clicks to each bidder i that must respect the budget at the given price; i.e., we have $p_i c_i \leq B_i$. The *revenue* of a mechanism is $\sum_i p_i c_i$. A mechanism is *truthful* if it is a weakly dominant strategy to declare one's true budget and max-cpc; i.e., for any bidder i, given any set of bids and budgets declared by the other bidders, declaring her true budget B_i and max-cpc m_i maximizes u_i. In this setting, a (pure strategy) Nash equilibrium is a set of declared bids and budgets such that no bidder wants to change her declaration of bid or budget, given that all other declarations stay fixed. An ε-*Nash equilibrium* is a set of bids and budgets where no bidder can increase her u_i by more than ε by changing her bid or budget.

Throughout the presentation we assume some arbitrary lexicographic ordering on the bidders, that does not necessarily match the subscripts. When we compare two bids b_i and $b_{i'}$ we say that $b_i \succ b_{i'}$ iff either $b_i > b_{i'}$, or $b_i = b_{i'}$ but i occurs first lexicographically.

We comment that for this problem one is tempted to apply a *Fisher Market* model: here m divisible goods are available to n buyers with money B_i, and $u_{ij}(x)$ denotes i's utility of receiving x amount of good j. It is known [6, 14, 11] that under certain conditions a vector of prices for goods exists (and can be found efficiently [12]) such that the *market clears*, in that there is no surplus of goods, and all the money is spent. The natural way to apply a Fisher model to a slot auction is to regard the slots as commodities and have the utilities be in proportion to the number of clicks. However this becomes problematic because there does not seem to be a way to encode the scheduling constraints in the Fisher model; this constraint could make an apparently "market-clearing" equilibrium infeasible.

4.4.1 Special Case: One Slot

In this section we consider the case $k = 1$, where there is only one advertising slot, with some number $D := D_1$ of clicks. A truthful mechanism for this case is derived by first considering the two extreme cases of infinite bids and infinite budgets.

Suppose all budgets $B_i = \infty$. Then, our input amounts to bids $b_1 \succ b_2 \succ \ldots \succ b_n$. The obvious mechanism is simply to give all the clicks to the highest bidder. We charge bidder 1 her full price $p_1 = b_1$. A simple argument shows that reporting the truth is a weakly dominant strategy for this mechanism. Clearly all bidders will report $b_i \leq m_i$, since the price is set to b_i if they win. The losing bidders cannot gain from decreasing b_i. The winning bidder can lower her price by lowering b_i, but this will not gain her any more clicks, since she is already getting all D of them.

Now suppose all bids $b_i = \infty$; our input is just a set of budgets $B_1, \ldots, B_n$, and we need to allocate D clicks, with no ceiling on the per-click price. Here we apply a simple rule known as *proportional sharing* (see [26, 25][11]): Let $\mathscr{B} = \sum_i B_i$. Now to each bidder i, allocate $(B_i/\mathscr{B})D$ clicks. Set all prices the same: $p_i = p = \mathscr{B}/D$. The mechanism guarantees that each bidder exactly spends her budget, thus no bidder will report $B_i' > B_i$. Now suppose some bidder reports $B_i' = B_i - \Delta$, for $\Delta > 0$. Then this bidder is allocated $D(B_i - \Delta)/(\mathscr{B} - \Delta)$ clicks, which is less than $D(B_i/\mathscr{B})$, since $n > 1$ and all $B_i > 0$.

Greedy First-Price Mechanism. A natural mechanism for the general single-slot case is to solve the associated "fractional knapsack" problem, and charge bidders their bid; i.e., starting with the highest bidder, greedily add bidders to the allocation, charging them their bid, until all the clicks are allocated. We refer to this as the *greedy first-price* (GFP) mechanism. Though natural (and revenue-maximizing as a function of bids) this is easily seen to be not truthful:

Example 4.1. [18] Suppose there are two bidders and $D = 120$ clicks. Bidder 1 has ($m_1 = \$2$, $B_1 = \$100$) and bidder 2 has ($m_2 = \$1$, $B_2 = \$50$). In the GFP mechanism, if both bidders tell the truth, then bidder 1 gets 50 clicks for \$2 each, and 50 of the remaining 70 clicks go to bidder 2 for \$1 each. However, if bidder 1 instead declares $b_1 = \$1 + \varepsilon$, then she gets (roughly) 100 clicks, and bidder 2 is left with (roughly) 20 clicks.

The problem here is that the high bidders can get away with bidding lower, thus getting a lower price. The difference between this and the unlimited-budget case above is that a lower price now results in more clicks. It turns out that in equilibrium, this mechanism will result in an allocation where a prefix of the top bidders are allocated, but their prices equalize to (roughly) the lowest bid in the prefix (as in the example above).

The Price-Setting Mechanism. An equilibrium allocation of GFP can be computed directly via the following mechanism, which [18] refers to as the *price-setting (PS) mechanism*. Essentially this is a descending price mechanism: the price stops descending when the bidders willing to pay at that price have enough budget to purchase all the clicks. We have to be careful at the moment a bidder is added to the pool of the willing bidders; if this new bidder has a large enough budget, then suddenly the willing bidders have *more* than enough budget to pay for all of the clicks. To compensate, the mechanism decreases this "threshold" bidder's effective budget until the clicks are paid for exactly.

---

[11] Nguyen and Tardos [37] give a generalization of [25] to general polyhedral constraints, and also discuss the application to sponsored search. Both their bidding language and utility function differ from [18], but it would be interesting to see if there are any connections between their approach and [18].

Price-Setting (PS) Mechanism (Single Slot) [18]
- Assume wlog that $b_1 \succ b_2 \succ \ldots \succ b_n \geq 0$.
- Let k be the first bidder such that $b_{k+1} \leq \sum_{i=1}^{k} B_i/D$. Compute price $p = \min\{\sum_{i=1}^{k} B_i/D, b_k\}$.
- Allocate B_i/p clicks to each $i \leq k-1$. Allocate $\hat{B}_k/p$ clicks to bidder k, where $\hat{B}_k = pD - \sum_{i=1}^{k-1} B_i$.

Example 4.2. [18] Suppose there are three bidders with $b_1 = \$2$, $b_2 = \$1$, $b_3 = \$0.25$ and $B_1 = \$100$, $B_2 = \$50$, $B_3 = \$80$, and $D = 300$ clicks. Running the PS mechanism, we get $k = 2$ since $B_1/D = 1/3 < b_2 = \$1$, but $(B_1 + B_2)/D = \$0.50 \geq b_3 = \$0.25$. The price is set to $\min\{\$0.50, \$1\} = \$0.50$, and bidders 1 and 2 get 200 and 100 clicks at that price, respectively. There is no threshold bidder.

Example 4.3. [18] Suppose now bidder 2 changes her bid to $b_2 = \$0.40$ (everything else remains the same as Example 4.2). We still get $k = 2$ since $B_1/D = 1/3 < b_2 = \$0.40$. But now the price is set to $\min\{\$0.50, \$0.40\} = \$0.40$, and bidders 1 and 2 get 250 and 50 clicks at that price, respectively. Note that bidder 2 is now a threshold bidder, does not use her entire budget, and gets fewer clicks.

Theorem 4.4. [18] The price-setting mechanism (single slot) is truthful.

Price-Setting Mechanism Computes Nash Equilibrium of GFP. Consider the greedy first-price auction in which the highest bidder receives B_1/b_1 clicks, the second B_2/b_2 clicks and so on, until the supply of D clicks is exhausted. It is immediate that truthfully reporting budgets is a dominant strategy in this mechanism, since when a bidder is considered, her reported budget is exhausted as much as possible, at a fixed price. However, reporting $b_i = m_i$ is *not* a dominant strategy. Nevertheless, it turns out that GFP has an equilibrium whose outcome is (roughly) the same as the PS mechanism. One cannot show that there is a plain Nash equilibrium because of the way ties are resolved lexicographically, so [18] proves instead that the bidders reach an ε-Nash equilibrium:

Theorem 4.5. *Suppose the PS mechanism is run on the truthful input, resulting in price p and clicks $c_1, \ldots, c_n$ for each bidder. Then, for any $\varepsilon > 0$ there is a pure-strategy ε-Nash equilibrium of the GFP mechanism where each bidder receives $c_i \pm \varepsilon$ clicks.*

4.4.2 Multiple Slots

Generalizing to multiple slots makes the scheduling constraint nontrivial. Now instead of splitting a pool of D clicks arbitrarily, we need to assign clicks that correspond to a feasible schedule of bidders to slots. The conditions under which this is possible add a complexity that needs to be incorporated into the mechanism.

As in the single-slot case it will be instructive to consider first the cases of infinite bids or budgets. Suppose all $B_i = \infty$. In this case, the input consists of bids only $b_1 \succ b_2 \succ \ldots \succ b_n$. Naturally, what we do here is rank by bid, and allocate the slots to the bidders in that order. Since each budget is infinite, we can always set the prices p_i equal to the bids b_i. By the same logic as in the single-slot case, this is easily seen to be truthful. In the other case, when $b_i = \infty$, there is a lot more work to do.

Without loss of generality, we may assume the number of slots equals the number of bids (i.e., $n' = n$); if this is not the case, then we add dummy bidders with $B_i = b_i = 0$, or dummy slots with $D_i = 0$, as appropriate. We keep this assumption for the remainder of the section.

Assigning Slots Using a Classical Scheduling Algorithm. First we give an important lemma that characterizes the conditions under which a set of bidders can be allocated to a set of slots, which turns out to be just a restatement of a classical result [24] from scheduling theory.

Lemma 4.3. [24, 18] Suppose we would like to assign an arbitrary set $\{1, \ldots, k\}$ of bidders to a set of slots $\{1, \ldots, k\}$ with $D_1 > \cdots > D_k$. Then, a click allocation $c_1 \geq \ldots \geq c_k$ is feasible iff

$$c_1 + \cdots + c_\ell \leq D_1 + \cdots + D_\ell \quad \text{for all } \ell = 1, \ldots, k. \tag{4.4}$$

Proof. In scheduling theory, we say a *job* with *service requirement* x is a task that needs x/s units of time to complete on a *machine* with *speed* s. The question of whether there is a feasible allocation is equivalent to the following scheduling problem: Given k jobs with service requirements $x_i = c_i$, and k machines with speeds $s_i = D_i$, is there a schedule of jobs to machines (with preemption allowed) that completes in one unit of time?

As shown in [24, 22], the optimal schedule for this problem (a.k.a. $Q|pmtn|C_{\max}$) can be found efficiently by the *level algorithm*, and the schedule completes in time $\max_{\ell \leq k}\{\sum_{i=1}^{\ell} x_i / \sum_{i=1}^{\ell} s_i\}$. Thus, the conditions of the lemma are exactly the conditions under which the schedule completes in one unit of time. ∎

A Multiple-Slot Budgets-Only Mechanism. The mechanism in [18] is roughly a descending-price mechanism where we decrease the price until a prefix of budgets fits tightly into a prefix of positions at that price, whereupon we allocate that prefix, and continue to decrease the price for the remaining bidders. More formally, it can be written as follows:

Price-Setting Mechanism (Multiple Slots, Budgets Only) [18]
- If all $D_i = 0$, assign bidders to slots arbitrarily and exit.
- Sort the bidders by budget and assume wlog that $B_1 \geq B_2 \geq ... \geq B_n$.
- Define $r_\ell = \sum_{i=1}^{\ell} B_i / \sum_{i=1}^{\ell} D_i$. Set price $p = \max_\ell r_\ell$.
- Let ℓ^* be the largest ℓ such that $r_\ell = p$. Allocate slots $\{1,...\ell^*\}$ to bidders $\{1,...,\ell^*\}$ at price p, using all of their budgets; i.e., $c_i = B_i/p$.
- Repeat the steps above on the remaining bidders and slots until all slots are allocated.

Note that the allocation step is always possible since for all $\ell \leq \ell^*$, we have $p \geq r_\ell = \sum_{i=1}^{\ell} B_i / \sum_{i=1}^{\ell} D_i$, which rewritten is $\sum_{i=1}^{\ell} c_i \leq \sum_{i=1}^{\ell} D_i$, and so we can apply Lemma 4.3. An example run of the price-setting mechanism is shown in Figure 4.4.

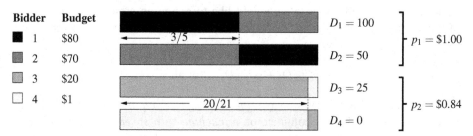

Bidder	Budget
1	$80
2	$70
3	$20
4	$1

Fig. 4.4 An example of the PS mechanism (multiple slots, budgets only). The first application of Find-Price-Block computes $r_1 = B_1/D_1 = 80/100$, $r_2 = (B_1 + B_2)/(D_1 + D_2) = 150/150$, $r_3 = (B_1 + B_2 + B_3)/(D_1 + D_2 + D_3) = 170/175$, $r_4 = (B_1 + B_2 + B_3 + B_4)/(D_1 + D_2 + D_3 + D_4) = 171/175$. Since r_2 is largest, the top two slots make up the first price block with a price $p_1 = r_2 = \$1$; bidder 1 gets 80 clicks and bidder 2 gets 70 clicks, using the schedule as shown. In the second price block, we get $B_3/D_3 = 20/25$ and $(B_3 + B_4)/(D_3 + D_4) = 21/25$. Thus p_2 is set to $21/25 = \$0.84$, bidder 3 gets $500/21$ clicks and bidder 4 gets $25/21$ clicks, using the schedule as shown.

Theorem 4.6. [18] The price-setting mechanism (multi-slot, budgets only) is truthful.

The Price-Setting Mechanism (General Case). The generalization of the multiple-slot PS mechanism to use both bids and budgets combines the ideas from the bids-and-budgets version of the single slot mechanism with the budgets-only version of the multiple-slot mechanism. As our price descends, we maintain a set of "active" bidders with bids at or above this price, as in the single-slot mechanism. These active bidders are kept ranked by *budget*, and when the price reaches the point where a prefix of bidders fits into a prefix of slots (as in the budgets-only mechanism) we allocate them and repeat. As in the single-slot case, we must be careful when a bidder enters the active set and suddenly causes an over-fit; in this case we again reduce the budget of this "threshold" bidder until it fits. For details on this mechanism and a proof that it is also truthful, we refer the reader to the paper [18].

Greedy First-Price Mechanism for Multiple Slots. In the multiple-slot case, as in the single-slot case, there is a natural *greedy first-price* (GFP) mechanism when the bidding language includes both bids and budgets: Order the bidders by bid $b_1 \succ b_2 \succ \ldots \succ b_n$. Starting from the highest bidder, for each bidder i compute the maximum possible number of clicks c_i that one could allocate to bidder i at price b_i, given the budget constraint B_i and the commitments to previous bidders $c_1, \ldots, c_{i-1}$. This reduces to the "fractional knapsack" problem in the single-slot case, and so one would hope that it maximizes revenue for the given bids and budgets, as in the single-slot case. This is not immediately clear, but does turn out to be true (see [18] for details). As in the single-slot case, the GFP mechanism is not a truthful mechanism. However, [18] give a generalization of Theorem 4.5 showing that the multiple-slot GFP mechanism does have a pure-strategy equilibrium, and that equilibrium has prices and allocation equivalent to the multiple-slot price setting mechanism.

4.4.3 Extensions

There are several natural generalizations of the *Online Ad Slot Scheduling* problem where it would be interesting to extend or apply the results of [18]:

- *Click-through rates.* To incorporate ad-specific click-through rates α_i into this model, we would say that a bidder i assigned to slot j for a time period of length $\tau - \sigma$ would receive $(\tau - \sigma)\alpha_i D_j$ clicks. All the results of [18] can be generalized to this setting by simply scaling the bids using $b'_i = b_i \alpha_i$. However, now the mechanism does not necessarily prefer more *efficient* solutions; i.e., ones that generate more overall clicks. It would be interesting to analyze a possible tradeoff between efficiency and revenue in this setting.
- *Multiple Keywords.* To model multiple keywords in this model, we could say that each query q had its own set of click totals $D_{q,1} \ldots D_{q,n}$, and each bidder is interested in a subset of queries. The greedy first-price mechanism is easily generalized to this case: maximally allocate clicks to bidders in order of their bid b_i (at price b_i) while respecting the budgets, the query preferences, and the click commitments to previous bidders. It would not be surprising if there was an equilibrium of this extension of the greedy mechanism that could be computed directly with a generalization of the PS mechanism.
- *Online queries, uncertain supply.* In sponsored search, allocations must be made online in response to user queries, and some of the previous literature has focused on this aspect of the problem (e.g., [34, 32]). Perhaps the ideas from [18] could be used to help make online allocation decisions using (unreliable) estimates of the supply, a setting considered in [32], with game-theoretic considerations.

4.5 The User's Point of View: a Markov Model for Clicks

In the GSP auction, by fixing the sort order, we leave out an important third party in sponsored search; i.e., the *search engine user*. Unfortunately, there is very little guidance on this in the literature, even though the user's behavior is the essential ingredient that defines *the commodity* the advertisers are bidding on, and its value. In [4] a different framework is suggested for principled understanding of sponsored search auctions:

- Define a suitable probabilistic model for search engine user behavior upon being presented the ads.
- Once this model is fixed, ask the traditional mechanism design questions of how do assign the ads to slots, and how to price them.
- Analyze the given mechanism from the perspective of the bidders (e.g., strategies) and the search engine (e.g., user satisfaction, efficiency and revenue).

There are certain well-accepted observations about the user's interaction with the sponsored search ads that should inform the model:

- The higher the ad is on the page, the more clicks it gets.
- The "better" the ad is, the more clicks it gets, where the "goodness" of an ad is related to the inherent quality of the ad, and how well it matches the user's query.

These properties govern not only how the auction is run but also how advertisers think about their bidding strategy (they prefer to appear higher and get more clicks). Thus it is important for an auction to have what we call *intuitive bidding*: a higher bid translates to a higher position and more clicks.

In [4], a natural Markov model is proposed for user clicks, taking the above observations into account. An algorithm is given to determine an optimal assignment of ads to positions in terms of economic efficiency. Together with VCG pricing, this gives a truthful auction. They further show that the optimal assignment under this model has certain monotonicity properties that allow for intuitive bidding. In what follows, we will describe these contributions in more detail.

Modeling the Search Engine User. Previous work on sponsored search has (implicitly) modeled the user using two types of parameters: ad-specific click-through rates α_i and position-specific visibility factors β_j. There are some intuitive user behavior models that express overall click-through probabilities in terms of these parameters. One possibility is "for each position j *independently*, the user looks at the ad i in that position with probability β_j then clicks on the ad with probability α_i." Alternatively: "The user picks a *single* position according to the distribution implied by the β_j's, and then clicks on the ad i in that position with probability α_i." Under both these models, it follows that the probability of an ad i in position j receiving a click is equal to $\alpha_i \beta_j$, which is the so-called *separability* assumption (see [5] or the discussion in Section 4.2). From separability it follows that GSP ordering of ads will be suitable, because GSP ordering maximizes the total advertiser value on the page.

In both these models there is no reason *a priori* that the position factors β_j should be decreasing; this is simply imposed because it makes sense, and it is verifiable empirically. Also, both suggested models assume that the probability of an ad getting clicked is independent of *other ads* that appear with it on the page, an assumption made without much justification. It is hard to imagine that seeing an ad, perhaps followed by a click, has no effect on the subsequent behavior of the user.

In designing a user model, we would like to have the monotonicity of the positions arise naturally. Also, each ad should have parameters dictating their effect on the user both in terms of clicking on that ad, as well as looking at other ads. In [4], a model is proposed of a user who starts to scan the list of ads from the top, and makes decisions (about whether to click, continue scanning, or give up altogether) based on what he sees. More specifically, the user is modeled as the following Markov process: "Begin scanning the ads from the top down. When position j is reached, click on the ad i with probability α_i. Continue scanning with probability q_i." In this model, if we try to write the click probability of an ad i in position j as $\alpha_i \beta_j$, we get that $\beta_j = \Pi_{i' \in A} q_{i'}$, where A is the set of ads placed above[12] position j. Thus the "position factor" in the click probability decreases with position, and does so naturally from the model. Also note that we do not have separability anymore, since β_j depends on which ads are above position j. Consequently, it can be shown that GSP assignment of ads is no longer the most efficient.

Auction with Markovian users. Given this new user model, we can now ask what the best assignment is of ads to slots. In [4], the most efficient assignment is studied; i.e., the one that maximizes total advertiser value derived from user clicks. It turns out that the structure of this assignment is different than that of GSP, and indeed is more sophisticated than any simple ranking. The presence of the q_i's requires a delicate tradeoff between the click probability of an ad and its effect on the slots below it. In [4], certain structural properties of the optimal assignment are identified and used to find such an optimal assignment efficiently, not only in polynomial time, but in near-linear time. Given this algorithm, a natural candidate for pricing is VCG [42, 10, 23], which is clearly truthful in this setting, at least under a profit-maximizing utility.

Intuitive Bidding. One of the reasons why GSP is successful is perhaps because bidding strategy is intuitive: Under GSP ranking, if an advertiser bids more, they get to a higher position, and consequently, if they bid more, their click probability increases. Now that we have defined a more sophisticated assignment function, even though VCG pricing is truthful, the auction still may not have these intuitive properties. The main technical result in [4] is to show that in the Markov user model, if a mechanism uses the most efficient assignment, indeed position and click probabilities are monotonic in an ad's bid (with all other bids fixed), thus preserving this important property. While not surprising, position-monotonicity turns out to be rather involved to prove, requiring some delicate combinatorial arguments, and insights into the optimal substructure of bidder assignments.

---

[12] Throughout the section, we will often refer to a position or an ad being "higher" or "above" another position or ad; this means that it is earlier on the list, and is looked at first by the user.

116   Jon Feldman and S. Muthukrishnan

In summary, sponsored search auctions are a three party process which can be studied by modeling the behavior of users first and then designing suitable mechanisms to affect the game theory between the advertiser and the search engine. The work of [4] sheds some light on the intricate connection between the user models and the mechanisms; for example, the sort order of GSP that is currently popular (sort by $b_i\alpha_i$) is not optimal under the Markov user model.

4.5.1 A Simple Markov User Click Model

We consider a sponsored search auction with n bidders $\mathscr{B} = \{1,\ldots,n\}$ and k positions. We will also refer to "ad i," meaning the advertisement submitted by bidder i. Each bidder $i \in \mathscr{B}$ has two parameters, α_i and q_i. The click-through-rate α_i is the probability that a user will click on ad i, given that they *look* at it. The continuation probability q_i is the probability that a user will look at the next ad in a list, given that they look at ad i.

Each bidder submits a bid b_i to the auction, representing the amount that they value a click. The quantity $\alpha_i b_i$ then represents the value of an "impression," i.e., how much they value a user looking at their ad. This is commonly referred to as their "ecpm."[13] Throughout, we will use the notation $e_i = \alpha_i b_i$ for convenience.

Given an assignment $(x_1,\ldots,x_k)$ of bidders to the k positions, the user looks at the first ad x_1, clicks on it with probability α_{x_1}, and then continues looking with probability q_{x_1}.[14] This is repeated with the second bidder, etc., until the last ad is reached, or some continuation test has failed. Thus the overall expected value of the assignment to the bidders is

$$e_{x_1} + q_{x_1}(e_{x_2} + q_{x_2}(e_{x_3} + q_{x_3}(\ldots q_{x_{n'-1}}(e_{x_n})))).$$

Now that we have defined the user model, and characterized the value of an assignment in that model, we can now define a new auction mechanism: First, the search engine computes an assignment of ads to positions that maximizes the overall expected value. Given this assignment, prices can then be computed using VCG [42, 10, 23]; for each assigned bidder we compute the change in others' value if that bidder were to disappear. This assures truthful reporting of bids under a profit-maximizing utility function.

---

[13] The acronym ecpm stands for "expected cost per thousand" impressions, where M is the roman numeral for one thousand. We will drop the factor of one thousand and refer to $\alpha_i b_i$ as the "ecpm."

[14] The click event and the continuation event could in principle have some correlation, and the results mentioned here will still hold.

4.5.2 Properties of Optimal Assignments for Markovian Users

Since the optimal assignment used by the mechanism is no longer simple ranking by ecpm, it is essential to understand the structure of this assignment. This understanding will allow us to compute the assignment more efficiently, and prove some important game-theoretic properties of the mechanism.

It turns out that the quantity $e_i/(1 - q_i)$, which we will refer to as the "adjusted ecpm (a-ecpm)," plays a central role in this model. Intuitively, this quantity is the impression value adjusted by the negative effect this ad has on the ads below it. We use $a_i = e_i/(1 - q_i)$ for convenience. The following theorem tells us how to assign a set of k selected ads to the k positions:

Theorem 4.7. [4] In the most efficient assignment, the ads that are placed are sorted in decreasing order of adjusted ecpm $a_i = e_i/(1 - q_i)$.

While this theorem tells us how to sort the ads selected, it does not tell us *which* k ads to select. One is tempted to say that choosing the top k ads by a-ecpm would do the trick; however the following example proves otherwise:

Example 4.4. [4] Suppose we have three bidders and two slots, and the bidders have the following parameters:

Bidder	e_i	q_i	$a_i = e_i/(1-q_i)$
1	$1	.75	4
2	$2	.2	2.5
3	$0.85	.8	4.25

Let's consider some possible assignments and their efficiency. If we use simple ranking by ecpm e_i, we get the assignment $(2, 1)$, which has efficiency $2 + .2(\$1) = \$2.20$. If we use simple ranking by a-ecpm a_i we get the assignment $(3, 1)$ with efficiency $\$0.85 + .8(\$1) = \$1.65$. It turns out that the optimal assignment is $(1, 2)$ with efficiency $\$1 + .75(\$2) = \$2.50$. The assigned bidders are ordered by a-ecpm in the assignment, but are not the top 2 bidders by a-ecpm.

Now suppose we have the same set of bidders, but now we have three slots. The optimal assignment in this case is $(3, 1, 2)$; note how bidder 3 goes from being unassigned to being assigned the first position.

In classical sponsored search with simple ranking, a bidder j can dominate another bidder i by having higher ecpm; i.e., bidder j will always appear whenever i does, and in a higher position. Example 4.4 above shows that having a higher ecpm (or a-ecpm) does not allow a bidder to dominate another bidder in our new model. However, we show that if she has higher ecpm *and* a-ecpm, then this does suffice. This is not only interesting in its own right, it is essential for proving deeper structural properties.

Theorem 4.8. [4] For all bidders i in an optimal assignment, if some bidder j is not in the assignment, and $a_j \geq a_i$ and $e_j \geq e_i$, then we may substitute j for i, and the assignment is no worse.

The following theorem shows some subset structure between optimal assignments to different numbers of slots. This theorem is used to prove position monotonicity, and is an essential ingredient of the more efficient algorithm for finding the optimal assignment. Let $\mathrm{OPT}(C,j)$ denote the set of all optimal solutions for filling j positions with bidders from the set C.

Theorem 4.9. [4] Let $j \in \{1,\ldots,k\}$ be some number of positions, and let C be an arbitrary set of bidders. Then, for all $S \in \mathrm{OPT}(C,j-1)$, there is some $S' \in \mathrm{OPT}(C,j)$ where $S' \supset S$.

Finally, we state a main technical theorem of [4], which shows that bidding is intuitive under a mechanism that maximizes value in the Markovian model.

Theorem 4.10. [4] With all other bids fixed, the probability of receiving a click in the optimal solution is non-decreasing in one's bid. In addition, the position of a particular bidder in the optimal solution is monotonic that bidder's bid.

This theorem, whose proof relies on all the previous results in this section, implies that from the perspective of a bidder participating in the auction, all the complexities of the underlying assignment still do not interfere with the intuitive nature of bidding; if you bid more, you still get more clicks, and get to a higher position.

4.5.3 Computing the Optimal Assignment

A simple algorithm for computing the optimal assignment proceeds as follows. First, sort the ads in decreasing order of a-ecpm in time $O(n\log n)$. Then, let $F(i,j)$ be the efficiency obtained (given that you reach slot j) by filling slots $(j,\ldots,k)$ with bidders from the set $\{i,\ldots,n\}$. We get the following recurrence:

$$F(i,j) = \max(F(i+1,j+1)q_i + e_i, F(i+1,j)).$$

Solving this recurrence for $F(1,1)$ yields the optimal assignment, and can be done in $O(nk)$ time. Using the properties about optimal assignments proved in the previous section, this can be improved to

Theorem 4.11. [4] Consider the auction with n Markovian bidders and k slots. There is an optimal assignment which can be determined in $O(n\log n + k^2\log^2 n)$ time.

4.6 Open Issues

We emphasize three open directions, besides the various game-theoretic and algorithmic open problems already proposed so far.

- *Estimating Parameters.* In order to run the basic auction and its extensions, the search companies need to estimate a number of parameters: ctr, position-specific factors, minimum bidder-specific reserve prices, etc. In addition, for operational reasons, search engines have to provide traffic estimates to potential advertisers, that is, for each keyword, they need to show landscape functions such as the ones in Section 3. An open research problem is, given a log of search and ad traffic over a significant period of time, design and validate efficient learning methods for estimating these parameters, and perhaps, even identify the models that fit the variation of these parameters over time. This is a significant research challenge since these parameters have intricate dependencies, and in addition, there is a long tail effect in the logs, that is, there is a significant amount of rare queries and keywords, as well as rare clicks for particular keywords.

- *Grand Simulation.* In order for the academic world to develop intuition into the world of sponsored search auctions and the associated dynamics, we need a grand simulation platform that can generate search traffic, ad inventories, ad clicks, and market specifics at the "Internet scale" that search engines face. Such a platform will help us understand the many tradeoffs: increasing keywords vs increasing budget for a campaign, making better bids vs choosing different search engines, choosing to bid for impressions vs clicks vs action, etc. Some auction programs are currently available[15], but a systematic, large scale effort by academia will have tremendous impact for research.

- *Grand Models.* In general, we need more detailed models for the behavior of users, advertisers as well as the impact of the search engine design on them. We described a highly preliminary effort here in which the users were Markovian, but more powerful models will also be of great interest. For example, a small extension is to make the continuation probability q_i a function of location as well, which makes the optimization problem more difficult. One can also generalize the Markov model to handle arbitrary configurations of ads on a web page (not necessarily the linear order in current search results page), or to allow various other user states (such as navigating a *landing* page, that is the page that is the target of an ad). Finally, since page layout can be performed dynamically, we could ask what would happen if the layout of a web page were a part of the model, which would combine both users as well as the search engine into a model. In general, there may be grand, unified models that capture the relationship between all the three parties in sponsored search.

4.7 Concluding Remarks

We have discussed algorithmic and game-theoretic issues in auctions for sponsored search.

---

[15] For example, see http://www.hss.caltech.edu/ jkg/jAuctions.html

Auctions are used for other products in Internet advertising, for example Google's *AdSense*, where an Internet publisher (like an online newspaper) can sign up with an ad network (in this case Google) to place ads on their site. Here, an additional aspect of the problem from the auctioneer's perspective is how to *target* ads, that is, how to choose the keywords from the surrounding context, to run auctions like the ones we discussed thus far. This also introduces the fourth player in the game, i.e., the *publisher*, and consequently, the game theory is more intricate and largely unexplored.

Internet ads like sponsored search or AdSense may combine different types of ads, i.e., text, image or video ads. Each has its own specifications in terms of dimensions, user engagement and effectiveness. How to combine them into a unified auction is an interesting challenge.

Beyond Internet ads, the Internet medium is also used for enabling ads in traditional media including TV, Radio, Print etc. In such cases, the auction problems may take on a richer combinatorial component, and also, a component based on ability to reserve ad slots ahead of time. The resulting algorithmic and game-theoretic problems are largely unexplored in the research community.

4.8 Acknowledgements

We gratefully thank numerous engineers and researchers at Google.

References

1. Z. Abrams and A. Ghosh. Auctions with revenue guarantees for sponsored search. In *Proc. Workshop on Internet and Network Economics (WINE)*, 2007.
2. Z. Abrams, O. Mendelevitch, and J. Tomlin. Optimal delivery of sponsored search advertisements subject to budget constraints. In *ACM Conference on Electronic Commerce*, 2007.
3. G. Aggarwal, J. Feldman, and S. Muthukrishnan. Bidding to the top: VCG and equilibria of position-based auctions. In Proc. Workshop on Approximation and Online Algorithms (WAOA), 2006.
4. G. Aggarwal, J. Feldman, S. Muthukrishnan, and M. Pál. Sponsored search auctions with Markovian users, 2008. Submitted.
5. G. Aggarwal, A. Goel, and R. Motwani. Truthful auctions for pricing search keywords. In *ACM Conference on Electronic Commerce (EC)*, 2006.
6. K. Arrow and G. Debreu. Existence of an equilibrium for a competitive economy. *Econometrica*, 22:265–290, 1954.
7. C. Borgs, J. Chayes, O. Etesami, N. Immorlica, K. Jain, and M. Mahdian. Dynamics of bid optimization in online advertisement auctions. In *Proc. WWW*, 2007.
8. C. Borgs, J. T. Chayes, N. Immorlica, M. Mahdian, and A. Saberi. Multi-unit auctions with budget-constrained bidders. In *ACM Conference on Electronic Commerce (EC)*, 2005.
9. M. Cary, A. Das, B. Edelman, I. Giotis, K. Heimerl, A. R. Karlin, C. Mathieu, and M. Schwarz. Greedy bidding strategies for keyword auctions. In *ACM Conference on Electronic Commerce*, 2007.
10. E. Clarke. Multipart pricing of public goods. *Public Choice*, 11:17–33, 1971.

11. X. Deng, C. Papadimitriou, and S. Safra. On the complexity of equilibria. In *Proceedings of ACM Symposium on Theory of Computing.*, 2002.
12. N. Devanur, C. Papadimitriou, A. Saberi, and V. Vazirani. Market equilibrium via a primal-dual-type algorithm, 2002.
13. B. Edelman, M. Ostrovsky, and M. Schwarz. Internet advertising and the generalized second price auction: Selling billions of dollars worth of keywords. In Second workshop on sponsored search auctions, 2006.
14. E. Eisenberg and D. Gale. Consensus of subjective probabilities: The pari-mutuel method. *Annals Of Mathematical Statistics*, 30:165–168, 1959.
15. E. Even-Dar, J. Feldman, Y. Mansour, and S. Muthukrishnan. Position auctions with bidder-specific minimum prices, 2008. Submitted.
16. E. Even-Dar, S. Mannor, and Y. Mansour. Pac bounds for multi-armed bandit and markov decision processes. In *COLT '02: Proceedings of the 15th Annual Conference on Computational Learning Theory*, pages 255–270, London, UK, 2002. Springer-Verlag.
17. J. Feldman, S. Muthukrishnan, M. Pál, and C. Stein. Budget optimization in search-based advertising auctions. In *ACM Conference on Electronic Commerce*, 2007.
18. J. Feldman, E. Nikolova, S. Muthukrishnan, and M. Pál. A truthful mechanism for offline ad slot scheduling. In *Proc. Symposium on Algorithmic Game Theory (SAGT)*, 2008. To appear.
19. G. Goel and A. Mehta. Adwords auctions with decreasing valuation bids. In *Proc. Workshop on Internet and Network Economics (WINE)*, 2007.
20. G. Goel and A. Mehta. Online budgeted matching in random input models with applications to adwords. In *Proc. Symposium on Discrete Algorithms (SODA)*, 2008.
21. Rica Gonen and Elan Pavlov. An adaptive sponsored search mechanism delta-gain truthful in valuation, time, and budget. In *Proc. Workshop on Internet and Network Economics (WINE)*, 2007.
22. T. Gonzalez and S. Sahni. Preemptive scheduling of uniform processing systems. *Journal of the ACM*, 25:92–101, January 1978.
23. T. Groves. Incentives in teams. Econometrica, 41(4):617–631, 1973.
24. E. C. Horvath, S. Lam, and R. Sethi. A level algorithm for preemptive scheduling. *J. ACM*, 24(1):32–43, 1977.
25. R. Johari and J.N. Tsitsiklis. Efficiency loss in a network resource allocation game. *Mathematics of Operations Research*, 29(3):407–435, 2004.
26. F. Kelly. Charging and rate control for elastic traffic. *European Transactions on Telecommunications*, 8:33–37, January 1997.
27. W. Labio, M. Rose, and S. Ramaswamy, May 2004. Internal Document, Google, Inc.
28. S. Lahaie. An analysis of alternative slot auction designs for sponsored search. In *ACM Conference on Electronic Commerce (EC)*, 2006.
29. S. Lahaie, D. Pennock, A. Saberi, and R. Vohra. *Sponsored Search Auctions*, chapter 28. Algorithmic Game Theory. Cambridge University Press, 2007.
30. L. Liang and Q. Qi. Cooperative or vindictive: Bidding strategies in sponsored search auction. In *WINE*, pages 167–178, 2007.
31. E. Dominowska M. Richardson and R. Ragno. Predicting clicks: Estimating the click-through rates for new ads. In WWW 2007, Track: Search, 2007.
32. M. Mahdian, H. Nazerzadeh, and A. Saberi. Allocating online advertisement space with unreliable estimates. In *ACM Conference on Electronic Commerce*, 2007.
33. M. Mahdian and A. Saberi. Multi-unit auctions with unknown supply. In *ACM conference on Electronic commerce (EC)*, 2006.
34. A. Mehta, A. Saberi, U. Vazirani, and V. Vazirani. AdWords and generalized online matching. In *FOCS*, 2005.
35. S. Muthukrishnan, M. Pál, and Z. Svitkina. Stochastic models for budget optimization in search-based advertising. In *Proc. Workshop on Internet and Network Economics (WINE)*, 2007.
36. M. Mahdian N. Immorlica, K. Jain and K. Talwar. Click fraud resistant methods for learning click-through rates. In Workshop on Internet and Network Economics (WINE), 2005.

37. T. Nguyen and E. Tardos. Approximately maximizing efficiency and revenue in polyhedral environments. In *ACM Conference on Electronic Commerce (EC)*, 2007.
38. Nielsen//NetRatings. Interactive advertising bureau (IAB) search branding study, August 2004. Commissioned by the IAB Search Engine Committee. Available at http://www.iab.net/resources/iab_searchbrand.asp.
39. P. Rusmevichientong and D. Williamson. An adaptive algorithm for selecting profitable keywords for search-based advertising services. In *Proc. 7th ACM conference on Electronic commerce (EC)*, 2006.
40. B. K. Szymanski and J.-S. Lee. Impact of roi on bidding and revenue in sponsored search advertisement auctions. In *2nd Workshop on Sponsored Search Auctions in ACM Conference on Electronic Commerce (EC)*, 2006.
41. H. Varian. Position auctions. *International Journal of Industrial Organization*, 25(6):1163–1178, December 2007.
42. W. Vickrey. Counterspeculation, auctions and competitive-sealed tenders. *Finance*, 16(1):8–37, 1961.
43. Y. Vorobeychik and D. M. Reeves. Equilibrium analysis of dynamic bidding in sponsored search auctions. In *Proc. Workshop on Internet and Network Economics (WINE)*, 2007.
44. J. Wortman, Y. Vorobeychik, L. Li, and J. Langford. Maintaining equilibria during exploration in sponsored search auctions. In *Proc. Workshop on Internet and Network Economics (WINE)*, 2007.
45. Y. Zhou and R. Lukose. Vindictive bidding in keyword auctions. In *ICEC '07: Proceedings of the ninth international conference on Electronic commerce*, pages 141–146, New York, NY, USA, 2007. ACM.

Part II
Scheduling and Control

Chapter 5
Advances in Oblivious Routing of Internet Traffic

M. Kodialam, T. V. Lakshman, and Sudipta Sengupta

Abstract Routing is a central topic in networking since it determines the connectivity between users. Recently, with the growing use of the Internet for a wide variety of bandwidth intensive applications, including peer-to-peer and on-demand/real-time multimedia, it has also become important that routing accounts for the quality-of-service needs of applications and users. A research problem of much current interest is traffic-oblivious routing for ensuring that the network provides the needed quality-of-service despite uncertain knowledge of the carried traffic. Oblivious routing involves using pre-determined paths to route between each ingress-egress node in the network (typically an Internet domain) that do not change with changing traffic patterns. By removing the need to detect changes in traffic in real-time or reconfigure the network in response to it, significant simplification in network management/operations and associated reduction in costs can be achieved. Moreover, oblivious routing has the potential to make the Internet much more robust and predictable in the face of rapidly varying and unpredictable traffic patterns. Theoretical advances in the area have shown that oblivious routing can provide these benefits without compromising capacity efficiency. We survey recent advances in oblivious routing with a view towards its application in (intra-domain) Internet routing.

5.1 Introduction

As the Internet continues to grow in size and complexity, it becomes increasingly difficult to predict future traffic patterns. Many emerging applications for the Inter-

M. Kodialam, T. V. Lakshman
Bell Laboratories, Alcatel-Lucent, Murray Hill, NJ, USA
e-mail: {muralik, lakshman}@alcatel-lucent.com

Sudipta Sengupta
Microsoft Research, Redmond, WA, USA
e-mail: sudipta@microsoft.com

net are characterized by highly variable traffic behavior over time. We have already
seen the emergence (or, migration) of many services over the public Internet carried
over the ubiquitous Internet Protocol (IP), including VoIP (voice-over-IP), peer-to-
peer file sharing, video streaming, and IPTV. The bandwidth requirements of these
applications are not only high but show marked variations, both temporally and
geographically, compared to traditional telephony voice traffic patterns. This has reduced the time-scales at which traffic changes dynamically, making it impossible to
extrapolate past traffic patterns to the future.

To enable such applications to operate seamlessly, it is imperative that the Internet routing infrastructure be reliable and robust and guarantee network performance
in the face of highly unpredictable and rapidly varying traffic patterns. Oblivious
routing, due to its lack of dependence on accurate traffic knowledge, has hence become an important topic of research. Traffic-oblivious routing has the potential to
make the Internet far more reliable and robust in the face of dynamically changing
traffic patterns.

An oblivious routing scheme is determined by a set of (multi-)path routes (with
traffic split ratios) for each source-destination pair in the network. Traffic is routed
along those paths regardless of the (current) traffic matrix. An instance of oblivious
routing is thus completely described by specifying how a unit flow is (splittably)
routed between each source-destination pair in the network. Computing an oblivious
routing scheme so as to minimize various performance metrics under a given traffic
variation model has been the underlying theme of research on this topic.

We classify the work in the literature on oblivious routing into two broad categories based on the traffic variation model. In the *unconstrained* traffic variation
model, the traffic matrix can vary arbitrarily and oblivious routing provides *relative*
guarantees for routing a given traffic matrix with respect to the best routing for that
matrix. In the *hose constrained* traffic variation model, the traffic matrix can vary
subject to aggregate network ingress-egress constraints and oblivious routing can
provide *absolute guarantees* for routing *all* such matrices.

For the hose model, oblivious routing schemes can be further classified depending on whether the routing from source to destination is along "direct" (possibly
multi-hop) paths or through a set of intermediate nodes (also called two-phase routing). In the first phase of two-phase routing, incoming traffic is sent from the source
to a set of intermediate nodes and then, in the second phase, from the intermediate nodes to the final destination. We point out the benefits of two-phase routing
in supporting statically provisioned optical layer in IP-over-Optical networks and
indirection in specialized service overlays. The origins of two-phase routing can
be traced back to Valiant's randomized scheme for communication among parallel processors interconnected in a hypercube topology, also known as Valiant Load
Balancing [36].

The paper is structured as follows. In Section 5.2, we discuss some aspects of the
inherent difficulty in measuring traffic and reconfiguring the network in response
to changes in it and bring out the need for oblivious routing. In Section 5.3, we
introduce the traffic variation and performance models. In Section 5.4, we cover
oblivious routing under the unconstrained traffic variation model. In Section 5.5,

we cover oblivious routing for the hose constrained traffic model. In Section 5.6, we cover two-phase (oblivious) routing for the hose constrained traffic model. We summarize in Section 5.7. Throughout the paper, we assume that the network is denoted by $G = (N, E)$ with node set N and (directed) edge (link) set E where each node in the network can be a source or destination of traffic. Let $|N| = n$ and $|E| = m$. The nodes in N are labeled $\{1, 2, \ldots, n\}$. We use T to represent a traffic matrix where t_{ij} is the traffic rate between nodes i and j.

5.2 The Need for Traffic Oblivious Routing

In an ideal network deployment scenario where complete traffic information is known and does not change over time, we can optimize the routing for that single traffic matrix – a large volume of research has addressed this problem. However, real-world traffic in Internet backbones is highly variable and largely unpredictable. In this section, we discuss some aspects of the inherent difficulty in measuring traffic and reconfiguring the network in response to changes in it. The most important innovation of oblivious routing schemes is the ability to handle traffic variability in a capacity efficient manner through static preconfiguration of the network and without requiring either (i) measurement of traffic in real-time or (ii) reconfiguration of the network in response to changes in it.

5.2.1 Difficulties in Measuring Traffic

Network traffic is not only hard to measure in real-time but even harder to predict based on past measurements. Direct measurement methods do not scale with network size as the number of entries in a traffic matrix is quadratic in the number of nodes. Moreover, such direct real-time monitoring methods lead to unacceptable degradation in router performance. In reality, only aggregate link traffic counts are available for traffic matrix estimation. SNMP (Simple Network Management Protocol) [8] provides this data via incoming and outgoing byte counts computed per link every 5 minutes. To estimate the traffic matrix from such link traffic measurements, the best techniques today give errors of 20% or more [28, 40, 37]. Moreover, many of these methods are not suitable for measuring traffic in real-time due to their computation intensive nature.

The emergence of new applications on the Internet, like P2P (peer-to-peer), VoIP (voice-over-IP), and video-on-demand has reduced the time-scales at which traffic changes dynamically, making it impossible to extrapolate past traffic patterns to the future. Currently, Internet Service Providers (ISPs) handle such unpredictability in network traffic by gross over-provisioning of capacity. This has led to ISP networks being under-utilized to levels below 30% [17].

5.2.2 Difficulties in Dynamic Network Reconfiguration

Even if it were possible to track changes in the traffic matrix in real-time, dynamic changes in routing in the network may be difficult or prohibitively expensive from a network management and operations perspective. In spite of the continuing research on network control plane and IP-Optical integration, network deployments are far away from utilizing the optical control plane to provide bandwidth provisioning in real-time to the IP layer. The unavailability of network control plane mechanisms for reconfiguring the network in response to and at time-scales of changing traffic further amplifies the necessity of the static preconfiguration property of a routing scheme in handling traffic variability.

5.3 Traffic Variation and Performance Models

There are two categories of traffic variation and associated performance models that have been considered in the literature in the context of oblivious routing. These models differ in the way they define the performance objective for evaluating the "quality" of a given oblivious routing scheme.

5.3.1 Unconstrained Traffic Variation Model

In this model, the traffic matrix to be routed by the network is arbitrary. Given (finite) link capacities in the network, there may not be any feasible routing scheme for a given traffic matrix. We define the optimal (non-oblivious or traffic-aware) routing for a given traffic matrix T to be the routing scheme that minimizes the maximum link utilization (or, equivalently, feasibly routes the matrix $\lambda \cdot T$ for the maximum possible value of the scalar λ). If the maximum link utilization achieved by the optimal scheme for routing T is greater than 1 (or, equivalently, $\lambda < 1$), then the traffic matrix T is infeasible for the network (under any routing scheme). However, we can still compare the performance of a given oblivious routing scheme to that of the optimal (non-oblivious) routing for a given traffic matrix, and use the worst performance gap (over all traffic matrices) as a measure of performance for oblivious routing. This *relative guarantee* is called the *oblivious performance ratio* and is described formally in Section 5.4. The objective is to pick an oblivious routing scheme with the best performance ratio.

5.3.2 Hose Constrained Traffic Variation Model

In the hose traffic model, the total amount of traffic that enters (leaves) each ingress (egress) node in the network is bounded by given values. This model was proposed by [12] and subsequently used by [10] as a method for specifying the bandwidth requirements of a Virtual Private Network (VPN). Note that the hose model naturally accommodates the network's ingress-egress capacity constraints.

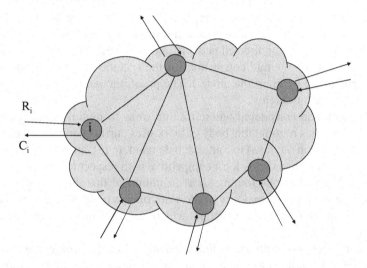

Fig. 5.1 Schematic of Network with Hose Constraints: Total ingress traffic at node i is upper bounded by R_i and total egress traffic at node i is upper bounded by C_i. Point-to-point traffic is not known.

Let the upper bounds on the total amount of traffic entering and leaving the network at node i be denoted by R_i and C_i respectively. This is illustrated in Figure 5.1. The point-to-point matrix for the traffic in the network is thus constrained by these ingress-egress capacity bounds. These constraints are the only known aspects of the traffic to be carried by the network, and knowing these is equivalent to knowing the row and column sum bounds on the traffic matrix. That is, any feasible traffic matrix $T = [t_{ij}]$ for the network must obey

$$\sum_{j\in N, j\neq i} t_{ij} \leq R_i, \quad \sum_{j\in N, j\neq i} t_{ji} \leq C_i \ \forall \ i \in N \qquad (5.1)$$

For given R_i and C_i values, denote the set of all such matrices that are partially specified by their row and column sums by $\mathscr{T}(\mathbf{R},\mathbf{C})$. We will use $\lambda \cdot \mathscr{T}(\mathbf{R},\mathbf{C})$ to denote the set of all traffic matrices in $\mathscr{T}(\mathbf{R},\mathbf{C})$ with their entries multiplied by λ. For the hose model, the throughput is defined as the maximum multiplier λ such that all matrices in $\lambda \cdot \mathscr{T}(\mathbf{R},\mathbf{C})$ can be feasibly routed under given link capacities (by some routing scheme). The objective then is to choose an oblivious routing scheme that maximizes the throughput. The problem of minimum cost network design has also been considered in which each link has associated costs per unit traffic. We will cover these problems in Sections 5.5 and 5.6.

5.4 Oblivious Routing under Unconstrained Traffic Model

The notion of oblivious routing was introduced by Räcke [29], in which demands are routed in an online manner and the objective is to minimize the maximum link utilization (or, congestion). Räcke proved the surprising result that it is possible to route obliviously in *any* undirected network and achieve a congestion that is within polylog(n) times the optimal congestion for the specific set of demands (the latter being computed in an offline model). The proof, though constructive, relies on solving $\mathcal{NP}$-hard problems.

Earlier work had considered online routing so as to minimize congestion – in contrast to oblivious routing, this body of work uses current network state information (e.g., congestion on links) to route each demand. In [3], an online algorithm for this problem is designed that is $\log n$ competitive with respect to congestion.

Computing an oblivious routing so as to minimize the oblivious performance ratio has been the focus of majority of the work on this topic. We define this objective next, using the notion of throughput which is the reciprocal of maximum link utilization.

Consider a network with given link capacities. Let the *throughput* $\lambda(T)$ of a given matrix T be defined as the maximum multiplier λ such that the matrix $\lambda \cdot T$ is feasible (under some routing) for the given link capacities. This can be computed using a *maximum concurrent flow formulation* [32]. Note that the reciprocal of $\lambda(T)$ can be interpreted as the minimum (over all routing choices) of the maximum link utilization for routing matrix T.

Given an oblivious routing f, let $\lambda_f(T)$ denote the throughput of routing matrix T under f. Clearly, it follows that $\lambda(T) \geq \lambda_f(T)$. The performance of routing f on matrix T is worse than the best possible (traffic dependent) routing by a factor of $\lambda(T)/\lambda_f(T)$. The oblivious performance ratio of routing f is defined as the maximum value of this ratio over all traffic matrices.

$$\text{OBLIVIOUS-PERFORMANCE-RATIO}(f) = \max_T \frac{\lambda(T)}{\lambda_f(T)}$$

Following up from the above oblivious routing result by Räcke, polynomial time algorithms for oblivious routing (in undirected and directed networks) so as to minimize the oblivious performance ratio were developed in [4, 16]. In [4], the authors give a linear programming formulation with an exponential number of constraints and a polynomial time separation oracle for the constraints, thus leading to a polynomial time solution using the ellipsoid algorithm for linear programming [13]. Subsequently, a polynomial *size* linear programming formulation was developed in

[2] by taking the dual of the separation oracle and using it to replace the exponential set of constraints.

The oblivious performance ratio has been extended to handle restoration of link and node failures in [1]. The authors provide linear programming formulations for three different restoration models: (i) rerouting on the new network after failure, (ii) end-to-end restoration of paths affected by failure, and (iii) local (span) restoration around a failed link.

5.5 Oblivious Routing of Hose Constrained Traffic

Oblivious routing has also been considered in the context of the hose constrained traffic model described in Section 5.3.2. Since the hose traffic model bounds ingress-egress traffic at each node, the traffic on a network link under any oblivious routing choice is bounded. Hence, the relevant optimization problems in this context are minimum cost network design and minimizing the maximum link utilization (also referred to as maximum throughput network routing, as explained in Section 5.3.2).

Constant factor approximation algorithms for minimum cost network design for *single-path* oblivious routing are provided in [25, 15]. For this problem, the traffic usage on a link, for a given oblivious routing, is the maximum carried traffic on that link over all hose matrices. Link costs per unit traffic are given, and the objective is to minimize the total cost over all links.

In [11], the authors consider the problem of minimum cost (multi-path) oblivious routing of hose traffic under given link costs *and* link capacities. They give a linear programming formulation with an exponential number of constraints (and, a polynomial size separation oracle linear program) that is suitable for solving using the ellipsoid method [13]. The ellipsoid method is primarily a theoretical tool for proving polynomial-time solvability – its running time is not feasible for practical implementations. The authors also give a cutting-plane heuristic for solving the exponential size linear program and obtain reasonable running times for the experiments reported. However, this cutting-plane heuristic can have exponential running times in the worst case. In [23], the authors give a polynomial *size* linear program for maximum throughput oblivious routing of hose traffic under given link capacities. Their technique can be used to obtain a polynomial size linear program for the minimum cost version of the problem also, thus improving the result in [11].

Allocating link capacity for restoration under link failures has also been considered for oblivious routing of hose traffic. When the links used for routing form a tree topology, the problem of computing backup paths for each link and allocating capacity under a single link failure model is considered in [19], where a constant factor approximation algorithm is provided for minimizing total bandwidth reserved on backup links.

5.6 Two-Phase (Oblivious) Routing of Hose Constrained Traffic

Two-phase routing has been recently proposed [20, 38] as an oblivious routing scheme for handling arbitrary traffic variations subject to aggregate ingress-egress constraints (i.e., the hose constrained traffic model as described in Section 5.3). We begin with an overview of the scheme. As is indicative from the name, the routing scheme operates in two phases:

- **Phase 1:** A predetermined fraction α_j of the traffic entering the network at any node is distributed to every node j *independent of the final destination of the traffic*.
- **Phase 2:** As a result of the routing in Phase 1, each node receives traffic destined for different destinations that it routes to their respective destinations in this phase.

In contrast to two-phase routing, the oblivious routing approach in Section 5.5 can be viewed as routing along "direct" source-destination (possibly multi-hop) paths (ie., without the requirement to go through specific intermediate nodes). Hence, when comparing with two-phase routing, we will refer to the latter as "direct source-destination path routing". (Note that the use of the term "direct" in this context does not necessarily mean a single-hop path from source to destination.)

The traffic split ratios $\alpha_1, \alpha_2, \ldots, \alpha_n$ in Phase 1 of the scheme are such that $\sum_{i=1}^{n} \alpha_i = 1$. A simple method of implementing this routing scheme in the network is to form *fixed bandwidth paths between the nodes*. In order to differentiate between the paths carrying Phase 1 and Phase 2 traffic, we will refer to them as Phase 1 and Phase 2 paths respectively (Figure 2). The critical reason the two-phase routing strategy works is that the *bandwidth required for these tunnels depends on the ingress-egress capacities R_i, C_i and the traffic split ratios α_j but not on the (unknown) individual entries in the traffic matrix*. Depending on the underlying routing architecture, the Phase 1 and Phase 2 paths can be implemented as IP tunnels, optical layer circuits, or Label Switched Paths in Multi-Protocol Label Switching (MPLS) [31].

A subtle aspect of the scheme may not be apparent from its above description. Notwithstanding the two-phase nature of the scheme, some fraction of the traffic is actually routed to its destination in one phase, i.e., directly from source to destination (this may not be necessarily on a single-hop path). To see this, consider the traffic originating from node i and destined to node j. The fraction α_i of this traffic that should go to (intermediate) node i in Phase 1 does not appear on the network because it originates at node i. Hence, this traffic is routed directly to its destination in Phase 2. Similarly, a fraction α_j of the traffic that goes to (intermediate) node j in Phase 1 actually reaches its final destination after Phase 1. Hence, this traffic does not appear on the network in Phase 2. Thus, for each source-destination pair (i,j), a fraction $\alpha_i + \alpha_j$ of the traffic between them is directly routed to its destination using only one of the phases (either Phase 1 or Phase 2).

The problem of maximizing directly routed traffic in two-phase routing under either local (at a node) or global traffic information is considered in [27], for the special case when the underlying topology is full-mesh, all ingress-egress capacities are equal, and all link capacities are equal.

We now derive the bandwidth requirement for the Phase 1 and Phase 2 paths. Consider a node i with maximum incoming traffic R_i. Node i sends $\alpha_j R_i$ amount of this traffic to node j during the first phase for each $j \in N$. Thus, the traffic demand from node i to node j as a result of Phase 1 routing is $\alpha_j R_i$. At the end of Phase 1, node i has received $\alpha_i R_k$ traffic from any other node k. Out of this, the traffic destined for node j is $\alpha_i t_{kj}$ since all traffic is initially split without regard to the final destination. The traffic that needs to be routed from node i to node j during Phase 2 is $\sum_{k \in N} \alpha_i t_{kj} \leq \alpha_i C_j$, where t_{kj} is the traffic rate from node k to node j. Thus, the traffic demand from node i to node j as a result of Phase 2 routing is $\alpha_i C_j$. This computation is shown in Figure 3.

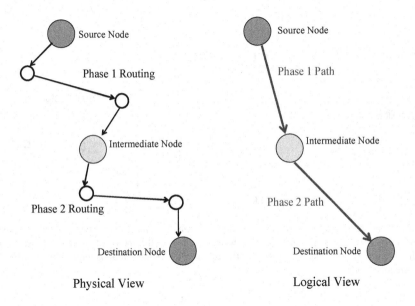

Fig. 5.2 A schematic figure of two-Phase Routing showing the physical and logical views. Note that the (logical) Phase 1 and Phase 2 paths can traverse multiple hops in the physical network.

Hence, the maximum demand from node i to node j as a result of routing in Phases 1 and 2 is $\alpha_j R_i + \alpha_i C_j$. Note that this does not depend on the matrix T. Two important properties of the scheme become clear from the above discussion. These are as follows:

Property 1 (Routing Oblivious to Traffic Variations): The routing of source-destination traffic is along fixed paths with predetermined traffic split ratios and *does not depend* on the current traffic matrix T.

Property 2 (Provisioned Capacity is Traffic Matrix Independent): The total demand from node i to node j as a result of routing in Phases 1 and 2 is $\alpha_j R_i + \alpha_i C_j$ and does not depend on the traffic matrix T but only on the aggregate ingress-egress capacities. The *bandwidth of the Phase 1 and Phase 2 paths* are *fixed*.

Property 2 implies that the scheme handles variability in traffic matrix T by effectively routing the fixed matrix $D = [d_{ij}] = [\alpha_j R_i + \alpha_i C_j]$ that depends only on aggregate ingress-egress capacities and the traffic split ratios $\alpha_1, \alpha_2, \ldots, \alpha_n$, and not on the specific matrix T. All that is required is that T be a feasible traffic matrix. This is what makes the routing scheme oblivious to changes in the traffic distribution.

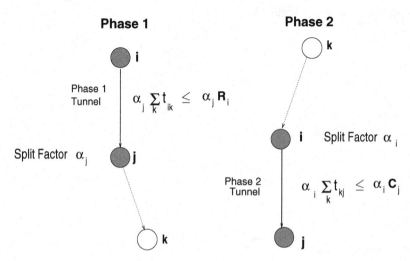

Fig. 5.3 Computing the bandwidth requirements for Phase 1 and Phase 2 paths between nodes i and j. In the bandwidth computation for Phase 1, node j is the intermediate node. In the bandwidth computation for Phase 2, node i is the intermediate node. Node k represents an arbitrary ingress/egress node.

We highlight below some additional properties of the two-phase routing scheme:

1. *Handling Indirection:* The routing decision at each source node in Phase 1 is independent of the final destination node of traffic. Hence, in addition to providing performance guarantees for variable traffic, two-phase routing is also ideally suited for providing bandwidth guaranteed services in architectures that decouple the sender from the receiver as in the *Internet Indirection Infrastructure* (i3) [35]. We discuss this further in Section 5.6.2.

2. *Multicast Traffic:* Two-phase routing can also naturally provide a *bandwidth guaranteed multicast* service. If the intermediate nodes can replicate packets for multicast, there is always sufficient bandwidth under two-phase routing to provide bandwidth guarantees for multicast traffic. The only requirement is that the ingress-egress capacity constraints of the hose model are satisfied by the total (unicast and multicast) traffic.

The origins of two-phase routing can be traced back to Valiant's randomized scheme for communication among parallel processors interconnected in a hyper-cube topology [36] where routing is through a *randomly and uniformly chosen intermediate node*. The two-phase routing scheme can be viewed as a deterministic scheme with possibly *unequal traffic split ratios* which can accommodate all traffic matrices within the network's natural ingress-egress capacity constraints. We will survey recent work on this scheme that has considered many new aspects arising from its potential application to routing Internet traffic in ISP backbone networks.

5.6.1 Addressing Some Aspects of Two-Phase Routing

We address some practical aspects of two-phase routing related to packet reordering and end-to-end delay and explain why they should not pose any hurdles in the deployment of the routing scheme in ISP networks.

Packet Reordering

In two-phase routing, the source node splits traffic to different intermediate nodes regardless of the final destination. Thus, packets belonging to the same end-to-end connection can arrive out of order at the destination node if the traffic is split within the same connection. The question arises whether this packet reordering is an issue that needs to be addressed.

The Internet standard for IP router requirements, RFC 1812, does not prohibit packet reordering in routers [5]. In fact, parallelism in router/OXC components and links causes packet reordering under normal operation and has been observed in the Internet [6, 18]. Packet reordering can affect the performance of TCP (Transmission Control Protocol) [9] and other traffic that relies on packet ordering. In its current version, TCP, which is used to carry most of the traffic in today's Internet, interprets packet reordering as a loss indicator. This triggers unnecessary retransmissions and TCP timeouts that cause a decrease in TCP throughput and increase in packet delay. Proposals have been made to make TCP more robust to packet reordering [7]. However, any new TCP feature requires protocol standardization and modification/upgrade of TCP software implementations running on hundreds of millions of client devices. Hence, it might be desirable to avoid packet reordering.

Packet reordering can be avoided in two-phase routing by splitting traffic at the application flow level at the source node (rather than at the packet level). An application level flow corresponds to a single end-to-end session of communication between two users on different machines and is commonly identified by a 5-tuple consisting of source IP address, destination IP address, source port number, destination port number, and protocol id [9]. In order to prevent congestion along the Phase 2 paths in two-phase routing, it is necessary to split the set of flows corresponding to each destination node among intermediate nodes in accordance with the traffic split ratios $\alpha_1, \alpha_2, \ldots, \alpha_n$.

The question then is whether two-phase routing with per-flow splitting can provide bandwidth guarantees to all traffic matrices within the network's natural ingress-egress capacity constraints. The answer, as we explain below, is in the affirmative. We are advocating this routing scheme for core networks where recent advances in DWDM (Dense Wavelength Division Multiplexing) transmission technologies [30] have resulted in link bandwidths of 10 Gbps and heading higher. Individual flows at best are in the Mbps range and hence small compared to link rates – tens of thousands of flows share a single 10 Gbps link. Moreover, TCP is not really good for gigabit flows – the throughput goes down as $1/(RTT * \sqrt{\text{random loss probability}})$ [9] and so very low random loss (due to bursty cross traffic) is needed to get gigabit throughputs for any reasonable RTT (round-trip time).

Increase in End-to-End Delay

Because of the two-phase nature of the routing scheme, packets might incur about twice the delay in end-to-end routing compared to direct source-destination path routing along shortest paths. However, for the portion of traffic that is routed directly to its destination (as explained in the description of the scheme), or when the intermediate node already lies on the shortest source-destination path, no additional delay is encountered, thus suggesting that the average delay may be less than a factor of two compared to that in direct source-destination path routing. In fact, experiments on actual ISP topologies collected for the Rocketfuel project [34] for maximum throughput two-phase routing indicate that the end-to-end hop count as a result of two-phase routing is about 1.4-1.6 times that of shortest path routing [33].

More importantly, this increase in delay may be tolerable for most applications. Consider an Internet backbone spanning the transcontinental US. A ping from MIT (US east coast) to UC Berkeley (US west coast) gives a round-trip time of about 90 msec. This round trip time includes two traversals of the long-haul network *and* two traversals each of Boston and Oakland metro access networks. Thus, the one-way end-to-end traversal time with two-phase routing deployed in the long-haul network can be expected to be much less than 90 msec. An end-to-end delay of up to 100 msec is acceptable for most applications.

Moreover, the bandwidth guarantees provided by two-phase routing under highly variable traffic reduce the delay variance (jitter). This reduction in jitter and the guarantee of predictable performance to unpredictable traffic provides a reasonable trade-off for the fixed increase in propagation delay. The effect of bursty traffic on jitter is mitigated by the source splitting of traffic to multiple intermediate nodes in two-phase routing.

Delay-sensitive traffic that cannot tolerate traversal of the core backbone twice can be routed along shortest paths in a hybrid architecture that accommodates both two-phase routing and direct source-destination path routing.

5.6.2 Benefits of Two-Phase Routing

In this section, we briefly discuss some properties of two-phase routing that differentiate it from direct source-destination path routing. We consider aspects of two different application scenarios to bring out the benefits of two-phase routing.

Static Optical Layer Provisioning in IP-over-Optical Networks

Core IP networks are often deployed by interconnecting routers over a switched optical backbone. When applied to such networks, direct source-destination path routing routes packets from source to destination along direct paths in the optical layer. Note that even though these paths are fixed a priori and do not depend on the traffic matrix, their *bandwidth requirements change* with variations in the traffic matrix. Thus, bandwidth needs to be deallocated from some paths and assigned to other paths as the traffic matrix changes. (Alternatively, paths between every source-destination pair can be provisioned a priori to handle the maximum traffic between them, but this leads to gross over-provisioning of capacity, since all source-destination pairs cannot simultaneously reach their peak traffic limit in the hose traffic model.) This necessitates (i) detection of changes in traffic patterns and (ii) *dynamic reconfiguration* of the provisioned optical layer circuits (i.e., change in bandwidth) in response to it. Both (i) and (ii) are difficult functionalities to deploy in current ISP networks, as discussed in Section 5.2. This amplifies the necessity of *static provisioning at the optical layer* in any scheme that handles traffic variability. Direct source-destination path routing does not meet this requirement.

To illustrate this point, consider the scenario in Figure 5.4 for direct source-destination routing in IP-over-Optical networks. Here, router A is connected to router C using 3 OC-48 connections and to Router D using 1 OC-12 connection, so as to meet the traffic demand from node A to nodes C and D of 7.5 Gbps and 600 Mbps respectively. Suppose that at a later time, traffic from A to C decreases to 5 Gbps, while traffic from A to D increases to 1200 Mbps. Then, the optical layer must be reconfigured so as to delete one OC-48 connection between A and C and creating a new OC-12 connection between A and D. As such, the *requirement of static provisioning at the optical layer is not met.*

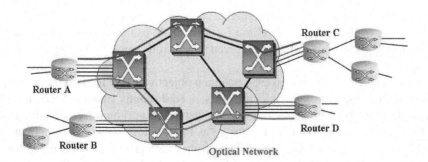

Fig. 5.4 Routing through direct optical layer circuits in IP-over-Optical networks.

Two-phase routing, as envisaged for IP-over-Optical networks, establishes the fixed bandwidth Phase 1 and Phase 2 paths at the optical layer. Thus, the *optical layer is statically provisioned* and does not need to be reconfigured in response to traffic changes. IP packets are routed end-to-end with *IP layer processing at a single intermediate node only*.

Indirection in Specialized Service Overlay Networks

The Internet Indirection Infrastructure (i3) was proposed in [35] to ease the deployment of services – like mobility, multicast and anycast – on the Internet. i3 provides a rendezvous-based communication abstraction through indirection – sources send packets to a logical identifier, and receivers express interest in packets sent to an identifier. The rendezvous points are provided by i3 servers that forward packets to all receivers that express interest in a particular identifier. The communication between senders and receivers is through these rendezvous points over an overlay network.

Two-phase routing can be used to provide bandwidth guarantees for variable traffic and support indirection in intra-ISP deployments of specialized service overlays like i3. (Note that we are not considering Internet-wide deployment here.) The intermediate nodes in the two-phase routing scheme are ideal candidates for locating i3 servers. Because we are considering a network whose topology is known, the two-phase routing scheme can be used to not only pick the i3 server locations (intermediate nodes) but also traffic engineer paths for routing with bandwidth guarantees between sender and receiver through i3 server nodes.

In service overlay models like i3, the *final destination of a packet is not known at the source* but only at the rendezvous nodes. Because the final destination of a packet needs to be known only at the intermediate nodes in two-phase routing, it is well-suited for specialized service overlays as envisaged above. In contrast, for direct source-destination path routing, the source needs to *know the destination of a packet* for routing it, thus rendering it unsuitable for such service overlay networks.

5.6.3 Determining Split Ratios and Path Routing

An instance of the scheme requires specification of the traffic split ratios $\alpha_1, \alpha_2, \ldots, \alpha_n$ and routing of the Phase 1 and Phase 2 paths. These can be picked and optimized for different performance objectives, given the network topology and ingress-egress constraints.

When link capacities are given, a common objective in the networking literature is to minimize the maximum link utilization, or equivalently, maximize the throughput. Linear programming based and combinatorial algorithms for computing the traffic split ratios and routing of paths so as to maximize network throughput are developed in [21]. The combinatorial algorithm uses a primal-dual technique based on a path-indexed linear programming formulation for the problem – it is simple to implement and involves a sequence of shortest path computations.

In [39], the authors consider the problem of minimizing the maximum *fanout* of any node when ingress-egress capacities are symmetric ($R_i = C_i$ for all i) and the underlying topology is full-mesh. The *fanout* of a node is defined as the ratio of its total outgoing link capacity to its ingress (egress) traffic capacity.

The problem of minimum cost network design (with the additional constraint of link capacities) can be formulated as a linear program and also admits solution by fast combinatorial algorithms [33].

5.6.4 Protecting Against Network Failures

We provide an overview of extensions to two-phase routing that can make the scheme resilient to network failures.

Router Node Failures in IP-over-Optical Networks

In an IP-over-Optical network where IP routers are interconnected over a switched optical backbone, the first and second phase paths are realized at the optical layer with router packet grooming at a single intermediate node only. IP routers are 200 times more unreliable than traditional carrier-grade switches and average 1219 minutes of down time per year [26]. Two-phase routing in IP-over-Optical networks can be made resilient against router node failures. (In the term "router node failure", node refers to an ISP PoP (Point-of-Presence), hence it includes the failure of all routers in a PoP.) When a router at a node f fails, any other node i cannot split any portion of its originating traffic to intermediate node f. Hence, it must redistribute the traffic split ratio α_f among other nodes $j \neq f$. In [22], the authors propose two different schemes for provisioning the optical layer to handle this redistribution of traffic – one that is failure node independent and static, and the other that is failure node dependent and dynamic.

Link Failures

Link failures can be caused by events like fiber cuts and malfunctioning of router/switch line cards. The two-phase routing scheme can be made resilient against link failures by protecting the first and second phase paths using *pre-provisioned* restoration mechanisms. By pre-provisioned, we mean that the backup paths are computed and "soft-reserved" a priori – the main action after failure is the rerouting of affected traffic on backup paths. The pre-provisioned nature of these mechanisms increases the reliability of the network by guaranteeing availability of backup resources after failure. It also allows fast restoration of traffic in an attempt to provide failure transparency to upper network layers. We discuss three such restoration mechanisms that have been considered in the literature for making two-phase routing resilient against link failures.

The first restoration mechanism [24] is local (or, link based) and consists of rerouting traffic around the failed link through pre-provisioned backup paths (link detours). The routing of traffic on portions of the primary path unaffected by the failure remains unchanged. Backup paths protecting different links can share band-width on their links so as to guarantee complete recovery against any single link failure.

The other two mechanisms [24, 33] are end-to-end (or, path based) and different in the way backup bandwidth is shared across different link failure scenarios. In *K-route path restoration*, a connection consists of $K \geq 2$ link disjoint paths from source to destination. One of these paths is designated as the backup path and the others as primary paths. The backup path carries traffic when any one of the primary paths fail due to a link failure.

In *shared backup path restoration*, a primary path is protected by a link disjoint backup path. Different backup paths can share bandwidth on common links so long as their primary paths are link disjoint. Thus, backup bandwidth is shared to provide completely recovery against single link failures. Shared backup path restoration has been shown to have lower restoration capacity overhead compared to the other two mechanisms described above [14].

Linear programming based and combinatorial algorithms for maximum through-put two-phase routing under the respective protection schemes are presented in [22, 24, 33].

Complete Node Failures

We discussed how to make two-phase routing resilient to router node failures in IP-over-Optical networks. Failure of optical switches at a node in an IP-over-Optical network or of routers at a node in a pure IP router architecture (IP routers directly connected to WDM systems) leads to failure of the node for routing Phase 1 and Phase 2 paths also (in addition to loss of intermediate node functionality). The handling of such complete node failures in two-phase routing poses additional challenges. Failure of non-intermediate nodes lying on Phase 1 or Phase 2 paths can be restored by extending the mechanisms for protecting against link failures and using detours around nodes in local restoration or node-disjoint paths in path restoration. The failure of intermediate nodes can be handled through redistribution of traffic to other intermediate nodes. Because a complete node failure can lead to both of the above scenarios, a combination of the corresponding mechanisms can be used to protect against such failures.

5.6.5 Generalized Traffic Split Ratios

The traffic split ratios α_i can be generalized to depend on source and/or destination nodes of the traffic, as proposed in [20]. In this formulation, a fraction α_k^{ij} of the traffic that originates at node i whose destination is node j is routed to node k in Phase 1. While this does not meet the indirection requirement of specialized service overlays like i3, it can potentially increase the throughput performance of the two-phase routing scheme for other application scenarios like IP-over-Optical networks.

The problem of minimum cost network design or maximum throughput routing with generalized traffic split ratios is considered in [23]. For each problem, the authors first give a linear programming formulation with an exponential set of constraints and a corresponding separation oracle (linear program of polynomial size), thus leading to a polynomial time solution using the ellipsoid algorithm for linear programming [13]. Then, by using the dual of the separation oracle linear program to replace the corresponding set of exponential constraints, they obtain a polynomial *size* linear program for the problem.

An example to illustrate the improvement in throughput when the traffic split ratios are generalized as above is given in [23]. In fact, the same example shows that the gap between the throughput values of two-phase routing with intermediate node dependent traffic split ratios α_k and generalized traffic split ratios α_k^{ij} can be made arbitrarily large. However, the 2-optimality result for two-phase routing, which we discuss in Section 5.6.6, uses only intermediate node dependent traffic split ratios and assumes $R_i = C_i$ for all i. Hence, it follows that such pathological examples where the throughput improvement with generalized split ratios is arbitrarily large (or, even greater than 2) do not exist when ingress-egress capacities are symmetric.

Moreover, the pathological example in [23] exploits asymmetric link capacities and asymmetric ingress-egress capacities ($R_i \neq C_i$ for some nodes i). There is empirical evidence that suggests when ingress-egress and link capacities are symmetric, the *throughput of two-phase routing with α_i traffic split ratios equals that with generalized traffic split ratios and matches the throughput of direct source-destination routing along fixed paths*. This is indeed the case for the Rocketfuel topologies [34] evaluated in [23]. The above remains an open and unsettled question. In particular, it would be interesting to identify the assumptions under which this might be universally true (e.g., symmetric ingress-egress and link capacities).

5.6.6 Optimality Bound for Two-Phase Routing

Two-phase routing specifies ratios for splitting traffic among intermediate nodes and Phase 1 and Phase 2 paths for routing them. Thus, two-phase routing is one form of oblivious routing. However, as explained in Section 5.6.2, it has the desirable property of static provisioning that a general solution of oblivious routing (e.g., direct source-destination path routing) may not have. Moreover, when the traffic split ratios in two-phase routing depend on intermediate nodes only, the scheme does not require a packet's final destination to be known as the source, an indirection property that is required of specialized service overlays like i3.

A natural subject of investigation, then, is: *Do the desirable properties of two-phase routing come with any resource (throughput or cost) overhead compared to (i) direct source-destination path routing, and (ii) optimal scheme among the class of all schemes that are allowed to make the routing dynamically dependent on the traffic matrix?* This question has been addressed from two approaches.

First, using the polynomial size linear programming formulations developed in [23], the authors compare the throughput of two-phase routing with that of direct source-destination path routing on actual ISP topologies. Using upper bounds on the throughput of the optimal scheme, they compare the throughput of two-phase routing with that of the optimal scheme.

Second, the authors in [23] analyze the throughput (and cost) requirements of two-phase routing from a theoretical perspective and establish a 2-optimality bound. That is, the throughput of two-phase routing is at least $1/2$ that of the best possible scheme in which the *routing can be dependent on the traffic matrix*. It is worth emphasizing the generality of this result – it compares two-phase routing with the *most general class of schemes* for routing hose traffic. We briefly discuss this result.

Characterization of Optimal Scheme

Consider the class of all schemes for routing all matrices in $\mathscr{T}(\mathbf{R}, \mathbf{C})$ where the routing can be made dependent on the traffic matrix. For any scheme $\mathscr{A}$, let $A(e, T)$ be the traffic on link e when matrix T is routed by $\mathscr{A}$. Then, the throughput λ_A of scheme $\mathscr{A}$ is given by

$$\lambda_A = \min_{e \in E} \frac{u_e}{\max_{T \in \mathscr{T}(\mathbf{R}, \mathbf{C})} A(e, T)}$$

The optimal scheme is the one that achieves the maximum throughput λ_{OPT} among all schemes. This is given by

$$\lambda_{OPT} = \max_{\mathscr{A}} \lambda_A$$

For each $T \in \mathscr{T}(\mathbf{R}, \mathbf{C})$, let $\lambda(T)$ be the maximum throughput achievable for routing the single matrix T. Then, the throughput of the optimal scheme can be expressed as

$$\lambda_{OPT} = \min_{T \in \mathscr{T}(\mathbf{R}, \mathbf{C})} \lambda(T)$$

At first glance, the optimal scheme that maximizes throughput appears to be hard to specify because it can route each traffic matrix differently, of which there are infinitely many in $\mathscr{T}(\mathbf{R}, \mathbf{C})$. However, because the link capacities are given in our throughput maximization model, (an) the optimal scheme can be characterized in a simple way from the proof of the lemma. Given a traffic matrix as input, route it in a manner that maximizes its throughput. Routing a single matrix so as to maximize its throughput is also known as the *maximum concurrent flow problem* [32] and is solvable in polynomial time. Clearly, the routing is dependent on the traffic matrix and can be different for different matrices.

The problem of computing λ_{OPT} can be shown to be $co\mathscr{N}\mathscr{P}$-hard [33]. Computing the cost of the optimal scheme for the minimum cost network design version of the problem is also known to be $co\mathscr{N}\mathscr{P}$-hard – the result is stated without proof in [15]. (An) The optimal scheme for minimum cost network design does not even appear to have a simple characterization like that for maximum throughput network routing.

2-Optimality Result for Two-Phase Routing

The 2-optimal bound for two-phase routing that we now discuss establishes that two-phase routing provides a 2-approximation to the optimal scheme *for both maximum throughput network routing and minimum cost network design*. This is as an useful theoretical result, given the computational intractability of the optimal schemes for both problems.

Even though this theoretical result shows that the throughput of two-phase routing, in the *worst case*, can be as low as $1/2$ that of the optimal scheme (and, hence that of direct source-destination path routing), the experiments reported in [23] indicate that two-phase routing performs much better in practice – *the throughput of two-phase routing matches that of direct source-destination path routing and is within 6% of that of the optimal scheme on all evaluated topologies*.

For the 2-optimality result, it is assumed that ingress-egress capacities are symmetric, i.e., $R_i = C_i$ for all nodes i. This is not a restrictive assumption because network routers and switches have bidirectional ports (line cards), hence the ingress and egress capacities are equal.

Theorem 5.1. *Let $R_i = C_i$ for all nodes i, and $R = \sum_{i \in N} R_i$. Consider the throughput maximization problem under given link capacities. Then, the throughput of the optimal scheme is at most*

$$2\left(1 - \frac{1}{R}\min_{i \in N} R_i\right)$$

times that of two-phase routing.

The following result for minimum cost network design is also established in [23].

Theorem 5.2. *Let $R_i = C_i$ for all nodes i, and $R = \sum_{i \in N} R_i$. Consider the minimum cost network design problem under given link costs for unit traffic. Then, the cost of two-phase routing is at most*

$$2\left(1 - \frac{1}{R}\min_{i \in N} R_i\right)$$

times that of the optimal scheme.

5.7 Summary

We surveyed recent advances in oblivious routing for handling highly dynamic and changing traffic patterns on the Internet with bandwidth guarantees. If deployed, oblivious routing will allow service providers to operate their networks in a quasi-static manner where both intra-domain paths and the bandwidths allocated to these paths is robust to extreme traffic variation. The ability to handle traffic variation without almost any routing adaptation will lead to more stable and robust Internet behavior. Theoretical advances in the area of oblivious routing have shown that it can provide these benefits without compromising capacity efficiency.

We classified the work in the literature on oblivious routing into two broad categories based on the traffic variation model – unconstrained traffic variation and hose traffic variation. For the hose model, we further classified oblivious routing schemes depending on whether the routing from source to destination is along "direct" (possibly multi-hop) paths or through a set of intermediate nodes (two-phase routing). Two-phase routing has the additional desirable properties of supporting (i) static optical layer provisioning in IP-over-Optical networks, and (ii) indirection in specialized service overlay models like i3.

References

1. D. Applegate, L. Breslau, and E. Cohen, "Coping with Network Failures: Routing Strategies for Optimal Demand Oblivious Restoration", *ACM SIGMETRICS 2004*, June 2004.
2. D. Applegate and E. Cohen, "Making Intra-Domain Routing Robust to Changing and Uncertain Traffic Demands: Understanding Fundamental Tradeoffs", *ACM SIGCOMM 2003*, August 2003.
3. J. Aspnes, Y. Azar, A. Fiat, S. A. Plotkin, and O. Waarts, "On-line routing of virtual circuits with applications to load balancing and machine scheduling", *Journal of the ACM*, 44(3):486504, 1997.
4. Y. Azar, E. Cohen, A. Fiat, H. Kaplan, and H. Räcke, "Optimal Oblivious Routing in Polynomial Time", *Journal of Computer and System Sciences*, 69(3):383-394, 2004.
5. F. Baker, "Requirements for IP Version 4 Routers", RFC 1812, June 1995.
6. J. C. R. Bennett, C. Partridge, and N. Shectman, "Packet Reordering is Not Pathological Network Behavior", *IEEE/ACM Transactions on Networking*, vol. 7, no. 6, pp. 789-798, December 1999.
7. E. Blanton and M. Allman, "On Making TCP More Robust to Packet Reordering", *ACM Computer Communication Review*, vol. 32, no. 1, pp. 20-30, January 2002.
8. J. Case, M. Fedor, M. Schoffstall, J. Davin, "Simple Network Management Protocol (SNMP)", RFC 1157, May 1990.
9. Douglas E. Comer, *Internetworking with TCP/IP Vol.1: Principles, Protocols, and Architecture*, Prentice Hall, 4th edition, January 2000.
10. N. G. Duffield, P. Goyal, A. G. Greenberg, P. P. Mishra, K. K. Ramakrishnan, J. E. van der Merwe, "A flexible model for resource management in virtual private network", *ACM SIGCOMM 1999*, August 1999.
11. T. Erlebach and M. Rüegg, "Optimal Bandwidth Reservation in Hose-Model VPNs with Multi-Path Routing", *IEEE Infocom 2004*, March 2004.
12. J. A. Fingerhut, S. Suri, and J. S. Turner, "Designing Least-Cost Nonblocking Broadband Networks", *Journal of Algorithms*, 24(2), pp. 287-309, 1997.
13. M. Grötschel, L. Lovász, and A. Schrijver, *Geometric Algorithms and Combinatorial Optimization*, Springer-Verlag, 1988.
14. W. D. Grover, *Mesh-based Survivable Transport Networks: Options and Strategies for Optical, MPLS, SONET and ATM Networking*, Prentice Hall, 2003.
15. A. Gupta, A. Kumar, M. Pal, and T. Roughgarden, "Approximation via cost sharing: Simpler and better approximation algorithms for network design", *Journal of the ACM (JACM)*, vol. 54, issue 3, June 2007.

16. C. Harrelson, K. Hildrum, S. Rao, "A Polynomial-time Tree Decomposition to Minimize Congestion", *Symposium on Parallelism in Algorithms and Architectures (SPAA)*, June 2003.
17. S. Iyer, S. Bhattacharyya, N. Taft, C. Diot, "An approach to alleviate link overload as observed on an IP backbone", *IEEE Infocom 2003*, March 2003.
18. S. Jaiswal, G. Iannaccone, C. Diot, J. Kurose, and D. Towsley, "Measurement and Classification of Out-of-Sequence Packets in a Tier-1 IP Backbone", *IEEE Infocom 2003*, March 2003.
19. G. Italiano, R. Rastogi, and B. Yener, "Restoration Algorithms for VPN Hose Model", *IEEE Infocom 2002*, 2002.
20. M. Kodialam, T. V. Lakshman, and Sudipta Sengupta, "Efficient and Robust Routing of Highly Variable Traffic", *Third Workshop on Hot Topics in Networks (HotNets-III)*, November 2004.
21. M. Kodialam, T. V. Lakshman, J. B. Orlin, and Sudipta Sengupta, "A Versatile Scheme for Routing Highly Variable Traffic in Service Overlays and IP Backbones", *IEEE Infocom 2006*, April 2006.
22. M. Kodialam, T. V. Lakshman, J. B. Orlin, and Sudipta Sengupta, "Preconfiguring IP-over-Optical Networks to Handle Router Failures and Unpredictable Traffic", *IEEE Journal on Selected Areas in Communications (JSAC)*, Special Issue on Traffic Engineering for Multi-Layer Networks, June 2007.
23. M. Kodialam, T. V. Lakshman, and S. Sengupta, "Maximum Throughput Routing of Traffic in the Hose Model", *IEEE Infocom 2006*, April 2006.
24. M. Kodialam, T. V. Lakshman, and Sudipta Sengupta, "Throughput Guaranteed Restorable Routing Without Traffic Prediction", *IEEE ICNP 2006*, November 2006.
25. A. Kumar, R. Rastogi, A. Silberschatz , B. Yener, "Algorithms for provisioning VPNs in the hose model", *ACM SIGCOMM 2001*, August 2001.
26. C. Labovitz, A. Ahuja, and F. Jahanian, "Experimental Study of Internet Stability and Backbone Failures", Proceedings of *29th International Symposium on Fault-Tolerant Computing (FTCS)*, Madison, Wisconsin, pp. 278-285, June 1999.
27. H. Liu and R. Zhang-Shen, "On Direct Routing in the Valiant Load-Balancing Architecture", *IEEE Globecom 2005*, November 2005.
28. A. Medina, N. Taft, K. Salamatian, S. Bhattacharyya, C. Diot, "Traffic Matrix Estimation: Existing Techniques and New Directions", *ACM SIGCOMM 2002*, August 2002.
29. H. Räcke, "Minimizing congestion in general networks", *43rd IEEE Symposium on Foundations of Computer Science (FOCS)*, 2002.
30. R. Ramaswami and K. N. Sivarajan, *Optical Networks: A Practical Perspective*, Morgan Kaufmann Publishers, 2002.
31. E. Rosen, A. Viswanathan, and R. Callon, "Multiprotocol Label Switching Architecture", RFC 3031, January 2001.
32. F. Shahrokhi and D. Matula, "The Maximum Concurrent Flow Problem", *Journal of ACM*, 37(2):318-334, 1990.
33. Sudipta Sengupta, *Efficient and Robust Routing of Highly Variable Traffic*, Ph.D. Thesis, Massachusetts Institute of Technology (MIT), December 2005.
34. N. Spring, R. Mahajan, D. Wetherall, and T. Anderson, "Measuring ISP Topologies with Rocketfuel", *IEEE/ACM Transactions on Networking*, vol. 12, no. 1, pp. 2-16, February 2004.
35. I. Stoica, D. Adkins, S. Zhuang, S. Shenker, S. Surana, "Internet Indirection Infrastructure", *ACM SIGCOMM 2002*, August 2002.
36. L. G. Valiant, "A scheme for fast parallel communication", *SIAM Journal on Computing*, 11(7), pp. 350-361, 1982.
37. Y. Zhang, M. Roughan, N. Duffield, A. Greenberg, "Fast Accurate Computation of Large-Scale IP Traffic Matrices from Link Loads", *ACM SIGMETRICS 2003*, June 2003.
38. R. Zhang-Shen and N. McKeown "Designing a Predictable Internet Backbone Network", *Third Workshop on Hot Topics in Networks (HotNets-III)*, November 2004.
39. R. Zhang-Shen and N. McKeown, "Designing a Predictable Internet Backbone with Valiant Load-Balancing", *Thirteenth International Workshop on Quality of Service (IWQoS 2005)*, June 2005.

40. Y. Zhang, M. Roughan, C. Lund, and D. Donoho, "An Information-Theoretic Approach to Traffic Matrix Estimation", *ACM SIGCOMM 2003*, August 2003.

Chapter 6
Network Scheduling and Message-passing

Devavrat Shah

Abstract Algorithms are operational building-blocks of a network. An important class of network algorithms deal with the scheduling of common resources among various entities such as packets or flows. In a generic setup, such algorithms operate under stringent hardware, time, power or energy constraints. Therefore, algorithms have to be extremely simple, lightweight in data-structure and distributed. Therefore, a network algorithm designer is usually faced with the task of resolving an acute tension between performance and implementability of the algorithm. In this chapter, we survey recent results on novel design and analysis methods for simple, distributed aka message-passing scheduling algorithms. We describe how the asymptotic analysis methods like fluid model and heavy traffic naturally come together with algorithm design methods such as randomization and belief-propagation (message-passing heuristic) in the context of network scheduling.

6.1 Introduction

We consider a queuing network in which there are constraints on which queues may be served simultaneously. Specifically, consider a collection of queues operating in discrete time. In each timeslot, queues are offered service according to a *service schedule* chosen from a specified set. For example, in a three-queue system, the set of allowed schedules might consist of "Serve 3 units of work each from queues A & B" and "Serve 1 unit of work each from queues A & C, and 2 units from queue B". New work may arrive in each timeslot; let each queue have a dedicated exogenous arrival process, with specified mean arrival rates. Once the work is served, it leaves the network.

This general model has been used to describe a wireless network in which radio interference limits the amount of service that can be given to each host. It has

Devavrat Shah
Massachusetts Institute of Technology, Cambridge MA 02139, e-mail: devavrat@mit.edu

been used to describe an input-queued switch, the device at the heart of high-end Internet routers, whose underlying silicon architecture imposes constraints on which traffic streams can be transmitted simultaneously. It has been used to describe the overall operation of congestion control in the Internet, whereby TCP assigns transmission rates to flows, subject to network constraints about the capacity on shared links. It can even describe road junctions, where the schedule of which lanes can move is controlled by traffic lights. Our general model is described in more detail in Section 6.2. We will use examples of switch scheduling and wireless scheduling throughout. We select these two examples, because (1) switch is the simplest nontrivial example of general scheduling problem and of great practical importance, (2) wireless network with scheduling constraints characterized by independent set on interference graph encapsulates a large class of scheduling problems.

We give the name *scheduling algorithm* to the procedure whereby a schedule is chosen for each timeslot. In such a setup, the basic question is about the characterization of an *optimal* scheduling algorithm. But before that, we need to understand the notion of *optimality*. In order to define *optimality*, we consider two important network performance metrics: throughput and delay or backlog (queue-size) on average[1]. Roughly speaking, throughput optimality corresponds to utilizing the network capacity to the fullest. Equivalently, an algorithm is called throughput optimal if whenever the network is *underloaded* the backlog in the network remains finite. The delay optimality of an algorithm is usually defined as the minimization of various norms of delay or queue-size. We will focus on minimization of the net queue-size in this chapter.

First, we will address the question of characterizing throughput and delay (queue-size) optimal algorithm. It should be noted that answering this question is quite non-trivial. The primary reason is that the algorithm has to be *online* (i.e. use only network-state information like queue-size or age of packet). However, the performance metrics like throughput and average queue-size are determined by the behavior of the network system over the entire time horizon (in principle infinite) it is operating. We will start with the description of the popular maximum-weight scheduling, called MW, introduced by Tassiulas and Ephremides [31]. It assigns a weight to each schedule, from summing the lengths of the queues that schedule proposes to serve, and choses the schedule with the largest weight. It was shown that the MW algorithm is throughput optimal for the general network model considered in this chapter (see Section 6.2). The MW algorithm is also known to induce reasonable (polynomial in network size) average queue-size for this model. But, it is not necessarily optimal in terms of average queue-size.

To understand the optimal algorithm both in terms of throughput and average queue-size, Keslassy and McKeown [14] considered a class of MW algorithms, called MW-α for $\alpha > 0$. Like MW algorithm, MW-α algorithm also uses the schedule with maximum weight. However, MW-α uses the queue-size to power α as weight instead of plain queue-size. Clearly, the MW algorithm is MW-α algorithm when $\alpha = 1$. The MW-α algorithm is throughput optimal for all $\alpha > 0$. The natural

---

[1] Due to general result like Little's law for stable system, we will use delay and queue-size or backlog interchangeably throughout.

question is: how does queue-size change with value of α? In [14], through an extensive empirical study in the context of input-queued switch, it was found that the average queue-size decreases monotonically as $\alpha \to 0^+$. This led them to conjecture that MW-0^+ is optimal in the class of MW-α algorithms, $\alpha > 0$. In Section 6.3, we will provide partial justification to this claim using the critical fluid model of the network. Specifically, an algorithm is called queue-size optimal if it induces minimal queue-size in its critical fluid model. The justification provided in this chapter shows that the MW-0^+ algorithm (i.e. limit of MW-α algorithm as $\alpha \to 0^+$) is queue-size optimal among all the scheduling algorithm, not just in the class of MW-α algorithm, in this critical fluid model. This justification holds for the general network model of this chapter, not just for input-queued switch. This result was recently established by Shah and Wischik [26].

The characterization of MW-0^+ as an optimal algorithm suggests that finding a good schedule requires solving a certain global (network-wide) combinatorial optimization problem every time. In order to be implementable, this necessitates the design of simple and distributed algorithms for such combinatorial optimization problems. In the second part of this chapter, we describe an extremely simple, randomized message-passing scheduling algorithm that is shown to be throughput optimal essentially for all known examples. This algorithm uses clever distributed summation algorithm along with a simple random sampler. The algorithm will be explained in detail through examples of switch scheduling and wireless scheduling in Section 6.4.

This randomized algorithm, though simple and throughput optimal, can induce very large (exponential in size of the network) average queue-size. Now, when scheduling constraints have simple structure (e.g. matching in switches), the algorithm performs very well even in terms of queue-size. However, when scheduling constraints have complex structure (e.g. independent set in wireless network), the algorithm induces exponentially (in network size) large queue-size. More generally, impossibility of any simple (polynomial time) centralized or distributed algorithm, that is throughput optimal and has low (polynomial size) delay, is established when scheduling constraints are complex enough (e.g. independent set) (see recent result by Shah, Tse and Tsitsiklis [24]).

Therefore, a pragmatic approach is to design simple, distributed algorithm that provides terrific performance when the underlying problem structure is simple and works as a reasonable heuristic when problem structure is hard. In the last part of this chapter in Section 6.5, we describe such an algorithm design method based on belief propagation (BP). The BP has recently emerged as a very successful heuristic for hard combinatorial problems. We present BP based scheduling algorithm for switches (matching) and wireless networks (independent set). These algorithms are exact when underlying problem have certain LP relaxation tight; and work as a reasonable heuristic otherwise.

We take note of the limitation of this chapter in that there is a lot of exciting work done in the past decade or two on the topic of network scheduling (e.g.[2, 11, 29, 20, 27]) and it is not discussed here for natural reasons. An interested reader is strongly encouraged to explore these results.

6.2 Model

This section describes an abstract model of the queuing network that we will consider. Though the model described here corresponds to *single-hop* network for convenience, most of the analytic and algorithmic results stated here should apply for general *multi-hop* network with appropriate changes. The examples of switch and wireless scheduling, which are special cases of the model, are described in detail and will be useful throughout the chapter.

6.2.1 Abstract formulation

Consider a collection of N queues. Let time be discrete, indexed by $\tau \in \{0, 1, \dots\}$. Let $Q_n(\tau)$ be the size of queue n at the beginning of timeslot τ, and write $\mathbf{Q}(\tau)$ for the vector $[Q_n(\tau)]_{1 \le n \le N}$. Let $\mathbf{Q}(0)$ be the prespecified vector of initial queue sizes.

In each timeslot, each queue is offered service subject to a *scheduling constraint* described below. If the amount of service offered to a queue is larger than the queue size, then we say that the queue has *idled*, otherwise it does not idle. Once work is served it leaves the network. New work may arrive in each timeslot; let each of the N queues have a dedicated exogenous arrival process.

The scheduling constraint is described by a finite set of *feasible schedules* $\mathscr{S} \subset \mathbb{R}_+^N$. In every timeslot a *schedule* $\pi \in \mathscr{S}$ is chosen; queue n is offered an amount of service π_n in that timeslot. For example, in the case of input-queued switch, $\mathscr{S}$ is the set of all matchings between input ports and output ports; in the case of wireless network, $\mathscr{S}$ is the set of independent sets in the interference graph. For simplicity, we will restrict ourselves to $\mathscr{S}$ such that $\mathscr{S} \subset \{0, 1\}^N$; that is, for any $\pi \in \mathscr{S}$, $\pi_n = 1$ (queue n has received unit amount of service) or 0 (queue n receives no service). We will also assume that $\mathscr{S}$ is *monotone*: if $\pi \in \mathscr{S}$ then for any $\sigma \le \pi$ component-wise, i.e. $\sigma_n \le \pi_n$ for all n, $\sigma \in \mathscr{S}$.

Let $S_\pi(\tau) \in \mathbb{R}_+$ be the total length of time up to the end of timeslot τ in which schedule π has been chosen, and let $S_\pi(0) = 0$. Let $Z_n(\tau)$ be the total amount of idling at queue n up to the end of timeslot τ, and let $Z_n(0) = 0$. Let $A_n(\tau)$ be the total amount of work arriving to queue n up to the end of timeslot τ, and $A_n(0) = 0$. We will take $\mathbf{A}(\cdot)$ to be a random process. Define the arrival rate vector λ by

$$\lambda_n = \lim_{\tau \to \infty} \frac{1}{\tau} A_n(\tau) \tag{6.1}$$

and assume that this limit exists almost surely for each queue. For simplicity, we will assume the following about the arrival process: $A_n(\tau + 1) - A_n(\tau)$ are independent across τ and n, identically distributed for a given n but different τ, have support on integer values only and are bounded. A simplest example of the above is $A_n(\cdot)$ being Bernoulli i. i. d. process with parameter λ_n.

We will use the convention that $\mathbf{Q}(\tau)$ is the vector of queue sizes at the beginning of timeslot τ, and then the schedule for timeslot τ is chosen and service happens, and then arrivals for timeslot τ happen. Define the cumulative offered service vector $\Sigma(\tau) = [\Sigma_n(\tau)]$ as $\Sigma(\tau) = \sum_{\pi \in \mathscr{S}} \pi S_\pi(\tau)$. Then,

$$Q_n(\tau) = Q_n(0) + A_n(\tau) - \Sigma_n(\tau) + Z_n(\tau) \tag{6.2}$$

$$Z_n(\tau) - Z_n(\tau - 1) = \max\left(0, \Sigma_n(\tau) - \Sigma_n(\tau - 1) - Q_n(\tau - 1)\right) \tag{6.3}$$

6.2.1.1 Notation

Finally, some notation. We will reserve bold letters for vectors in $\mathbb{R}^N$. Let $\mathbf{0}$ be the vector of all 0s, and $\mathbf{1}$ be the vector of all 1s. Let $1_{\{.\}}$ be the indicator function, $1_{\text{true}} = 1$ and $1_{\text{false}} = 0$. Let $x \wedge y = \min(x,y)$ and $x \vee y = \max(x,y)$ and $[x]^+ = x \vee 0$. When x is a vector, the maximum is taken componentwise. Use the norm $|x| = \max_i |x_i|$ for vectors x. For vectors $\mathbf{u}$ and $\mathbf{v}$ and functions $f : \mathbb{R} \to \mathbb{R}$, let

$$\mathbf{u} \cdot \mathbf{v} = \sum_{n=1}^{N} u_n v_n, \quad \text{and} \quad f(\mathbf{u}) = \left[f(u_n) \right]_{1 \le n \le N}$$

Let $\mathbb{N}$ be the set of natural numbers $\{1, 2, \dots\}$, let $\mathbb{Z}_+ = \{0, 1, 2, \dots\}$, let $\mathbb{R}$ be the set of real numbers, and let $\mathbb{R}_+ = \{x \in \mathbb{R} : x \ge 0\}$.

6.2.2 Scheduling algorithms

For our purposes, one scheduling algorithm is particularly interesting: the Maximum Weight (MW) scheduling algorithm, which works as follows. Let $\mathbf{Q}(\tau)$ be the vector of queue sizes at the beginning of timeslot τ. Define the weight of a schedule $\pi \in \mathscr{S}$ to be $\pi \cdot \mathbf{Q}(\tau)$. The algorithm then chooses for timeslot τ a scheduling with the greatest weight (breaking ties arbitrarily). This algorithm can be generalized to choose a schedule which maximizes $\pi \cdot \mathbf{Q}(\tau)^\alpha$, where the exponent is taken componentwise for some $\alpha > 0$; call this the MW-α algorithm. In this paper, we will study the MW-α algorithm in detail. More generally, one could choose a schedule π such that

$$\pi \cdot f(\mathbf{Q}(\tau)) = \max_{\rho \in \mathscr{S}} \rho \cdot f(\mathbf{Q}(\tau)) \tag{6.4}$$

for some function $f : \mathbb{R}_+ \to \mathbb{R}_+$; call this the MW-$f$ algorithm. We will assume the following about f.

Assumption 1 *Assume f is differentiable and strictly increasing with $f(0) = 0$. Assume also that for any $\mathbf{q} \in \mathbb{R}_+^N$ and $\pi \in \mathscr{S}$, with $m(\mathbf{q}) = \max_{\rho \in \mathscr{S}} \rho \cdot f(\mathbf{q})$,*

$$\pi \cdot f(\mathbf{q}) = m(\mathbf{q}) \quad \Longrightarrow \quad \pi \cdot f(\kappa \mathbf{q}) = m(\kappa \mathbf{q}) \;\; \textit{for all } \kappa \in \mathbb{R}_+.$$

The MW-f algorithm is *myopic*, i.e. it chooses a schedule based only on the current queue sizes and doesn't need to try to learn traffic parameters etc. An important reason for the popularity of the MW algorithm is that MW-f is the only class of myopic scheduling algorithms known to have the largest possible stability region, for a large class of constrained scheduling problems. The MW algorithm was first proposed by Tassiulas and Ephremides [31]. Later, it was proposed by McKeown, Ananthram and Walrand in the context of switches [16]. The MW-f algorithm has been studied in detail by various researchers, including [22, 14, 1].

6.2.3 Input-queued switch

Here we describe input-queue switch as a special instance of the abstract network model. An Internet router has several input ports and output ports. A data transmission cable is attached to each of these ports. Packets arrive at the input ports. The function of the router is to work out which output port each packet should go to, and to transfer packets to the correct output ports. This last function is called *switching*. There are a number of possible switch architectures; we will consider the commercially popular input-queued switch architecture.

Figure 6.1 illustrates an input-queued switch with three input ports and three output ports. Packets arriving at input i destined for output j are stored at input port i, in queue $Q_{i,j}$. The switch operates in discrete time. In each timeslot, the switch fabric can transmit a number of packets from input ports to output ports, subject to the two constraints that each input can transmit at most one packet and that each output can receive at most one packet. In other words, at each timeslot the switch can choose a *matching* from inputs to outputs. Figure 6.1 shows two possible matchings. In the left hand figure, the matching allows a packet to be transmitted from input port 3 to output port 2, but since $Q_{3,2}$ is empty no packet is actually transmitted. The specific matching of inputs to outputs in each timeslot is chosen by the scheduling algorithm.

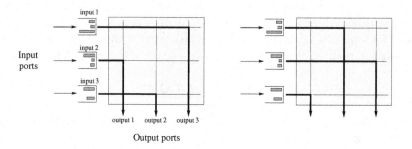

Fig. 6.1 An input-queued switch, and two example matching of inputs to outputs.

To connect back to the abstract formulation, note that an N-port switch has $n = N^2$ queues; in the context of switch, we will always use notation of Q_{ij} instead of notation of Q_n so as to be clear in referencing the corresponding input and output for a queue. The set of all feasible schedules $\mathscr{S}$ correspond to the set of all complete matchings in an $N \times N$ complete bipartite graph. Formally,

$$\mathscr{S} = \left\{ \pi = [\pi_{ij}] \in \{0,1\}^{N \times N} : \sum_{k=1}^{N} \pi_{ik} = 1, 1 \leq i \leq N; \sum_{k=1}^{N} \pi_{kj} = 1, 1 \leq j \leq N \right\}.$$

The MW (or MW-1) scheduling algorithm, therefore chooses a matching as the schedule that is one of the possibly many solutions of the following combinatorial optimization problem: let $\mathbf{Q}(\tau) = [Q_{ij}(\tau)]$ be queue-sizes at timeslot τ, then the schedule $\pi(\tau)$ at timeslot τ solves:

$$\text{maximize} \quad \sum_{i,j=1}^{N} \pi_{ij} Q_{ij}(\tau) \quad \text{over} \quad \pi_{ij} \in \{0,1\}, 1 \leq i, j \leq N \qquad (6.5)$$

$$\text{subject to} \quad \sum_{k=1}^{N} \pi_{ik} = 1, \ 1 \leq i \leq N; \quad \sum_{k=1}^{N} \pi_{kj} = 1, \ 1 \leq j \leq N.$$

The above optimization problem is the well-known Maximum Weight Matching(MWM) problem. Therefore, designing MW scheduling algorithm will involve solving this optimization problem every timeslot.

Some notes on the input-queued switch architecture. (1) We have illustrated a switch with as many inputs as outputs. It may be that some of these do not actually carry any traffic; thus there is no loss of generality in assuming as many inputs as outputs. (2) In the Internet, packets may have different sizes. Before the packet reaches the switch fabric, it will be fragmented into a collection of smaller packets (called cells) of fixed size. (3) There will typically be a block of memory at each input port for the queues, and one packet's worth of memory at each output port to hold the packet as it is serialized onto the outgoing cable. Memory access speeds are a limiting factor, and indeed the time it takes to read or write a packet from memory is what determines the length of a timeslot. There are switches which perform several matchings per timeslot—but then the timeslots need to last several times longer, to give time for the extra reads and writes.

6.2.4 Wireless networks

Consider several wifi networks close to each other and sharing the same frequency. If two devices close to each other transmit at the same time, then there is interference and the data may be lost; whereas two devices far from each other may successfully transmit at the same time. A popular way to model this sort of interference is to draw a graph with a node for each device and an edge between two nodes if they can interfere with each other; in other words a transmission from a node is successful only if none of its neighbors in the network graph is transmitting at the same time. (This is called the *independent set* model for interference.)

Figure 6.2 illustrates a wireless network of three nodes operating under interference constraints. Here, like switch packets arriving at node i and destined for node j are stored at node i in queue $Q_{i,j}$. For example, the queue $Q_{2,3}$ shown in the Figure 6.2 stores packet destined for node 3 arrived at node 2. The independent set constraint on scheduling, in our example, implies that at a given timeslot at most one of the three node can transmit. Figure 6.2 shows that node 3 is selected for transmission while other two nodes remain silent; and node 3 transmits packet to node 2.

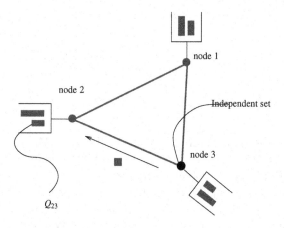

Fig. 6.2 A wireless network operating under interference constraint, and an example independent set (node 3) schedule for transmission from 3 to 2.

In a general wireless network, the interference network graph is represented as $G = (V, E)$ with vertices corresponding to nodes, $V = \{1, \ldots, N\}$ and edges corresponding to interference, that is

$$E = \{(i, j) : i \text{ and } j \text{ interfere with each other}\}.$$

An implicit assumption here is that any node $i \in V$ can transmit packets to node j only if $(i, j) \in E$. We will consider a single-hop wireless network, that is each packet arrives at one node, gets transmitted to one of its neighbors and then departs the network. In such setup, if a node i transmits (to any of its neighbors), then all of i's neighbors must be silent. Therefore, the real constraint lies in deciding whether i transmits or not; but not in which node it transmits. Therefore, for simplicity we will ignore the finer classification of queue-sizes as Q_{ij} but instead consider $Q_i = \sum_j Q_{ij}$ here for the purpose of scheduling. In this setup, the set of schedules is the set of independent sets in G. Formally,

$$\mathscr{S} = \left\{ \sigma = [\sigma_i] \in \{0,1\}^N : \sigma_i + \sigma_j \leq 1, \text{ for all } (i,j) \in E \right\}.$$

The MW (or MW-1) scheduling algorithm, therefore chooses an independent set as the schedule that is one of the possibly many solutions of the following combinatorial optimization problem: let $\mathbf{Q}(\tau) = [Q_i(\tau)]$ be queue-sizes at timeslot τ, then the schedule $\sigma(\tau)$ at timeslot τ solves:

$$\text{maximize} \quad \sum_i^N \sigma_i Q_i(\tau) \quad \text{over} \quad \sigma_i \in \{0,1\}, 1 \leq i \leq N, \tag{6.6}$$

$$\text{subject to} \quad \sigma_i + \sigma_j \leq 1, \text{ for all } (i,j) \in E.$$

The above optimization problem is the well-known Maximum Weight Independent Set(MWIS) problem. Therefore, designing MW scheduling algorithm will involve solving this optimization problem every timeslot.

Some notes on the described wireless network. (1) In the multi-hop network, the MW scheduling corresponds to solving MWIS problem with somewhat different weights (e.g. Back-pressure algorithm [31]). Therefore, for the purpose of scheduling algorithm design, the above model captures the essence. (2) The above describe model of interference is general in the following sense. Many of the combinatorial interference models such as 2-hop matching model (secondary interference model) can be represented as an independent set model by representing transmission edges as nodes; and such transformations are computationally equivalent (formally, they are reductions). (3) We note that there are other models of interference (e.g. SINR model) that can not be captures by *hard* constraints of the type of independent set model.

6.3 Characterization of optimal algorithm

This section presents characterization of optimal scheduling algorithms first in terms of throughput and then in terms of queue-size. The algorithms considered here are part of the maximum weight (MW) family. Interestingly enough, as explained in this section, considering this class of algorithm is sufficient for the purpose of finding throughput and queue-size optimal algorithm. This section will utilize fluid-model technique. The contents of this section can be found in a recent paper by Shah and Wischik [26]. We note that fluid model for MW scheduling algorithm was first introduced in the context of switch by Dai and Prabhakar [9] and later used by Andrews et. al. [1].

6.3.1 Throughput optimality

Here, we will establish that all the MW-f algorithms are throughput optimal as long as f satisfies Assumption 1. First, some necessary definitions.

Admissible arrival rates. At each timeslot, a schedule $\pi \in \mathscr{S}$ must be chosen. Let Θ be the convex hull of $\mathscr{S}$,

$$\Theta = \left\{ \sum_{\pi \in \mathscr{S}} \alpha_\pi \pi : \sum_{\pi \in \mathscr{S}} \alpha_\pi = 1, \text{ and } \alpha_\pi \geq 0 \text{ for all } \pi \right\}. \qquad (6.7)$$

We say that an arrival rate vector λ is *admissible* if $\lambda \in \Lambda$ where

$$\Lambda = \left\{ \lambda \in \mathbb{R}_+^N : \lambda \leq \sigma \text{ componentwise, for some } \sigma \in \Theta \right\}. \qquad (6.8)$$

Intuitively, this means that there is some combination of feasible schedules which permits all incoming work to be served. Also define

$$\Lambda^\circ = \left\{ \lambda \in \Lambda : \lambda \leq \sum_{\pi \in \mathscr{S}} \alpha_\pi \pi, \text{ where } \sum_{\pi \in \mathscr{S}} \alpha_\pi < 1 \text{ and } \alpha_\pi \geq 0 \text{ for all } \pi \right\}$$

$$\partial \Lambda = \Lambda \setminus \Lambda^\circ.$$

Say that λ is *strictly admissible* if $\lambda \in \Lambda^\circ$, and that λ is *critical* if $\lambda \in \partial \Lambda$.

Fluid model. The fluid model is essentially the first-order deterministic description of the network. To obtain this formally, we need to consider the fluid scaling of the original system. Next, we describe a scaling procedure to obtain a sequence of (network) systems from the given system, indexed by $r \in \mathbb{N}$. Write $X^r(\tau) = (\mathbf{Q}^r(\tau), \mathbf{A}^r(\tau), \mathbf{Z}^r(\tau), S^r(\tau))$, $\tau \in \mathbb{Z}_+$, for the rth system. Define the scaled system $x^r(t) = (\mathbf{q}^r(t), \mathbf{a}^r(t), \mathbf{z}^r(t), s^r(t))$ for $t \in \mathbb{R}_+$ by

$$\mathbf{q}^r(t) = \mathbf{Q}^r(rt)/r \qquad\qquad \mathbf{a}^r(t) = \mathbf{A}^r(rt)/r$$
$$\mathbf{z}^r(t) = \mathbf{Z}^r(rt)/r \qquad\qquad s_\pi^r(t) = S_\pi^r(r't)/r'$$

after extending the domain of $X^r(\cdot)$ to $\mathbb{R}_+$ by linear interpolation in each interval $(\tau - 1, \tau)$. We describe fluid model equations, which are essentially satisfied by limiting system $X^r(\cdot)$ as $r \to \infty$. We say that the process $x(\cdot) = (\mathbf{q}(\cdot), \mathbf{a}(\cdot), \mathbf{z}(\cdot), s(\cdot))$ satisfies the fluid model for the MW-f scheduling algorithm if

$$\mathbf{a}(t) = \lambda t \qquad (6.9)$$

$$\mathbf{q}(t) = \mathbf{q}(0) + \mathbf{a}(t) - \sum_{\pi} s_\pi(t)\pi + \mathbf{z}(t) \qquad (6.10)$$

$$\sum_{\pi \in \mathscr{S}} s_\pi(t) = t \qquad (6.11)$$

each $s_\pi(\cdot)$ and $z_n(\cdot)$ is increasing (not necessarily strictly increasing) $\qquad$ (6.12)

all the components of $x(\cdot)$ are absolutely continuous $\qquad$ (6.13)

for almost all t, all n, $\dot{z}_n(t) = 0$ if $q_n(t) > 0$ $\qquad$ (6.14)

for almost all t, all $\pi \in \mathscr{S}$, $\dot{s}_\pi(t) = 0$ if $\pi \cdot f(\mathbf{q}(t)) < \max_{\rho \in \mathscr{S}} \rho \cdot f(\mathbf{q}(t))$ $\qquad$ (6.15)

Our goal is to establish that the dynamics of $x^r(t)$, for t in a fixed interval $[0,T]$, as $r \to \infty$ satisfies the above stated fluid model equations. We make the following necessary assumption in addition to the setup described so far: the initial size is non-random and that it converges,

$$\mathbf{q}^r(0) \to \mathbf{q}_0 \quad \text{for some } \mathbf{q}_0 \in \mathbb{R}_+^N. \qquad (6.16)$$

Theorem 6.1 (Theorem 5.1[26]). *Make assumption (6.16). Let FMS^2 be the set of all processes $x(t)$ over $t \in [0,T]$ which satisfy the appropriate fluid model equations, namely*

- *equations (6.9)–(6.14), for any scheduling algorithm,*
- *equation (6.15) in addition if the network is running MW-f and Condition 1 holds,*
- *$\mathbf{q}(0) = \mathbf{q}_0$ in addition, if (6.16) holds.*

Let FMS_ε be the ε-fattening

$$FMS_\varepsilon = \left\{ x : \sup_{t \in [0,T]} |x(t) - y(t)| < \varepsilon \text{ for some } y \in FMS \right\}.$$

Then for any $\varepsilon > 0$, $\mathbb{P}(x^r(\cdot) \in FMS_\varepsilon) = 1 - o(R(r))$, where $R(r) \to 0$ as $r \to \infty$.

Fluid stability and throughput optimality. A fluid model is said to be *stable* if there is some draining time $H \in \mathbb{R}_+$ such that every fluid model with bounded initial queue size $|\mathbf{q}(0)| \leq 1$ ends up with $\mathbf{q}(t) = \mathbf{0}$ for all $t \geq H$. It is said to be *weakly stable* if every fluid model with empty initial queues $\mathbf{q}(0) = \mathbf{0}$ remains at $\mathbf{q}(t) = \mathbf{0}$ for all $t \geq 0$. In lecture notes by Dai[8], Section 2.6 describes the relationship between stability of the fluid model and stability of the original (unscaled) stochastic process. Theorem 6.1 stated above suggests the spirit of the relationship. In our setup, the weakly stable fluid model implies that the system is *rate stable*. That is, let $\mathbf{D}(\tau) = [\mathbf{D}_n(\tau)]$ denote the vector of cumulative number of packets that has departed from from queues till timeslot τ. Then, weakly stable fluid model implies

----
[2] The abbreviation FMS is used for "fluid model solution".

$$\lim_{\tau \to \infty} \mathbf{D}(\tau) = \lambda, \text{ with probability 1.}$$

Here, we will seek weak stability only and we will call an algorithm *throughput optimal* if it is weakly stable. However, it should be noted that under our assumptions on arrival process, the strong stability[3] holds (and can be established either using the fluid model or discrete Foster-Lyapunov criteria). We will obtain weak stability for networks by considering the Lyapunov function

$$L(\mathbf{q}) = F(\mathbf{q}) \cdot \mathbf{1} \quad \text{where} \quad F(x) = \int_0^x f(y) \, dy. \tag{6.17}$$

The first claim of Lemma 6.1, together with the fact that $L(\mathbf{q}) = 0 \iff \mathbf{q} = \mathbf{0}$, implies that the fluid model for MW-f is weakly stable for $\lambda \in \Lambda$. Further, it can be shown that the fluid model is stable for $\lambda \in \Lambda^\circ$; this can be proved by writing an explicit bound for $\dot{L}(\mathbf{q}(t))$ in terms of $\max_\pi \pi \cdot \mathbf{q}(t)$, then using the technique of [28].

Lemma 6.1. *For $\lambda \in \Lambda$, every fluid model solution satisfies $\frac{dL(\mathbf{q}(t))}{dt} \leq 0$. For $\lambda \in \Lambda^\circ$, every fluid model solution satisfies $\frac{dL(\mathbf{q}(t))}{dt} < 0$. Furthermore,*

$$\frac{dL(\mathbf{q}(t))}{dt} = \lambda \cdot f(\mathbf{q}(t)) - \max_{\pi \in \mathscr{S}} \pi \cdot f(\mathbf{q}(t))$$

and

$$\lambda \cdot f(\mathbf{q}) - \max_{\pi \in \mathscr{S}} \pi \cdot f(\mathbf{q}) \leq 0 \quad \text{for all } \mathbf{q} \in \mathbb{R}_+^N.$$

Proof.

$$\frac{d}{dt} L(\mathbf{q}(t)) = \frac{d\mathbf{q}(t)}{dt} \cdot f(\mathbf{q}(t))$$

$$= \left(\lambda - \sum_{\pi \in \mathscr{S}} \dot{s}_\pi(t) \pi + \dot{\mathbf{z}}(t) \right) \cdot f(\mathbf{q}(t)) \quad \text{by differentiating (6.10)}$$

$$= \left(\lambda - \sum_\pi \dot{s}_\pi(t) \pi \right) \cdot f(\mathbf{q}(t)) \quad \text{by (6.14), using } f(0) = 0$$

$$= \lambda \cdot f(\mathbf{q}(t)) - \max_{\rho \in \mathscr{S}} \rho \cdot f(\mathbf{q}(t)) \quad \text{by (6.15).}$$

When $\lambda \in \Lambda$, we can write $\lambda \leq \sigma$ componentwise for some $\sigma = \sum_\pi \alpha_\pi \pi$ with $\alpha_\pi \geq 0$ and $\sum \alpha_\pi = 1$. This yields $\frac{dL(\mathbf{q}(t))}{dt} \leq 0$. When $\lambda \in \Lambda^\circ$, the same holds except with $\sum \alpha_\pi < 1$, which yields $\frac{dL(\mathbf{q}(t))}{dt} < 0$. □

When we use this result, we almost always implicitly pair it with a standard fact which is worth stating here: if $f : \mathbb{R}_+ \to \mathbb{R}$ is an absolutely continuous function, and $\dot{f}(t) \leq 0$ at almost all t, then $f(t) \leq f(0)$ for all $t \geq 0$.

---

[3] We call a network strongly stable if it is positive recurrent.

6.3.2 *Queue-size optimality*

The above results suggest that there is a large class of algorithms that are throughput optimal. Here, we will search for an algorithm that produces optimal performance in terms of queue-size as well. Clearly, identifying such an algorithm[4] in an absolute sense is a challenging question and is an open problem worth pursuing.

In this chapter, we will rely on fluid model characterization to seek an asymptotic answer to this question. We will restrict our search to special subclass of MW-f algorithms, the MW-α algorithms for $\alpha \in \mathbb{R}_+$. Recall that the MW-α algorithm uses $f(x) = x^\alpha$ as the weight function. The reason for this restriction is two fold. First, the average queue-size performance of MW-α scheduling algorithms was extensively studied (empirically) in the context of input-queued switch by Keslassy and McKeown [14]. They had observed that as $\alpha \to 0^+$, the average queue-size descreases. This led them to conjecture that MW-0^+ algorithm is an optimal (in the class of MW-α) algorithm with respect to its performance in terms of average queue-size. Second, the MW-α are a large class of algorithms and lend themselves to analytic tractability. Therefore, an optimist would take the conjecture of [14] one step ahead by hoping that MW-0^+ algorithm is optimal among all possible scheduling algorithms.

As we shall see, an optimist's perspective is indeed true; not only for switch, but for the general setup of network considered in this chapter. We again take note of the following limitation of the details provided in the remainder of this section. The justification of the optimality of MW-0^+ is *partial*, because the optimality is established for the fluid scaled queue-size. However, it is non-trivially important for two reasons. First, if MW-0^+ is optimal in terms of, say average (not fluid scaled) queue-size then it ought to be optimal with respect to fluid scaled queue-sizes as well. Second, optimality with respect to fluid scaling does imply[5] an approximate optimality in terms of average queue-size at the original scaling.

The presentation in this section follows [26] very closely. In what follows, we will formally introduce critical fluid model and queue-size optimality. Then, we will indulge into a minor digression by introducing various definitions in order to be able to state the main result of this section formally. An impatient and curious reader may skip this digression in the first read and jump directly to the Theorem 6.2. Finally, we will discuss the implications of this result in terms of the structure of the optimal algorithm.

Critical fluid model. Consider the network operating under MW-α scheduling algorithm with arrival rate $\lambda \in \Lambda$. Let $\mathbf{q}(t)$ denote the fluid scaled queue-size vector. That is, $\mathbf{q}(t)$ satisfies the fluid model equations (6.9)–(6.15) (with $f(x) = x^\alpha$) starting with some finite initial queue-size vector $\mathbf{q}_0$ at $t = 0$. We are interested in the net

---

[4] This algorithm should be online, i.e. utilize only the history of the network.

[5] This is not immediate and an interested reader will have to *dig through* the proof of Theorem 6.1. In particular, the approximation error introduced by fluid models in approximating the original system need to be quantified. Of course, it will lead to "probabilistically approximately correct" characterization which will depend on distributional characterization of arrival process in our setup.

queue-size of the network, that is $\sum_n \mathbf{q}_n(t)$, which we will denote by $\mathbf{1} \cdot \mathbf{q}(t)$. Now, suppose $\lambda \in \Lambda^\circ$. Then Lemma 6.1 suggests that as $t \to \infty$, the Lypanov function value $L(\mathbf{q}(t)) \to 0$ under MW-α algorithm for any $\alpha > 0$. Therefore, $\mathbf{1} \cdot \mathbf{q}(t) \to 0$ for MW-α algorithm for any $\alpha > 0$. Thus, using fluid model the performance of MW-α algorithms, in terms of the net queue-size at all time t, can not be differentiated if $\lambda \in \Lambda^\circ$. Therefore, in order to obtain any conclusive statement using fluid model, we need to restrict our attention to $\lambda \in \partial \Lambda$. We will call such a system *critically loaded* as λ is on the *boundary* of the capacity region of the system.

The fluid model obtained for such a critically loaded system is called the critical fluid model. Apart from the use of critical fluid model for studying queue-size scaling as in this chapter, the critical fluid model has been utilized as an important technical tool to establish the so called *state-space collapse property* under heavy traffic asymptotic. This turns out to be an important intermediate step to obtain the heavy traffic characterization of networks (an interested reader is strongly recommended to check an excellent sequel of papers by Bramson and Williams [7, 33] to find out more about this).

Queue-size optimality: a formal definition. Now, we formally define the notion of *queue-size optimality* for the purpose of this chapter. Consider a scheduling algorithm $\mathscr{A}$. By Theorem 6.1, there exists vector of queue-sizes $\mathbf{q}^{\mathscr{A}}(t)$ satisfying (6.9)–(6.14) for any $\lambda \in \partial \Lambda$ with some initial queue-size vector $\mathbf{q}^{\mathscr{A}}(0) = \mathbf{q}_0 \in \mathbb{R}_+^N$. We call the algorithm $\mathscr{A}$ as a $(1 + \phi)$-approximation algorithm, $\phi \geq 0$, if the following holds: for any other scheduling algorithm $\mathscr{B}$ with the same initial condition and arrival process, its (fluid scaled) queue-size vector $\mathbf{q}^{\mathscr{B}}(t)$ is such that for all $t \geq 0$,

$$\mathbf{1} \cdot \mathbf{q}^{\mathscr{A}}(t) \leq (1 + \phi) \mathbf{1} \cdot \mathbf{q}^{\mathscr{B}}(t), \tag{6.18}$$

for all choices of $\lambda \in \partial \Lambda$ and all initial configuration $\mathbf{q}_0 \in \mathbb{R}_+^N$.

We call an algorithm *queue-size optimal*, if it is 1-approximation algorithm. In what follows, we will state that MW-α algorithm is $N^{\frac{\alpha}{1+\alpha}}$-approximation algorithm. Therefore, it is $(1 + \delta)$ approximation when $\alpha = \ln(1 + \delta)/\ln N \approx \delta/\ln N$ for $\delta > 0$. Thus, as $\alpha \to 0^+$ the MW-α algorithm becomes 1^+-approximation algorithm and hence essentially optimal.

Some necessary definitions. Here, we state some necessary definitions in order to state the main result about MW-α algorithms's approximate performance formally. Given $\lambda \in \Lambda$, first consider the optimization problem PRIMAL(λ):

minimize	$\sum_{\pi \in \mathscr{S}} \alpha_\pi$
over	$\alpha_\pi \in \mathbb{R}_+$ for all $\pi \in \mathscr{S}$
such that	$\lambda \leq \sum_{\pi \in \mathscr{S}} \alpha_\pi \pi$ componentwise

This problem asks whether it is possible to find a combination of schedules which can serve arrival rates λ; clearly λ is admissible if and only if the solution to the primal is ≤ 1. Now consider its dual problem DUAL(λ):

maximize	$\xi \cdot \lambda$
over	$\xi \in \mathbb{R}^N_+$
such that	$\max_{\pi \in \mathscr{S}} \xi \cdot \pi \leq 1$

The solution is clearly attained when the constraint is tight. Given a queue size vector $\mathbf{Q}$ and any dual-feasible ξ satisfying the constraint with equality, call $\xi \cdot \mathbf{Q}$ the *workload* at the *virtual resource* ξ. The virtual resource specifies a combination of several actual resources (namely the queues themselves). The long-run rate at which work arrives at the virtual resource is $\xi \cdot \lambda$, and the maximum rate at which it can be served is 1.

A concrete example. Consider a system with $N = 2$ queues, A and B. Suppose the set $\mathscr{S}$ of possible schedules consists of "serve three packets from queue A" (schedule 1) and "serve one packet each from A and B" (schedule 2). Let λ_A and λ_B be the arrival rates at the two queues, measured in packets per second.

PRIMAL description. Schedule 2 is the only action which serves queue B, so we need to perform schedule 2 at least λ_B times per second. There's no point performing schedule 2 any more than this. This allows for serving λ_B packets per second from queue A, so we additionally need to perform schedule 1 at a rate of $[\lambda_A - \lambda_B]^+/3$ times per second. If we're only allowed to choose one schedule per second, we require $\lambda_B \leq 1$ and $\lambda_A/3 + 2\lambda_B/3 \leq 1$.

DUAL description Define a virtual resource W as follows. Every time a packet arrives to queue A put $\zeta_A \geq 0$ tokens into W; every time a packet arrives to queue B put $\zeta_B \geq 0$ tokens into W. The most tokens that schedule 1 can remove from W is $3\zeta_A$, and the most tokens that schedule 2 can remove from W is $\zeta_A + \zeta_B$. We may as well normalize (ζ_A, ζ_B) so that the largest of these is 1. The total rate at which tokens arrive is $\lambda_A \zeta_A + \lambda_B \zeta_B$. If we're only allowed to choose one schedule per second, we need this to be ≤ 1.

  Set $\zeta_A = 1/3$ and $\zeta_B = 2/3$, and we recover the PRIMAL constraint that $\lambda_A/3 + 2\lambda_B/3 \leq 1$. Set $\zeta_A = 0$ and $\zeta_B = 1$, and we recover the PRIMAL constraint that $\lambda_B \leq 1$.

Critical workloads. Both problems are soluble so, by strong duality, the solutions to both problems are equal. Clearly the solutions to the optimization problems is ≤ 1 for any $\lambda \in \Lambda$. For $\lambda \in \Lambda^\circ$ it is < 1, and for $\lambda \in \partial\Lambda$ it is $= 1$. When this is so, we call the solutions to the dual problem the *critically-loaded virtual resources*.

  Let $\mathscr{S}^* = \mathscr{S}^*(\lambda)$ be the set of all critically loaded virtual resources that are extreme points of the feasible region. Call these the *principal* critically-loaded virtual resources. Note that the feasible region is a polytope, therefore $\mathscr{S}^*$ is finite; and that the feasible region is convex, therefore any critically-loaded virtual resource ζ can be written

$$\zeta = \sum_{\xi \in \mathscr{S}^*} x_\xi \xi \quad \text{with} \quad \sum x_\xi = 1 \text{ and all } x_\xi \geq 0. \tag{6.19}$$

The critical workloads have a useful property. Suppose $\lambda \in \Lambda$, and $\lambda \leq \sigma$ for some $\sigma \in \Sigma$, as per the definition of Λ. Then

$$\xi_n > 0 \text{ for some critically-loaded } \xi \implies \lambda_n = \sigma_n \tag{6.20}$$

In words, if queue n is critical, then it is not possible to reduce it without increasing some other queue. To see this, pick some critically-loaded ξ with $\xi_n > 0$. Then $\xi \cdot \sigma \geq \xi \cdot \lambda$ since $\sigma \geq \lambda$. Also $\xi \cdot \lambda = 1$ since ξ is critical, and $\xi \cdot \sigma \leq 1$ since ξ is feasible for DUAL(σ), and PRIMAL(σ) ≤ 1. Therefore there is equality, therefore $\lambda_n = \sigma_n$.

Example: input-queued switch. Consider a switch with N input ports and N output ports. Let λ_{ij} be the arrival rate at the queue at input port i of packets destined for output port j, $\lambda \in \mathbb{R}_+^{N \times N}$. This means there are N^2 queues in total, not N. This fits with the notation used to describe the input-queued switch in the earlier section, and it is more convenient than the notation for the general network from Section 6.2. The set $\mathscr{S}$ is the set of all matching in $N \times N$ complete bipartite graph or $N \times N$ permutation matrices. The Birkhoff–von-Neumann decomposition result says that any doubly substochastic matrix is less than or equal to a convex combination of permutation matrices, which gives us

$$\Lambda = \left\{ \lambda \in [0,1]^{N \times N} : \sum_{j=1}^N \lambda_{\hat{i},j} \leq 1 \text{ and } \sum_{i=1}^N \lambda_{i,\hat{j}} \leq 1 \quad \text{for all } \hat{i}, \hat{j} \right\}.$$

It is easy to check that

$$\partial \Lambda = \left\{ \lambda \in \Lambda : \sum_{j=1}^N \lambda_{\hat{i},j} = 1 \text{ or } \sum_{i=1}^N \lambda_{i,\hat{j}} = 1 \quad \text{for at least one } \hat{i} \text{ or } \hat{j} \right\}$$

We propose the following set $\mathscr{S}^*$ of principal critically-loaded virtual resources. This set is obtained from the row and column indicators $\mathbf{r}_{\hat{i}}$ and $\mathbf{c}_{\hat{j}}$, defined by $(\mathbf{r}_{\hat{i}})_{i,j} = 1_{i=\hat{i}}$ and $(\mathbf{c}_{\hat{j}})_{i,j} = 1_{j=\hat{j}}$. We also need

$$\mathscr{N} = \left\{ \mathbf{n} \in \{0,1\}^{N \times N} : n_{i,j} = 1 \text{ if } \lambda_{i,j} > 0 \right\}$$

Then

$$\mathscr{S}^* = \left\{ \mathbf{r}_{\hat{i}} \mathbf{n} \text{ for } \mathbf{n} \in \mathscr{N} \text{ and } \hat{i} \text{ such that } \sum_j \lambda_{\hat{i},j} = 1 \right\} \cup$$

$$\left\{ \mathbf{c}_{\hat{j}} \mathbf{n} \text{ for } \mathbf{n} \in \mathscr{N} \text{ and } \hat{j} \text{ such that } \sum_i \lambda_{i,\hat{j}} = 1 \right\}$$

The virtual resource $\mathbf{r}_1$, for example, corresponds to the constraint that at most one packet can be served from input port 1 in any timeslot, therefore the total arrival rate at input port 1 must be ≤ 1. If say $\lambda_{1,3} = 0$ then the total arrival rate to the remaining $N - 1$ queues at input port 1 must also be ≤ 1, and this corresponds to the virtual resource $\mathbf{r}_1 \mathbf{n}$ for $n_{i,j} = 1_{i>1 \text{ or } j\neq3}$.

It is easy to see that every $\xi \in \mathscr{S}^*$ is a critically-loaded virtual resource, and it is not hard to check that they are all extreme as well. To show (6.19) requires some more work.

First, we remark upon a dual to the Birkhoff–von-Neumann decomposition. Let

$$\mathscr{D} = \{\mathbf{r}_{\hat{i}} \text{ for all } \hat{i}\} \cup \{\mathbf{c}_{\hat{j}} \text{ for all } \hat{j}\}.$$

Then, given any vector $\zeta \in \mathbb{R}_+^{N \times N}$ for which $\max_{\pi \in \mathscr{S}} \zeta \cdot \pi \leq 1$, we can find some ζ' which is a convex combination of elements of $\mathscr{D}$ such that $\zeta \leq \zeta'$ componentwise. This is because $\text{DUAL}(\zeta) \leq 1$ when taken with respect to the schedule set $\mathscr{D}$, by the condition on ζ; and ζ' is then obtained from $\text{PRIMAL}(\zeta)$.

Now suppose that ζ is any critically-loaded virtual resource for $\text{DUAL}(\lambda)$. We need to show that (6.19) holds. First, use the dual decomposition above to write

$$\zeta = \sum_{\hat{i}} x_{\hat{i}} \mathbf{r}_{\hat{i}} + \sum_{\hat{j}} y_{\hat{j}} \mathbf{c}_{\hat{j}} - \mathbf{z}.$$

Note that $\mathbf{r}_{\hat{i}} \cdot \lambda \leq 1$ with equality only if $\mathbf{r}_{\hat{i}} \in \mathscr{S}^*$, and similarly for $\mathbf{c}_{\hat{j}}$. Since ζ is assumed to be critically loaded, $\zeta \cdot \lambda = 1$; it must therefore be that the coefficients $x_{\hat{i}}$ and $y_{\hat{j}}$ are 0 unless the corresponding virtual resource is in $\mathscr{S}^*$, and also that $z_{i,j} > 0$ only when $\lambda_{i,j} = 0$.

To recap, we have found

$$\zeta = \sum_{\xi \in \mathscr{S}^*} a_\xi \xi - \mathbf{z}$$

where $\sum a_\xi = 1$ and $a_\xi \geq 0$, and $z_{i,j} > 0$ only when $\lambda_{i,j} = 0$. It remains to dispose of $\mathbf{z}$. Suppose $z_{k,l} > 0$ for some k, l, and define $\mathbf{n}^{k,l}$ by $n_{i,j}^{k,l} = 1_{i\neq k \text{ or } j\neq l}$; note that $\mathbf{n}^{k,l} \in \mathscr{N}$ by the condition on $\mathbf{z}$. Also note that $\zeta \in \mathbb{R}_+^{N \times N}$, and so $\sum a_\xi \xi_{k,l} \geq z_{k,l}$. Now we can rewrite

$$\zeta = \frac{z_{k,l}}{\sum a_\xi \xi_{k,l}} \sum a_\xi \xi + \left(1 - \frac{z_{k,l}}{\sum a_\xi \xi_{k,l}}\right) \sum a_\xi \xi \mathbf{n}^{k,l} - \mathbf{z} \mathbf{n}^{k,l}.$$

Continuing in this way we can remove all non-zero elements of $\mathbf{z}$, until we are left with an expression of the form (6.19).

Main result: queue-size optimality of MW-0^+. The following result establishes the claim about queue-size optimality of MW-0^+ (see Theorem 10.2, [26] for detailed proof.)

Theorem 6.2. *Let $\lambda \in \partial\Lambda$ be such that there is a critically-loaded virtual resource which assigns equal wait to each queue (i.e. $1/\max_\pi \mathbf{1} \cdot \pi$ is a critical virtual resource). Then, MW-α algorithm is $N^{\alpha/(1+\alpha)}$-approximation algorithm.*

Theorem 6.2 implies that for $\alpha = \ln(1 + \delta)/\ln N$, the MW-$\alpha$ algorithm is $(1 + \delta)$-approximation for any $\delta > 0$. Thus, as $\alpha \to 0^+$ the MW-0^+ becomes 1^+-approximation and hence optimal.

Remark. In the example of input-queued switch, an example of the requirement that there be a critically-loaded virtual resource which assigns equal weight to all queues is satisfied by the requirement that either there is some set of critically loaded input ports (i.e. $\sum_k \lambda_{ik} = 1$ for some collection of i) and $\lambda_{i,j} = 0$ for all input ports i which are not critical; or that there is some set of critically loaded output ports and $\lambda_{i,j} = 0$ for all output ports j which are not critical.

Discussion: optimal algorithm. The above is an evidence based on critical fluid model of the optimality of limiting algorithm MW-0^+. There a second piece of (intuitive) evidence based on the *structure* of effective state space of the algorithm in the case of switch. It essentially suggests that as $\alpha \to 0^+$, the effective state space becomes largest possible and hence the algorithm does *not idle* unless essentially required – thus, being least *wasteful* and hence optimal. Due to space constraint, we do not discuss this in further detail. An interested reader is encourage to read [26] for furter details.

Given these two pieces of evidence, it is tempting to speculate about a formal limit of MW-α as $\alpha \to 0$. Since MW-α chooses a schedule π to maximize $\pi \cdot \mathbf{q}^\alpha$, and since

$$x^\alpha \approx \begin{cases} 1 + \alpha \log x & \text{if } x > 0 \\ 0 & \text{if } x = 0 \end{cases}$$

we make the following conjecture:

Conjecture 6.1. Consider the MW-0^+ scheduling algorithm, which at each timeslot looks at all maximum-size schedules (i.e. those $\pi \in \mathscr{S}$ for which $\sum_n \pi_n 1_{q_n > 0}$ is maximal), and among these picks one which has maximal log-weight (i.e. for which $\sum_{n:q_n > 0} \pi_n \log q_n$ is maximal), breaking ties arbitrarily. We conjecture that this algorithm is stable for $\lambda \in \Lambda^\circ$, and that it minimizes the total amount of idling in both the fluid limit and the heavy traffic limit for $\lambda \in \partial \Lambda$.

Key message on optimal algorithm. In [16], McKeown et. al. showed that maximum-size matching (without use of weights to break ties) is not stable for certain $\lambda \in \Lambda^\circ$, for an input-queued switch. However, the above conjecture (and MW-0^+ algorithm) suggests that the maximum-size schedule with (logarithmic) weights used to break ties is optimal. This suggests that the role of using *weight information* is in getting the *throughput maximized* while the role of *maximum-size* is in *minimizing delay*. This property is implicitly achieved by the MW-α algorithm for $\alpha \to 0^+$.

6.4 Message-passing: throughput optimality

The previous section argued that a maximum weight scheduling rule, with weights as an appropriate function of queue-size, leads to optimal performance both in terms of throughput and delay. Therefore, such a scheduling algorithm is required to solve a combinatorial optimization problem of finding a maximum weighted schedule, out of all possible choices, every timeslot.

Though the problem of finding maximum weight scheduling is a solvable (because number of scheduling choices are finite in our setup), if the scheduling constraints are complex (e.g. independent set in wireless network example), then designing efficient scheduling can become challenging (or may be impossible) in general. In most of scheduling applications, such as the input-queued switch and the wireless network considered here, the algorithms for finding schedule are highly constrained due to various engineering limitations: (a) they need to perform few logical operations either because of time-limitation or limited computational resources; (b) they need to operate in totally distributed manner while exchanging as little information as possible due to physical or architectural reasons; and (c) they need to maintain only little amount of data-structure. Such considerations lead to the fundamental question: is it possible to design *implementable* (as in satisfying the above stated qualitative requirements) scheduling algorithms that have good performance, both in terms of throughput and queue-size (delay), for any instance of the setup described here?

In this section, we will present an extremely simple, randomized distributed and hence implementable algorithm that is throughput optimal for any instance of the setup describe here. However, this algorithm can have very poor queue-size performance depending upon the complexity of the underlying problem structure. This algorithm (in centralized setup) was first proposed by Tassiulas [30] in the context of switch. The distributed implementation of this algorithm was discussed in [18, 13]. First, we present the generic algorithm and its throughput property. Then, we will explain it in the context of input-queued switch (matching) and wireless network (independent set). Finally, we will discuss its performance in terms of queue-size.

6.4.1 Throughput optimality through randomization and message-passing

The algorithm essentially uses the following key insights: (1) if a schedule $\pi \in \mathscr{S}$ has *high* weight (say, weight is equal to queue-size) at certain time-instance, then it is likely to have *high* weight at the next time-step as long as the weight is a linear or sub-linear function of queue-size; (2) in order to achieve throughput optimality, it is sufficient to have the weight of the schedule *close to* optimal, not necessarily optimal. Now, we describe the algorithm for any scheduling instance of our setup. But, before that we describe two sub-routines that the algorithm will utilize.

Sub-routine **RND**. It produces a random schedule $\sigma \in \mathscr{S}$ such that any schedule in $\mathscr{S}$ has strictly positive probability of being produced. That is, there exists $\omega > 0$ such that for any $\sigma \in \mathscr{S}$

$$\mathbf{Pr}(\mathbf{RND} \text{ outputs } \sigma) > \omega. \qquad (6.21)$$

Sub-routine **CNT**$(\sigma, \mathbf{w}, \varepsilon, \delta)$. Given parameters $\varepsilon, \delta > 0$ and schedule $\sigma \in \mathscr{S}$, with node-weights $\mathbf{w} = (w_i)$ (here, queue-size or function of queue-size), the algorithm returns a random number W such that

$$\mathbf{Pr}\left((1-\varepsilon)w(\sigma) \leq W \leq (1+\varepsilon)w(\sigma)\right) \geq 1-\delta, \qquad (6.22)$$

where $w(\sigma) = \sum_i \sigma_i w_i$.

ALGO I(ε, δ). Here, we describe the generic form of the algorithm. The distributed implementation of this algorithm will follow by explaining the distributed implementation of the subroutines **RND** and **CNT**, which is done later.

---

0. Let $\sigma(\tau)$ be the schedule used at time $\tau \geq 0$ and $\mathbf{Q}(\tau)$ denote the queue-size vector at time τ.
1. Initially, at $\tau = 0$ we have $\mathbf{Q}(0) = \mathbf{0}$ and choose $\sigma(0)$ at random using **RND**.
2. The schedule $\sigma(\tau+1)$ at time $\tau+1$ is computed from $\sigma(\tau)$ as follows.

   (a) Produce a random schedule $R(\tau+1)$ using **RND**.
   (b) Compute weights,
   $$W(\sigma(\tau)) = \mathbf{CNT}(\sigma(\tau), \mathbf{Q}(\tau+1), \varepsilon/8, \delta), \text{ and}$$
   $$W(R(\tau+1)) = \mathbf{CNT}(R(\tau+1), \mathbf{Q}(\tau+1), \varepsilon/8, \delta).$$
   (c) If $W(R(\tau+1)) \geq \frac{(1+\varepsilon/8)}{(1-\varepsilon/8)}W(\sigma(\tau))$, then $\sigma(\tau+1) = R(\tau+1)$, else retain $\sigma(\tau+1) = \sigma(\tau)$.

Remark. The above algorithm is an *approximation* of MW-1 algorithm. The result stated next about its throughput optimality should not be affected if we were approximating MW-α algorithm for $\alpha \in (0,1)$. That is, if instead of weight being $\mathbf{Q}(\tau)$, it were $\mathbf{Q}^\alpha(\tau)$, then the above algorithm will still have good throughput property. This is primarily because $f(x) = x^\alpha$ is a Lipschitz continuous function (with Lipschitz constant ≤ 1) for all $\alpha \in (0,1]$.

Performance of ALGO I(ε, δ). Here, we state the result that establishes (essentially) throughput optimality of the **ALGO I**.

Theorem 6.3. *Consider any strictly admissible* $\lambda \in \Lambda^\circ$. *Then, there is a* $\varepsilon > 0$ *such that* $(1-2\varepsilon)^{-1}\lambda \in \Lambda^\circ$. *Then, under the algorithm ALGO I*$(\varepsilon, \omega 3^{-N})$,

$$\limsup_{\tau \to \infty} \mathbb{E}\left[\|\mathbf{Q}(\tau)\|_1\right] < \infty.$$

The proof of this result follows from Foster-Lyapunov criteria [17] by considering the quadratic Lyapunov function $L(\tau) = \sum_i Q_i^2(\tau)$ and establishing *negative drift* over large enough finite horizon. We skip details here. An interested reader can reconstruct the proof from [18] or [13].

Cost of ALGO I($\varepsilon, \omega 3^{-N}$). As Theorem 6.3 suggests, we need to design distributed algorithms **RND** and **CNT**($\varepsilon, \omega 3^{-N}$) that are efficient (i.e. do computations in say *polynomial* in N distributed operations). We describe such distributed algorithms next. As we shall find, the **RND**, which is described for matching and independent set, takes $O(N)$ total computation (or $O(1)$ *rounds*[6]); the **CNT**($\varepsilon, \omega 3^{-N}$) takes $O(\varepsilon^{-2} N^2 \log 3^N / \omega)$ total computation (or $O(\varepsilon^{-2} N \log 3^N / \omega)$ *rounds*). Thus, net computation cost of the **ALGO I**($\varepsilon, \omega 3^{-N}$) will boil down to $O(\varepsilon^{-2} N \log 3^N / \omega)$ rounds or $O(\varepsilon^{-2} N^2 \log 3^N / \omega)$ total distributed operations. It should be noted that the number of *message* exchanged scales in the same manner as the number of distributed operations. As we shall see, $\omega = 1/N! \approx 2^{-N \log N}$ for matching and $\omega = 2^{-N}$ – thus, the cost (in terms of rounds) in case of matching is $O(\varepsilon^{-2} N^2 \log N)$ and $O(\varepsilon^{-2} N^2)$ in case of independent set.

Remark. It should be noted that we can slow down our schedule computation algorithm by factor $O(\varepsilon^{-2} N \log 3^N / \omega)$ – thus, spending $O(1)$ computation per timeslot – and retain the throughput optimality as is. This fact follows directly from the Lyapunov-Foster's criteria. However, it increases the average queue-size and thus degrades performance. An interested reader will find a detailed study of this aspect of scheduling algorithms in the context of input-queued switch in [23].

Description of RND. Here, we describe the distributed algorithm **RND** for two examples: matching and independent set. The algorithm for any instance of our setup can be obtained as long as the constraints corresponding to the feasibility of a schedule is checkable *locally*; which happens to be the case for matching and independent set.

First, consider **RND** for finding a random matching or a random schedule in the case of input-queued switch. Each input node i, uniformly at random selects an output node, say $r(i)$, and sends a request to $r(i)$. An output node, say j, upon receiving multiple requests, selects one of the inputs at random and sends it notification of acceptance. Input node i, upon receiving accept matches the output and upon not receiving accept (i.e. receiving reject) does not connect to any output.

It can be easily checked that all complete matchings are likely to be chosen with probability at least $1/N!$, for switch of size N, under this **RND**. Further, it involves only two rounds of distributed computation. Thus, it satisfies our required condition (6.21).

Next, we describe a similar description for independent set. Here, in the network graph $G = (V, E)$, each node (vertex) chooses to become *active* with probability $1/2$. An *active* node, becomes *inactive* if any of its neighbor is *active*. All the remaining

---

[6] By a round, we mean an iteration of distributed computation where each node gets to perform $O(1)$ exchanges.

active nodes declare them to be part of the independent set while others (*inactive*) keep out.

Again, it is easy to check that the nodes that decide to be part of independent set, indeed form an independent set. Further, any independent set has probability at least $1/2^N$ of being chosen for network of size N. As description suggests, it is a simple two-round algorithm.

Description of CNT($\varepsilon, \omega 3^{-N}$). The purpose of algorithm is to compute summation of node weights (approximately) for a given schedule – equivalently, given N numbers in the network graph G, compute their summation approximately. The standard averaging algorithm (cf. [32, 6]) will not work here, because we need an algorithm that will produce exactly the *same* estimation at all the nodes so that local decisions (i.e. whether to choose new schedule $R(\tau+1)$ or to choose an old schedule $\sigma(\tau)$) are globally consistent. And, averaging algorithm does not posses this property. Here, we will describe an approximate summation procedure based [19]. The algorithm is based on the following probabilistic facts:

> **F1.** Let $X_1, \ldots, X_k$ be independent random variables with exponential distribution and parameters $r_1, \ldots, r_k$. Then, $X_* = \min_{1 \leq i \leq k} X_i$ has exponential distribution with parameter $\sum_{i=1}^{k} r_i$.
>
> **F2.** Let $Y_1, \ldots, Y_m$ be independent exponential random variables with parameter r. Let $S_m = \frac{1}{m} \sum_{i=1}^{m} Y_i$. Then, for $\gamma \in (0, 1/2)$
>
> $$\mathbf{Pr}\left(S_m \notin (1-\gamma)r^{-1}, (1+\gamma)r^{-1}\right) \leq 2\exp\left(-\gamma^2 m/2\right).$$

F1 is well-known about exponential distribution; **F2** follows from Cramer's Theorem [10] about large deviation estimation for exponential distribution.

Now, the algorithm. Given node weights $W = [W_v]$, **F1** and **F2** can be used to compute $\bar{W} = \sum_v W_v$ approximately as follows: each node $v \in V$ draws an independent exponential random variable with parameter W_v (nodes with $W_v = 0$ do not participate in generating numbers); then all nodes together compute minimum, say X_* of these random numbers in distributed fashion by iteratively asking their neighbors for their estimates of minimum. Nodes should terminate this process after $\Theta(n)$ transmissions. Repeat this for m times to obtain minimums $X_*(i), 1 \leq i \leq m$. Now set $S_m = \frac{1}{m} \sum_{i=1}^{m} X_*(i)$ and declare $Z_m = 1/S_m$ as an estimate summation of $\bar{W}$.

Now, given small enough ε it follows from **F1**, **F2** that by selecting $m = O(\varepsilon^{-2} \log 3^N / \omega)$, we obtain estimate of summation, say $\hat{W}$ such that

$$\mathbf{Pr}\left(\hat{W} \notin ((1-\varepsilon)\bar{W}, (1+\varepsilon)\bar{W})\right) \leq \omega 3^{-N}. \tag{6.23}$$

Computation of a single minimum over the network can be done in a distributed manner in many ways. We skip the details here in interest of space. However, we refer an interested reader to see [19] for interesting account on such algorithms. The minimum computation takes total $O(N^2)$ or $O(N)$ per node message exchanges. This completes the description of desired **CNT($\varepsilon, \omega 3^{-N}$)** algorithm.

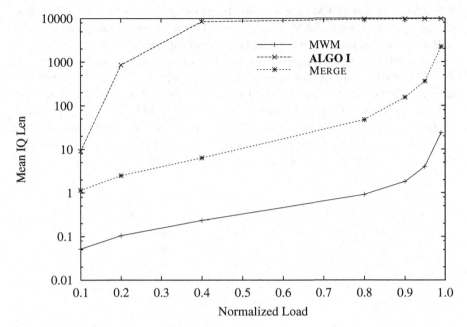

Fig. 6.3 An illustration of impact of MERGE on Performance.

6.4.2 Performance in terms of queue-size

The **ALGO I** is a simple, randomized message-passing algorithm that is through-put optimal for almost all reasonable instances of our setup. Now, we consider its performance in terms of queue-size. We will consider the cases of matching (switch scheduling) and independent set (wireless scheduling) to establish existence of the following dichotomy: for some scheduling problem, it is possible to have simple algorithms that are throughput optimal and have small queue-size; for other scheduling problems we can only hope for throughput optimal simple algorithms with very large queue-size.

ALGO I for switches: a simple modification. The basic version of the **ALGO I** described above is likely to induce very large queue-size. However, a simple modification of the **ALGO I** can lead to smaller queue-size[7] as described here. To exemplify this, we present a sample simulation in Figure 6.3 which plots average queue-size (on Y-axis) with respect to the varying load (on X-axis) for three algorithms: MW scheduling (MWM), the **ALGO I**, and MERGE (which is the modification of **ALGO I** for matching). The figure shows that the queue-sizes are very large under **ALGO**

---

[7] We make note of the following: while the modification presented here seem to reduce queue-size drastically (see [12] for detailed simulations) and there are arguments based on toy-model (again, see [12]) to justify this, the problem of establishing average queue-size being *polynomial* in size of switch N, under algorithm using MERGE remains an important open problem.

I , but MERGE and MWM have very small and comparable queue-sizes. The modification presented here, the MERGE algorithm, is based on the results described in [12] and a later adaption of it for distributed algorithm design in [18].

The main insight is as follows. In **ALGO I**, every time either we choose schedule $R(\tau+1)$ or $\sigma(\tau)$ entirely. However, some parts of $R(\tau+1)$ are likely to be higher weights while some other parts of $\sigma(\tau)$ are likely to be of higher weights. Therefore, a better approach towards designing such algorithm would be to choose *a mixture* of the best parts of these two schedules. In general, not all scheduling constraint structures allow for this. However, matching constraint allows for this possibility. Below, we describe this formally as the Merge procedure.

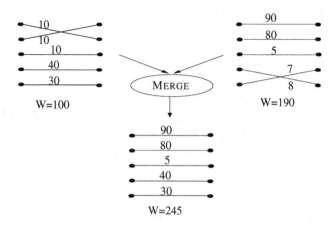

Fig. 6.4 An example of MERGE procedure.

Consider a switch bipartite graph with **Q** matrix as its edge weights. Given two matchings π^1 and π^2, define

$$\mathscr{S}(\pi^1,\pi^2) = \{\pi \in \mathscr{S} : \pi_{ij} = 1 \text{ only if } \pi_{ij}^1 = 1 \text{ or } \pi_{ij}^2 = 1\}.$$

The MERGE procedure, when applied to π^1 and π^2 with weights given by **Q**, returns a matching $\tilde{\pi}$ such that

$$\tilde{\pi} = \arg \max_{\pi \in \mathscr{S}(\pi(1),\pi(2))} \{\sum_{ij} \pi_{ij} Q_{ij}\}. \qquad (6.24)$$

The MERGE finds such matching using only $2n$ addition and subtraction. It is described as follows: Color the edges of π^1 as red and the edges of π^2 as green. Start at output node j_1 and follow the red edge to an input node, say i_1. From input node i_1 follow the (only) green edge to its output node, say j_2. If $j_2 = j_1$, stop. Else continue to trace a path of alternating red and green edges until j_1 is visited again. This gives a "cycle" in the subgraph of red and green edges.

Suppose the above cycle does not cover all the red and green edges. Then there exists an output j outside this cycle. Starting from j repeat the above procedure to find another cycle. In this fashion find all cycles of red and green edges. Suppose there are ℓ cycles, $C_1, ..., C_\ell$ at the end. Then each cycle, C_i, contains two matchings: G_i which has only green edges, and R_i which has only red edges. For each cycle C_i, the MERGE chooses R_i if the sum of the queue-size corresponding to these edges is higher than that of the G_i. Else, MERGE chooses G_i. It is easy to show that the final matching as chosen above is precisely the one claimed in (6.24). Figure 6.4 illustrates the MERGE procedure.

Finally, the MERGE is used in place of choosing $R(\tau + 1)$ or $\sigma(\tau)$ entirely. Note that, in order to construct the schedule for MERGE, essentially we need to compute the weights of schedules only restricted to the "cycles" as described above. However, this can be done in a totally distributed manner using the same **CNT** procedure since the membership to a cycle (or paths) is by definition defined locally. Note that this modification *does not* increase the (bound on the) cost of the algorithm. We refer interested readers to [18] for details.

ALGO I for independent set: impossibility of low queue-size. The above simple modification for matching reduces queue-sizes drastically and makes the algorithms comparable to MW scheduling. However, it utilizes the structure of matching crucially. Therefore, question remains whether it is possible to modify **ALGO I** to obtain small queue-size for any scheduling problem. Here, we will state an impossibility result in the context of independent set based scheduling which implies that, (a) **ALGO I** has exponentially large, in problem size N, average queue-size and (b) it is not possible to have simple modification of **ALGO I** to obtain smaller queue-sizes. This is based on a recent work [24].

To this end, we consider a wireless network operating under independent set constrained model. We assume that the network graph G can be arbitrary. Let Λ be its admissible arrival rate region and $c\Lambda = \{c\lambda : \lambda \in \Lambda\}$ for $c > 0$. Here, $c\Lambda$ means fraction c of the capacity region: e.g. for $c = 0.1$, it will be 10% of the capacity region. The following impossibility result implies that for any $\varepsilon > 0$, there is no simple algorithm that can achieve small average queue-size for all network instances. Thus, the problem of scheduling for low queue-size is inherently hard !

Theorem 6.4. *Consider any $\varepsilon > 0$. Then, there is no (centralized or distributed, deterministic or randomized) algorithm that runs in polynomial (in N) time and induces polynomial (in N) average queue-size for all $\lambda \in \varepsilon\Lambda$ unless certain computational hypothesis[8] is false.*

Key message on simple, randomized message-passing algorithm. The randomized algorithm **ALGO I** described here is a simple, message-passing mechanism that is essentially throughput optimal for any scheduling instance that allows for checking feasibility of a schedule through local constraints

---

[8] The precise computational hypothesis is NP $\not\subset$ BPP.

(e.g. matching, independent set). However, the queue-sizes induced are very large. The simpler problem structures, like matching allow for minor (problem dependent) modification of the **ALGO I**, to obtain lower queue-sizes while retaining the high throughput. However, for hard problem structures, like independent set it is impossible to obtain simultaneously high-throughput and low queue-sizes under arbitrary setup. Thus, *obtaining high-throughput is relatively simple, and meanwhile maintaining low queue-size is quite hard.*

6.5 Message-passing: low queue-size or delay

In essence, we have learnt so far that in order to retain small queue-size a known effective way is to design excellent approximation algorithm of maximum weight scheduling – in case of matching, we could do it since it is an easy problem, but in case of independent set we could not since it is a hard problem. The modification of randomized algorithm **ALGO I** to obtain small queue-size for matching is very problem specific. Ideally, we would like to have a generic method. Specifically, in this section we would like to design general message-passing algorithmic method that has the following properties: (a) for easy problem, allows for fine-control to trade-off performance with implementation cost; and (b) for hard problem, works well when problem posses special structure (like solvable through linear program) and gives a reasonable heuristic otherwise.

We will present two, somewhat surprisingly very related, approaches for algorithm design: (a) the classical optimization based method of co-ordinate descent algorithm and (b) the recently emerging heuristic from Statistical Physics and Artificial Intelligence, called belief propagation (also known as max-product for optimization problem). The presentation here is based on [3], [4] and [21]. We will explain these two methods in the context of input-queued switch (matching) and wireless network (independent set).

6.5.1 Input-queued switch: message-passing algorithm

Here, we describe two algorithms for input-queued switch. The first algorithm is a direct adaptation of the Auction algorithm by Bertsekas [5]. The second algorithm is based on belief propagation (max-product).

Auction algorithm. For ease of explanation, we introduce some notation. Consider an N port input-queued switch with N input ports and N output ports. Denote the N input ports by $\alpha_1, \ldots, \alpha_N$ and the N output ports by $\beta_1, \ldots, \beta_N$. As described earlier in Section 6.2, there are N^2 queues, one per distinct input-output pair. Let

At time τ the weight of an edge (α_i, β_j) will be $Q_{ij}(\tau - 1)$ and the weight of the matching π is $\sum_{i=1}^{n} Q_{i\pi(i)}(\tau - 1)$. Recall that the Maximum Weight Matching $\pi^*(\tau)$ at time τ is such that

$$\pi^*(\tau) \in \arg\max_{\pi \in \mathscr{S}} \sum_{i=1}^{n} Q_{i\pi(i)}(\tau - 1).$$

Now we describe the auction algorithm with parameter $\varepsilon > 0$. In the description of the algorithm, we drop reference to time τ for the queue-size. Readers familiar with the iSLIP [15] algorithm may notice a striking syntactic similarity between the iSLIP and the auction algorithms: both algorithms iterate between inputs proposing and outputs accepting/refusing. This similarity suggests that the auction algorithm is likely to very close to be implementable.

○ *Phase 0: Initialization.* Given queue-size matrix $\mathbf{Q}$, let $Q^* = \max_{ij} Q_{ij}$ which is determined as follows:

- Each output β_j computes $Q^*_{\cdot j} = \max_{k=1}^{n} Q_{kj}$.
- Each input α_i obtains $Q^*_{\cdot j}$ from all outputs β_j and computes $Q^* = \max_j Q^*_{\cdot j}$.
- Each output β_j contacts input α_j to obtain Q^*.
- Set $\delta = \varepsilon Q^*/n$.
- Initially, the set of matched inputs-outputs $S = \emptyset$; the set of unassigned inputs $I = \{\alpha_1, \ldots, \alpha_n\}$, and parameters $p_j = 0$ for $1 \le j \le n$.
- Algorithm finds matching of interest in two phases, described next.

○ *Phase 1: Bidding* For all $\alpha_i \in I$,

(1) Find the 'weight' maximizing output β_j. Let,

$$j_i = \arg\max_j \{Q_{ij} - p_j\}, \ v_i = \max_j \{Q_{ij} - p_j\}, \quad (6.25)$$

$$\text{and } u_i = \max_{j \ne j_i} \{Q_{ij} - p_j\}. \quad (6.26)$$

(2) Compute the 'proposal' of input α_i, denoted by $b_{\alpha_i \to \beta_{j_i}}$ as follows:
$$b_{\alpha_i \to \beta_{j_i}} = Q_{ij_i} - u_i + \delta.$$

○ *Phase 2: Assignment.* For each output β_j,

(3) Let $P(j)$ be the set of inputs from which β_j received a 'proposal'. If $P(j) \ne \emptyset$, increase p_j to the highest bid, i.e.
$$p_j = \max_{\alpha_i \in P(j)} b_{\alpha_i \to \beta_j}.$$

(4) Remove the maximum proposing input α_{i_j} from I and add (α_{i_j}, β_j) to S. If $(\alpha_k, \beta_j) \in S$, $k \ne i_j$, then put α_k back in I.

Performance of Auction algorithm. The auction algorithm described above is a slight variant of Bertsekas' auction algorithm. Given a fixed weighted bipartite graph, the behavior of the auction algorithm is well understood. However, the algorithm converges only if all the weights are finite. In our setup, weights are given by $\mathbf{Q}(\cdot)$. Hence, it is not clear if the above described algorithm will maintain finite queue-sizes $Q^*(\cdot)$ with probability 1. Specifically, the size of $Q^*(\cdot)$ directly affects the number of iterations required by the algorithm to converge. We state the following result (Theorem 1, [4]).

Theorem 6.5. *Given $\varepsilon > 0$, let $\lambda = \sum_k \alpha_k \pi_k$ be such that $\sum_k \alpha_k \le 1 - 2\varepsilon$. Then, for a switch operating under the Auction algorithm with parameter ε,*

$$\limsup_{\tau \to \infty} \mathbb{E}\left[\sum_{ij} Q_{ij}(\tau)\right] = O(n^2/\varepsilon).$$

Further, the algorithm takes $O(n^2/\varepsilon)$ iterations to compute the schedule.

Now, we consider a natural variant of the Auction algorithm to utilize the slowly varying nature of the switch. Specifically, at any time slot $\tau + 1$ the parameter p_j for $1 \le j \le n$ instead of being initiated with zero starts with its final value from the time slot τ. The intuition behind this modification is the following. At the end of the time slot τ the parameters p_j are optimal for the queue sizes $Q_{ij}(\tau - 1)$. Since, queue-size only changes by ± 1 in a time slot, one expects the parameters p_j to be near optimal at time $\tau + 1$ as well. Therefore, we expect algorithm to converge quickly starting from thus chosen new initial condition – this is confirmed by simulations presented next.

Representative simulation results. We describe simulation results for an 8×8 input queued switch with a non-uniform admissible arrival matrix. The traffic load takes one of the values from the set $\{.65, 8, .9, .95, .98\}$. All simulations are done for one million time slots. Here, "auction(c)" denotes the auction algorithm with $\delta = c$ where c is a constant. For the ε-Auction algorithm we use $\varepsilon = 1$ and hence denote it by 1-Auction. We compare the performance of auction algorithm with MWM and iSLIP algorithm – iSLIP is the popular heuristic used in practice. When the number of iterations of the iSLIP algorithm is not mentioned it is understood to have run all the way to the end, i.e. it runs $n = 8$ iterations.

Figure 6.5 shows that the 1-Auction algorithm performs much better than the iSLIP algorithm and is as good as MWM. The next plot, Figure 6.6, shows that 1-Auction with memory has better performance than 1-Auction.

Figures 6.7 and 6.8 show the trade-off achieved by tuning the parameter δ: the higher the value of δ, the poorer the performance and the fewer iterations required to find solution. Here the value $\delta = B/N$ takes one of the values $1, 10, 50$. As mentioned before larger values of δ yield less number of iterations but at the expense of greater queue sizes. Figure 6.9 shows a comparison between 1-Auction and iSLIP when both run only three iterations in each time slot. In practice sometimes only a few iterations of the iSLIP algorithm are used instead of the full iSLIP. This figure

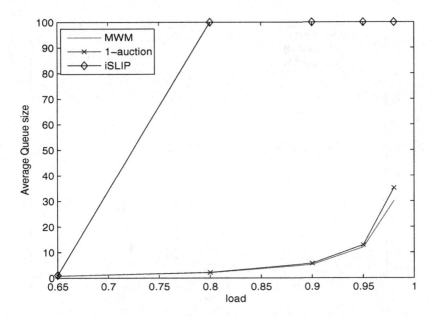

Fig. 6.5 Average queue sizes for MWM, 1-Auction and iSLIP.

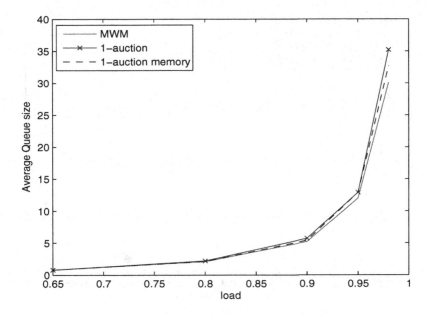

Fig. 6.6 Average queue sizes MWM, 1-Auction and 1-Auction with memory.

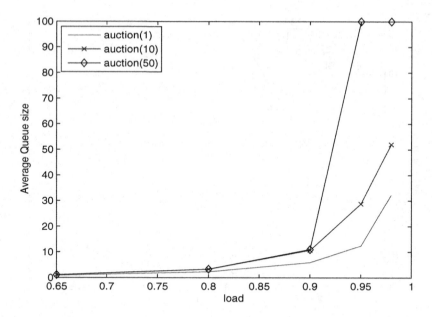

Fig. 6.7 Average queue sizes for auction(1), auction(10), auction (50)

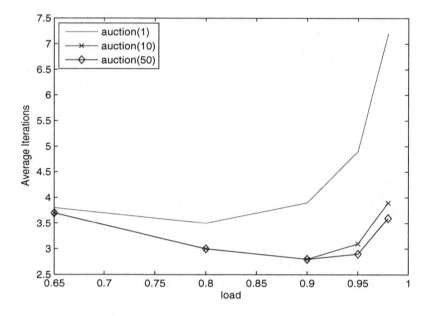

Fig. 6.8 Average iterations to converge for auction(1), auction(10), auction(50)

shows that the 1-Auction algorithm can also be used for a fewer number of iterations and it still outperforms iSLIP.

Belief propagation(BP) for matching. In a switch, the partition in the bipartite graph is well known. However, in general graph, even if it is bipartite such partition may not be known – for example, wireless ad-hoc network operating under *primary interference constraints*. In such cases, Auction algorithm, which requires prior partitioning and is not symmetric in its response to partitioning, is not very attractive. Instead, we would like to have a scalable approach that *does not* require prior knowledge of the bipartition and operates symmetrically. That is, we need an algorithm, that treats nodes of the two partitions in the same manner. Next, we describe such an algorithm based on the (Max-Product) Belief propagation algorithm.

The following algorithm is an adaption of the (Max-Product) Belief Propagation algorithm described in [3] that operates very similarly to the auction algorithm.

---

o Let $Q^* = \max_{ij} Q_{ij}$, which can be quickly computed in a distributed manner. Set $\delta = \varepsilon Q^*/n$.
o Given queue-size matrix $\mathbf{Q}$, define a symmetric weight matrix $\mathbf{W} = [W_{ij}]$ as follows: for all $(i,j) \notin E$, set $W_{ij} = 0$ and for all $(i,j) \in E$ set $W_{ij} = \max\{Q_{ij}, Q_{ji}\} + \delta_{ij}$. Where δ_{ij} is a randomly chosen number from the interval $(0, \delta)$ and can be selected by one communication between i, j.
o The algorithm variables are messages that are exchanged between neighboring nodes. Let $\hat{m}^k_{i\to j} \in \mathbb{R}$ denote message from node i to node j in iteration k.
o Initialize $k = 0$ and set the messages as follows: $\hat{m}^0_{i\to j} = W_{ij}$; $\hat{m}^0_{j\to i} = W_{ij}$.
o Algorithm is iterative, as described next.
o For $k \geq 1$, iterate as follows:

(a) Update messages as follows:

$$\hat{m}^k_{\alpha_i\to\beta_j} = W_{ij} - \max_{\ell\neq j}\hat{m}^{k-1}_{\beta_\ell\to\alpha_i},$$
$$\hat{m}^k_{\beta_j\to\alpha_i} = W_{ij} - \max_{\ell\neq i}\hat{m}^{k-1}_{\alpha_\ell\to\beta_j}. \qquad (6.27)$$

(b) The estimated MWM at the end of iteration k is π^k, where $\pi^k(i) = \arg\max_{j\in\mathcal{N}(i)}\{\hat{m}^k_{\beta_j\to\alpha_i}\}$ for $1 \leq i \leq n$. But when $\max_{j\in\mathcal{N}(i)}\{\hat{m}^k_{\beta_j\to\alpha_i}\} < 0$ then let $\pi^k(i) = $"null" which means node i chooses not to connect to any of its neighbors.
(c) Repeat (a)-(b) till $\pi^k(i)$ converges, i.e. for each $1 \leq i \leq n$, $\pi^k(\pi^k(i)) = i$ or $\pi^k(i) = $"null" for all k large enough.

Performance of Belief Propagation(BP). Let $\mathbf{Q}' = [Q'_{ij}]$ be a symmetric matrix of queue seizes defined by $Q'_{ij} = \max\{Q_{ij}, Q_{ji}\}$. Also, let π^* denote the MWM of matrix $\mathbf{Q}'$ and let W^* denote weight of π^*. We will prove the following result.

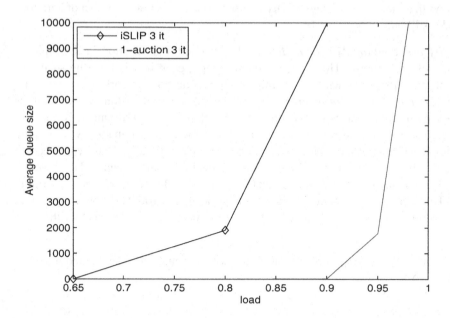

Fig. 6.9 Average queue sizes for iSLIP with 3 iterations and 1-Auction with 3 iterations

Theorem 6.6. *Given $\varepsilon > 0$, with probability one BP will converge to a matching with weight at least $W^* - \varepsilon Q^*$. The algorithm takes $O(n^2/\varepsilon\rho)$ iterations to converge with high probability, where ρ is some function of n.*

The BP algorithm performs very similar to the auction algorithm. Here, we provide a simulation run that confirms this as shown in Figure 6.10.

6.5.2 Wireless scheduling: message-passing scheduling

Here we describe message-passing algorithm for finding maximum weight independent set in order to obtain schedule in wireless networks. Clearly, it is not possible to find such an algorithm for all possible graph structures. We describe an algorithm, based on co-ordinate descent along with a combinatorial method, that works perfectly for bipartite graphs. We will end with a heuristic based on BP, very similar to the first algorithm, that is likely to provide very good performance on other graphs. The most of the results presented in this section are from [21].

Exact algorithm: bipartite graph. Here, we describe an algorithm for finding maximum weight independent set in a given graph $G = (V, E)$ with node weights represented by $w = [w_i]$. The algorithm is essentially a modification of the standard co-ordinate descent algorithm for a "dual" of an appropriate linear programming

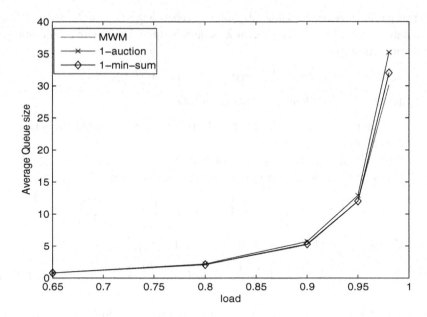

Fig. 6.10 Average queue sizes for MWM, 1-Auction and 1-min-sum

relaxation of the integer program of maximum weight independent set. We refer an interested reader to [21] for further details. The basic algorithm, described below, invokes two sub-routines which are described next.

(o) Given (small enough) positive parameter ε, δ, run sub-routine DESCENT(ε, δ) results in an output $\lambda^{\varepsilon, \delta} = (\lambda_{ij}^{\varepsilon, \delta})_{(i,j) \in E}$ upon convergence (or close to convergence).

(i) Next, using (small enough) $\delta_1 > 0$, use EST$(\lambda^{\varepsilon, \delta}, \delta_1)$, to produce an estimate for the MWIS as an output of the algorithm.

Algorithm DESCENT. Here, we describe the DESCENT algorithm.

(o)The parameters are variables λ_{ij}, one for each edge $(i,j) \in E$. We will use
notation that $\lambda_{ij}^t = \lambda_{ji}^t$. The vector λ is iteratively updated, with t denoting the
iteration number.

  ○ Initially, set $t = 0$ and $\lambda_{ij}^0 = \max\{w_i, w_j\}$ for all $(i,j) \in E$.

(i) In iteration $t+1$, update parameters as follows:

  ○ Pick an edge $(i,j) \in E$. The edge selection is done in a round-robin manner
    over all edges.
  ○ For all $(i',j') \in E, (i',j') \neq (i,j)$ do nothing, i.e. $\lambda_{i'j'}^{t+1} = \lambda_{i'j'}^t$.
  ○ For edge (i,j), nodes i and j exchange messages as follows:

$$\gamma_{i \to j}^{t+1} = \left(w_i - \sum_{k \neq j, k \in \mathcal{N}(i)} \lambda_{ki}^t \right)_+ , \quad \gamma_{j \to i}^{t+1} = \left(w_j - \sum_{k' \neq i, k' \in \mathcal{N}(j)} \lambda_{k'j}^t \right)_+ .$$

  ○ Update λ_{ij}^{t+1} as follows: with $a = \gamma_{i \to j}^{t+1}$ and $b = \gamma_{j \to i}^{t+1}$,

$$\lambda_{ij}^{t+1} = \left(\frac{a + b + 2\varepsilon + \sqrt{(a-b)^2 + 4\varepsilon^2}}{2} \right)_+ . \qquad (6.28)$$

(ii) Update $t = t + 1$ and repeat till algorithm converges within δ for each component.
(iii) Output the vector λ, denoted by $\lambda^{\varepsilon,\delta}$, when the algorithm stops.

Remark. It can be established that the update (6.28) turns out to be

$$\lambda_{ij}^{t+1} = \beta\varepsilon + \max\left\{ -\beta\varepsilon, \left(w_i - \sum_{k \in \mathcal{N}(i) \setminus j} \lambda_{ik}^t \right), \left(w_j - \sum_{k \in \mathcal{N}(j) \setminus i} \lambda_{kj}^t \right) \right\},$$

where for some $\beta \in (1,2]$ with its precise value dependent on $\gamma_{i \to j}^{t+1}, \gamma_{j \to i}^{t+1}$.

***Algorithm* EST.** The algorithm EST estimates the assignment of nodes in the
maximum weight independent set based on the converged messages of the DE-
SCENT algorithm.

(o) The algorithm iteratively estimates $\mathbf{x} = (x_i)$ given λ (expected to be a dual optimal solution).

(i) Initially, color a node i *gray* and set $x_i = 0$ if $\sum_{j \in \mathcal{N}(i)} \lambda_{ij} > w_i$. Color all other nodes with *green* and leave their values unspecified. The condition $\sum_{j \in \mathcal{N}(i)} \lambda_{ij} > w_i$ is checked as whether $\sum_{j \in \mathcal{N}(i)} \lambda_{ij} \geq w_i + \delta_1$ or not.

(ii) Repeat the following steps (in any order) till no more changes can happen:

  o if i is *green* and there exists a *gray* node $j \in \mathcal{N}(i)$ with $\lambda_{ij} > 0$, then set $x_i = 1$ and color it *orange*. The condition $\lambda_{ij} > 0$ is checked as whether $\lambda_{ij} \geq \delta_1$ or not.

  o if i is *green* and some *orange* node $j \in \mathcal{N}(i)$, then set $x_i = 0$ and color it *gray*.

(iii) If any node is *green*, say i, set $x_i = 1$ and color it *red*.

(iv) Produce the output $\mathbf{x}$ as an estimation.

Overall performance of algorithm ALGO. Here, we state the convergence, correctness and bound on convergence time of the ALGO using parameters $(\varepsilon, \delta, \delta_1)$.

Theorem 6.7. *The algorithm* ALGO *with parameters* ε, δ *converges for any choice of* $\varepsilon, \delta > 0$ *and for any G. The solution obtained by it is correct if G is bipartite with unique maximum weight independent set solution and* $\varepsilon, \delta > 0, \delta_1$ *are small enough. The convergence happens exponentially fast (constant dependent on problem size and weights through reasonable function).*

BP heuristic. We end this section, with brief description of the BP heuristic for maximum weight independent set. Many interesting properties of BP are known (see [21] for details). A reader is suggested to observe the extreme similarity between BP and the DESCENT algorithm.

(o) The parameters are variables $\gamma_{i \to j}^t, \gamma_{j \to i}^t$, for each $(i, j) \in E$ and iteration t. Initially, all of them are set to 0.

(i) In iteration $t + 1$, update parameters as follows: for each $(i, j) \in E$,

$$\gamma_{i \to j}^{t+1} = \left(w_i - \sum_{k \neq j, k \in \mathcal{N}(i)} \gamma_{k \to i}^t \right)_+ ,$$

$$\gamma_{j \to i}^{t+1} = \left(w_j - \sum_{k' \neq i, k' \in \mathcal{N}(j)} \gamma_{k' \to j}^t \right)_+ .$$

(ii) In iteration $t + 1$, estimate assignment for $i \in V$ in independent set as $\hat{x}_i^{t+1} = 1$, if $w_i > \sum_{k \in \mathcal{N}(i)} \gamma_{k \to i}^t$, and $\hat{x}_i^{t+1} = 0$, otherwise.

(iii) Update $t = t + 1$ and repeat till convergence.

Key message on message-passing algorithms. The algorithmic method based on co-ordinate descent and Belief Propagation provides extremely simple, message-passing algorithms that require very little data structure (few numbers at each node) and perform few simple (addition, maximum) logical operations. Such algorithms naturally allow trade-off between performance and implementation cost by varying the number of iterations and the tuning algorithm parameters. In that sense, this provides a *universal algorithmic architecture* for a large class of scheduling problems. One may imagine running a message-passing scheduler all the time and when required network can read-off schedule based on the current message-values – thus, providing excellent pipelineability along with simple, distributed and parallel implementation.

6.6 Discussion and future direction

We surveyed the current state-of-art in the field of scheduling algorithms for networks with input-queued switch and wireless networks as running examples. In summary, we note three important points: (1) optimal scheduling algorithm is the MW-0^+ which can be interpreted as maximum weight maximum size scheduling; (2) designing throughput optimal simple, distributed algorithm for any problem instance is easy but obtaining small queue-size in addition is impossible for all problems; and (3) belief propagation and co-ordinate descent provide very attractive message-passing algorithmic architecture for scheduling problems.

The future work involves progress in the direction of design and analysis of scheduling algorithms. An important question in terms of analysis lies in identifying optimal algorithm beyond the fluid model scaling. In terms of design, the question lies in designing better algorithms and heuristic methods for message-passing and simple implementation. Specifically, algorithms with easily tunable performance in various dimensions would be extremely useful.

Acknowledgements I am very grateful to all my collaborators on the topic of scheduling; without those collaborations it would not be possible for me to write this survy. I would particularly like to thank Balaji Prabhakar and Damon Wischik for numerous enlightening conversations on the topic of scheduling and network algorithms over many years: in person, on phone and more recently through skype. Finally, I would like to thank Cathy Xia and Zhen Liu for carefully reading the chapter and providing feedback to improve the readability of this chapter. I would like to acknowledge support by NSF CAREER from CNS division (on scheduling algorithms) and NSF Theoretical Foundation grant (on flow-level models) while preparing this manuscript.

References

1. Andrews, M. and Kumaran, M. and Ramanan, K. and Stolyar, A. and Vijayakumar, R. and Whiting, P. : Scheduling in a queueing system with asynchronously varying service rates. *Probability in the Engineering and Informational Sciences*, Vol. 18 (2): 191–217, (2004).

2. Bambos, N. and Walrand, J. : Scheduling and stability aspects of a general class of parallel processing systems. *Advances in Applied Probability*, Vol. 25(1) :176–202, (1993).

3. Bayati, M. and Shah, D. and Sharma, M. : Max-product for maximum weight matching: convergence, correctness and LP duality. *IEEE Information Theory Transactions*, Vol. 54 (3): 1241–1251, (2008). Preliminary versions appeareared in IEEE ISIT, (2005) and (2006).

4. Bayati, M. and Prabhakar, B. and Shah, D. and Sharma, M. : Iterative scheduling algorithms. IEEE Infocom, (2007).

5. Betsekas, D. : The auction algorithm: a distributed relaxation method for the assignment problem. *Annals of operations research*, Vol. 14: 105–123., (1988).

6. Boyd, S. and Ghosh, A. and Prabhakar, B. and Shah, D. : Gossip algorithms: design, analysis and application. In proceedings of IEEE Infocom, (2005).

7. Bramson, M. : State space collapse with application to heavy traffic limits for multiclass queueing networks. Queueing Systems **30** 89–148, (1998).

8. Dai, J. G. "Jim" : Stability of fluid and stochastic processing networks. MaPhySto Lecture Notes, (1999). http://www.maphysto.dk/cgi-bin/gp.cgi?publ=70

9. Dai, J. and Prabhakar, B. : The throughput of switches with and without speed-up. In proceedings of IEEE Infocom, (2000).

10. Dembo, A. and Zeitouni, O. : Large Deviations Techniques and Applications, 2nd edition, Springer, (1998).

11. Eryilmaz, A. and Srikant, R. and Perkins, J. R. : Stable scheduling policies for fading wireless channels. *IEEE/ACM Trans. Networking*, Vol. 13(2):411–424, (2005).

12. Giaccone, P. and Prabhakar, B and Shah, D. : Randomized scheduling algorithms for high-aggregate bandwidth switches. IEEE J. Sel. Areas Commun., 21(**4**), 546- 559, (2003).

13. Jung, K. and Shah, D. : Low Delay Scheduling in Wireless Network. In Proceedings of IEEE ISIT, (2007).

14. Keslassy, I. and McKeown, N. : Analysis of Scheduling Algorithms That Provide 100% Throughput in Input-Queued Switches. In proceedings of Allerton Conference on Communication, Control and Computing, (2001).

15. McKeown, N. : The iSLIP scheduling algorithm for input-queued switches. IEEE/ACM Transactions on Networking, **7**(**2**), 188 – 201, (1999).

16. McKeown, N. and Anantharam, V. and Walrand, J.: Achieving 100% throughput in an input-queued switch. In Proceedings of IEEE Infocom, 296–302 (1996).

17. Meyn, S. P. and Tweedie, R. L. : Markov Chains and Stochastic Stability. Springer-Verlag, London, (1993). http://probability.ca/MT/

18. Modiano, E. and Shah, D. Zussman, G. : Maximizing Throughput in Wireless Network via Gossiping. In Proceedings of ACM SIGMETRIC/Performance, (2006).

19. Mosk-Aoyama, D. and Shah, D. Computing separable functions via gossip. In Proceedings of ACM PODC, (2006). Longer version to appear in *IEEE Transaction on Information Theory*, (2008).

20. Tassiulas, L. and Ephremides, A.: Dynamic server allocation to parallel queues with randomly varying connectivity. *IEEE Transactions on Information Theory*, Vol. 39(2), 466-478, (1993).

21. Sanghavi, S. and Shah, D. and Willsky, A. : Message-passing for Maximum Weight Independent Set. Submitted. In Proceedings of NIPS, (2007).

22. Shah, D. : Stable algorithms for Input Queued Switches. In Proceedings of Allerton Conference on Communication, Control and Computing, (2001).

23. Shah, D. and Kopikare, M. : Delay bounds for the approximate Maximum Weight matching algorithm for input queued switches. In Proceedings of IEEE Infocom, (2002).

24. Shah, D. and Tse, D. and Tsitsiklis, J. N. : On hardness of low delay scheduling. Pre-print, (2008).

25. Shah, D. and Wischik, D. J. : Optimal scheduling algorithms for input-queued switches. In Proceedings of IEEE Infocom, (2006).
26. Shah, D. and Wischik, D. J. : Heavy traffic analysis of optimal scheduling algorithms for switches networks. Submitted. Preliminary version appeared in proceedings of IEEE Infocom, (2006). http://www.cs.ucl.ac.uk/staff/D.Wischik/Research/netsched.html
27. Shakkottai, S. and Srikant, R. and Stolyar, A. L. : Pathwise Optimality of the Exponential Scheduling Rule for Wireless Channels. *Advances in Applied Probability*, Vol. 36(4), 1021–1045, (2004).
28. Stolyar, A. L. : On the stability of multiclass queueing networks: A relaxed sufficient condition via limiting fluid processes. Markov Processes and Related Fields, 491–512, (1995).http://cm.bell-labs.com/who/stolyar/stabil_mprf.pdf
29. Stolyar, A. L. : Maxweight scheduling in a generalized switch: State space collapse and workload minimization in heavy traffic. *Annals of Applied Probability*, Vol. 14(1), 1–53, (2004).
30. Tassiulas, L. : Linear complexity algorithms for maximum throughput in radio networks and input queued switches. In Proceedings of IEEE INFOCOM'98, (1998).
31. Tassiulas, L. and Ephremides, A. : Stability properties of constrained queueing systems and scheduling policies for maximum throughput in multihop radio networks. IEEE Transactions on Automatic Control, **37**, 1936–1948 (1992).
32. Tsitsiklis, J. N. : Problems in decentralized decision making and computation. Ph.D. Thesis, Department of EECS, MIT, (1984).
33. Williams, R. : iffusion approximations for open multiclass queueing networks: sufficient conditions involving state space collapse. Queueing Systems **30** 27–88, (1998).

Chapter 7
Introduction to Control Theory
And Its Application to Computing Systems

Tarek Abdelzaher, Yixin Diao, Joseph L. Hellerstein,
Chenyang Lu, and Xiaoyun Zhu

Abstract Feedback control is central to managing computing systems and data networks. Unfortunately, computing practitioners typically approach the design of feedback control in an ad hoc manner. Control theory provides a systematic approach to designing feedback loops that are stable in that they avoid wild oscillations, accurate in that they achieve objectives such as target response times for service level management, and settle quickly to their steady state values. This paper provides an introduction to control theory for computing practitioners with an emphasis on applications in the areas of database systems, real-time systems, virtualized servers, and power management.

7.1 Introduction

Feedback control is central to managing computing systems and networks. For example, feedback (or closed loop systems) is employed to achieve response time objectives by taking resource actions such as adjusting scheduling priorities, memory allocations, and network bandwidth allocations. Unfortunately, computing practitioners typically employ an ad hoc approach to the design of feedback control, often

Tarek Abdelzaher
Dept. of Comp. Sci., University of Illinois, Urbana-Champaign, IL, e-mail: zaher@cs.uiuc.edu

Yixin Diao
IBM T. J. Watson Research Center, Hawthorne, NY, e-mail: diao@us.ibm.com

Joseph L. Hellerstein
Developer Division, Microsoft Corp, Redmond, WA, e-mail: joehe@microsoft.com

Chenyang Lu
Dept. of Comp. Sci. and Eng., Washington University, St. Louis, MO, e-mail: lu@cse.wustl.edu

Xiaoyun Zhu
Hewlett Packard Laboratories, Hewlett Packard Corp., Palo Alto, CA, e-mail: xiaoyun.zhu@hp.com

with undesirable results such as large oscillations or slow adaptation to changes in workloads.

In other mechanical, electrical, aeronautical and other engineering disciplines, control theory is used to analyze and design feedback loops. Control theory provides a systematic approach to designing closed loop systems that are stable in that they avoid wild oscillations, are accurate in that they achieve the desired outputs (e.g., response time objectives), and settle quickly to steady state values (e.g., to adjust to workload dynamics). Recently, control theory has been used in the design of many aspects of computing. For example, in data networks control theory has been applied to flow control [18] and to the design of new versions of TCP/IP [17].

This paper provides an introduction to control theory for computer scientists with an emphasis on applications. Section 2 discusses key concepts and fundamental results in control theory. Section 3 describes how control theory has been applied to self-tuning memory management in IBM's DB2 Universal Data Base Management System. Section 4 addresses the use of model-predictive control in distributed real-time systems. Section 5 discusses automated workload management in virtualized data centers. Section 6 details the use of control theory for managing power and performance in data centers. Our conclusions and research challenges are presented in Section 7.

7.2 Control Theory Fundamentals

This section provides a brief overview of control theory for computer scientists with little background in the area. The focus is on key concepts and fundamental results.

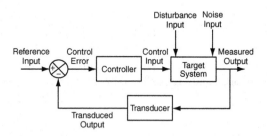

Fig. 7.1 *Block diagram of a feedback control system.*

Karl Astrom, one of the most prolific contributors to control theory, states that the "magic of feedback" is that it can create a system that performs well from components that perform poorly [2]. This is achieved by adding a new element, the controller, that dynamically adjusts the behavior of one or more other elements based on the measured outputs of the system. We use the term target system to refer to the elements that are manipulated by one or more controllers to achieve desired outputs.

The elements of a closed loop system are depicted in Figure 7.1. Below, we describe these elements and the information, or signals, that flow between elements. Throughout, time is discrete and is denoted by k. Signals are a functional of time.

- The reference input $r(k)$ is the desired value of the measured output (or transformations of them), such as CPU utilization. For example, $r(k)$ might be 66%. Sometimes, the reference input is referred to as the desired output or the set point.
- The control error $e(k)$ is the difference between the reference input and the measured output.
- The control input $u(k)$ is the setting of one or more parameters that manipulate the behavior of the target system(s) and can be adjusted dynamically.
- The controller determines the setting of the control input needed to achieve the reference input. The controller computes values of the control input based on current and past values of control error.
- The disturbance input $d(k)$ is any change that affects the way in which the control input influences the measured output (e.g., running a virus scan or a backup).
- The measured output $y(k)$ is a measurable characteristic of the target system such as CPU utilization and response time.
- The noise input $n(k)$ changes the measured output produced by the target system. This is also called sensor noise or measurement noise.
- The transducer transforms the measured output so that it can be compared with the reference input (e.g., smoothing stochastics of the output).

In general, there may be multiple instances of any of the above elements. For example, in clustered systems, there may be multiple load balancers (controllers) that regulate the loads on multiple servers (target systems).

To illustrate the foregoing, consider a cluster of three Apache Web Servers. The Administrator may want these systems to run at no greater than 66% utilization so that if any one of them fails, the other two can absorb the load of the failed server. Here, the measured output is CPU utilization. The control input is the maximum number of connections that the server permits as specified by the MaxClients parameter. This parameter can be manipulated to adjust CPU utilization. Examples of disturbances are changes in arrival rates and shifts in the type of requests (e.g., from static to dynamic pages). Control theory provides design techniques for determining the values of parameters such as MaxClients so that the resulting system is stable and settles quickly in response to disturbances.

Controllers are designed for some intended purpose or control objective. The most common objectives are:

- **regulatory control**: Ensure that the measured output is equal to (or near) the reference input. For example, in a cluster of three web servers, the reference input might be that the utilization of a web server should be maintained at 66% to handle fail-over. If we add a fourth web server to the cluster, then we may want to change the reference input from 66% to 75%.
- **disturbance rejection**: Ensure that disturbances acting on the system do not significantly affect the measured output. For example, when a backup or virus

scan is run on a web server, the overall utilization of the system is maintained at 66%. This differs from regulator control in that we focus on changes to the disturbance input, not to the reference input.

- **optimization**: Obtain the "best" value of the measured output, such as optimizing the setting of `MaxClients` in the Apache HTTP Server so as to minimize response times. Here, there is no reference input.

There are several properties of feedback control systems that should be considered when comparing controllers for computing systems. Our choice of metrics is drawn from experience with commercial information technology systems. Other properties may be of interest in different settings. For example, [21] discusses properties of interest for control of real-time systems.

Below, we motivate and present the main ideas of the properties considered.

- A system is said to be *stable* if for any bounded input, the output is also bounded. Stability is typically the first property considered in designing control systems since unstable systems cannot be used for mission critical work.

- The control system is *accurate* if the measured output converges (or becomes sufficiently close) to the reference input in the case of regulatory control and disturbance rejection, or the measured output converges to the optimal value in the case of an optimization objective. Accurate systems are essential to ensuring that control objectives are met, such as differentiating between gold and silver classes of service and ensuring that throughput is maximized without exceeding response time constraints. Typically, we do not quantify accuracy. Rather, we measure inaccuracy. For a system in steady state, its inaccuracy, or **steady state error** is the steady state value of the control error $e(k)$.

- The system has *short settling times* if it converges quickly to its steady state value. Short settling times are particularly important for disturbance rejection in the presence of time-varying workloads so that convergence is obtained before the workload changes.

- The system should achieve its objectives in a manner that *does not overshoot*. The motivation here is that overshoot typically leads to undershoot and hence to increased variability in the measured output.

Much of our application of control theory is based on the properties of stability, accuracy, settling time, and overshoot. We refer to these as the **SASO** properties.

To elaborate on the SASO properties, we consider what constitutes a stable system. For computing systems, we want the output of feedback control to converge, although it may not be constant due to the stochastic nature of the system. To refine this further, computing systems have operating regions (i.e., combinations of workloads and configuration settings) in which they perform acceptably and other operating regions in which they do not. Thus, in general, we refer to the stability of a system within an operating region. Clearly, if a system is not stable, its utility is severely limited. In particular, the system's response times will be large and highly variable, a situation that can make the system unusable.

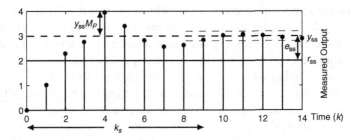

Fig. 7.2 *Response of a stable system to a step change in the reference input. At time 0, the reference input changes from 0 to 2. The system reaches steady state when its output always lies between the light weight dashed lines. Depicted are the steady state error (e_{ss}), settling time (k_s), and maximum overshoot (M_P).*

If the feedback system is stable, then it makes sense to consider the remaining SASO properties—accuracy, settling time, and overshoot. The vertical lines in Figure 7.2 plot the measured output of a stable feedback system. Initially, the (normalized) reference input is 0. At time 0, the reference input is changed to $r_{ss} = 2$. The system responds and its measured output eventually converges to $y_{ss} = 3$, as indicated by the heavy dashed line. The steady state error e_{ss} is -1, where $e_{ss} = r_{ss} - y_{ss}$. The settling time of the system k_s is the time from the change in input to when the measured output is sufficiently close to its new steady state value (as indicated by the light dashed lines). In the figure, $k_s = 9$. The maximum overshoot M_p is the (normalized) maximum amount by which the measured output exceeds its steady state value. In the figure, the maximum value of the output is 3.95 and so $(1 + M_p)y_{ss} = 3.95$, or $M_p = 32\%$.

The properties of feedback systems are used in two ways. The first is for analysis to assess the SASO properties of a system. The second is as design objectives. For the latter, we construct the feedback system to have acceptable values of steady state error, settling time, and maximum overshoot. More details on applying control theory to computing systems can be found in [16].

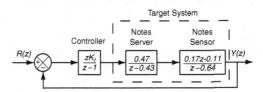

Fig. 7.3 *Block diagram of a feedback system to control RPCs in System for the IBM Lotus Notes Domino Server.*

We describe the essentials of control design using the IBM Lotus Domino Server in [26]. The feedback loop is depicted in Figure 7.3. It consists of the Controller, the Notes Server, and the Notes Sensor. The control objective is regulation, which is motivated by administrators who manage the reliability of Notes Servers by regulating the number of remote procedure calls (RPCs) in the server. This quantity, which we denote by *RIS*, roughly corresponds to the number of *active users* (those with requests outstanding at the server). Administrators choose a setting for *RIS* that balances the competing goals of maximizing throughput by having high concurrency levels with maximizing server reliability by reducing server loads.

RIS is measured by periodically reading a server log file, which we call the Notes Sensor. Regulation is accomplished by using the MaxUsers tuning parameter that controls the number of *connected users*. The correspondence between MaxUsers and *RIS* changes over time, which means that MaxUsers must be updated almost continuously to achieve the control objective. The controller automatically determines the value of MaxUsers based on the objective for *RIS* and the measured value of *RIS* obtained from the Notes Sensor.

Our starting point is to model how MaxUsers affects *RIS* as output by the Notes Server. We use $u(k)$ to denote the k-th of MaxUsers, and $y(k)$ to denote the k-th value of RIS. (Actually, $u(k)$ and $y(k)$ are offsets from a desired operating point.) We construct an empirical model that relates $y(k)$ to $u(k)$ by applying least squares regression to data obtained from off-line experiments. (Empirical models can also be constructed in real time using on-line data.) The resulting model is

$$y(k) = 0.43y(k-1) + 0.47u(k-1) \tag{7.1}$$

To better facilitate control analysis, Equation (7.1) is put into the form of a transfer function, which is a Z-transform representation of how MaxUsers affects *RIS*. Z-transforms provide a compact representation for time varying functions, where z represents a time shift operation. The transfer function of Equation (7.1) is

$$G(z) = \frac{0.47}{z - 0.43}$$

Note that the equation for $G(z)$ appears in the box in Figure 7.3 that corresponds to the Notes Server since $G(z)$ describes the essential control properties of the server. The poles of a transfer function are the values of z for which the denominator is 0. It turns out that the poles determine the stability of the system, and poles largely determine settling times as well. $G(z)$ has one pole, which is 0.43. The effect of this pole on settling time is clear if we solve the recurrence in Equation (7.1). The resulting expression for $y(k)$ has terms with $0.43^k, 0.43^{k-1}, \cdots$. Thus, if the absolute value of the pole is greater than one, the system is unstable. And the closer the pole is to 0, the shorter the settling time. A pole that is negative (or imaginary) indicates an oscillatory response.

The transfer function of a system provides another quantity of interest–steady state gain. Steady state gain quantifies how a change in the input affects the output, a critical consideration in assessing control accuracy. This can be calculated by evaluating $G(z)$ at $z = 1$. A steady state gain of 1 means that the output is equal to the input at steady state.

With this background, we outline how to do control design. We want to construct a controller for the system in Figure 7.3 that results in a closed loop system that is stable, accurate, and has short settling times. First, observe that the closed loop system itself has a transfer function that relates the reference input to the measured output. We denote this transfer function by $F(z)$. Translating the design objectives into properties of $F(z)$, we want the poles of $F(z)$ to be close to 0 (which achieves both stability and short settling times), and we want $F(z)$'s steady state gain to be 1 (which ensures accuracy since the measured output will be equal to the reference input). These objectives are achieved by choosing the right Controller.

We proceed as follows. First, we construct a transfer function $S(z)$ for the Notes Sensor in the same way as was done with the Notes Server. Next, we choose a parameterized controller. We use an integral controller, which provides incremental adjustments in MaxUsers. Specifically, $u(k+1) = u(k) + K_I e(k)$, and its transfer function is $K(z) = \frac{zK_I}{z-1}$. With these two transfer functions, it is straight forward to construct $F(z)$ [16]. It turns out that an integral controller guarantees that $F(z)$ has a steady state gain of 1. Thus, the control design reduces to choosing K_I such that the poles of $F(z)$ are close to 0.

The theory discussed so far addresses linear, time-invariant, deterministic (LTI) systems with a single input (e.g., MaxUsers) and a single output (e.g., RIS). There are many extensions to LTI theory. Adaptive control (e.g., [4]) provides a way to automatically adapt the controller in response to changes in the target system and/or workloads. Stochastic control (e.g., [3]) is a framework for going beyond deterministic systems. State space and hybrid systems (e.g., [24]) provide a way to address multiple inputs and multiple outputs as well as complex phase changes. Non-linear control provides a way to address complex relationships between inputs and outputs [29].

7.3 Application to Self-Tuning Memory Management of A Database System

This section describes a feedback control approach that achieves the optimization objective. We study such an approach in the context of memory management in IBM's DB2 Universal Database Management System. The feedback controller manages memory allocation in real time to respond to workload variation and minimize system response time.

Figure 7.4 shows the architecture and system operations of a database server that works with multiple memory pools. The database clients interact with the database server through the database agents which are computing elements that coordinate access to the data stored in the database. Since disk accesses are much slower relative to main memory accesses, database systems use memory pools to cache disk pages so as to reduce the number and time of disk input/output operations needed. The in-memory data are organized in several pools, which are dedicated for different purposes and can be of different types and characteristics (e.g., buffer pools, package cache, sort memory, lock list).

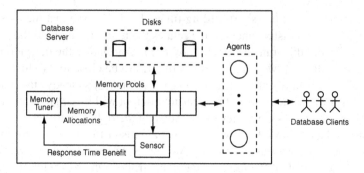

Fig. 7.4 *Architecture of database memory management.*

The management of these pools, especially in terms of determining their optimal sizes, is a key factor in tuning and determining database system performance. However, several challenges are associated with self-tuning memory management.

- Interconnection: In the database memory management problem, the total size of all memory pools is fixed. Increasing the size of one pool necessarily means decreasing the size of another. Although memory pool size increase can drastically reduce its response time to access disk data (since there is a higher probability that a copy of the data is cached in memory), its impact to other memory pools need to be considered as well.
- Heterogeneity: Buffer pools that store data pages or index pages exhibit different data access patterns. Furthermore, besides saving the I/O time, a larger size of memory pool can also lower the CPU time. For example, a larger sort memory increases the width of a merge tournament tree and reduces the number of merge passes so that the time spent in performing tournament merge can be reduced. These dissimilar usage characteristics make memory pool trade offs difficult.
- Adaptation and robustness: Each customer has its unique database configuration, a self-tuning memory controller is required to work out of the box without on-site adjustment. The controller is also required to automatically adjust itself in real time in response to database workload variation. On the other hand, robustness is of great concern to database administrators. Furthermore, for a database server, oscillations in the size of buffer pools is highly undesirable because it reduces throughput as a result of increased I/O rates to write dirty pages and to read new data.
- Cost of control: Care must be taken not to change memory pools too frequently since excessive adjustments introduce substantial resizing overheads that can decrease throughput and increase response time.

We start controller design from identifying the three key signals in a feedback control system: control input, measured output, and reference input (as depicted in Figure 7.1). The control input, $u_i(k), i = 1, 2, \ldots, N$, consists of the sizes of all N memory pools subject to self-tuning.

Although we could use system throughput or response time as measured output, they are not proper choices, because they can be affected not only by memory allocation but by many other factors (e.g., indexes and query plans) and their corresponding controllers (e.g., index advisor, query optimizer). Since the direct effect of having memory pools is to reduce the disk access time (and CPU computation time), we only focus on the saved response time in this sense. Specifically, we define measured output, $y_i(k)$, as the response time reduction caused by memory size increase. We refer to this as the *response time benefit* (or simply *benefit*), which is also known as the marginal gain. We measure benefit in units of seconds per page.

The response time benefit is measured dynamically by a special sensor. This sensor uses a "ghost buffer" that estimates the reduction in disk I/Os for a buffer pool if the the size of that buffer pool had been larger. The response time benefit is calculated as the saved disk access time divided by the size of the ghost buffer.

For the database memory problem, the control objective is optimization. Specifically, this is a constrained optimization problem where the objective is to maximize the total saved response time subject to the constraint of the total available memory [9] [11].

We introduce some notation. The scalar performance function is:

$$J = f(u_1, u_2, \dots, u_N) \tag{7.2}$$

The scalar equality constraint on total memory is:

$$g(u_1, u_2, \dots, u_N) = \sum_{i=1}^{N} u_i - U = 0 \tag{7.3}$$

Further, there may be N scalar inequality constraints imposed on the memory pools:

$$h_i(u_i) = u_i - \underline{u}_i \geq 0 \tag{7.4}$$

where $\underline{u}_i$ is the minimum size for memory pool i.

Note that for each memory pool, saved response time is increasing in memory size, and saved response time becomes saturated when the pool memory is large enough to hold the entire data block (so that there is no further I/O involved and no additional time can be saved). We assume the relationship between the pool size u_i and saved response time x_i is approximated by $x_i = a_i(1 - e^{-b_i u_i})$. We further assume that the interactions between memory pools are negligible so that the objective function is separable and convex. This gives $f = \sum_{i=1}^{N} x_i = \sum_{i=1}^{N} a_i(1 - e^{-b_i u_i})$ and its partial derivative (i.e., measured output) is $y_i = \frac{\partial f}{\partial u_i} = \frac{dx_i}{du_i} = a_i b_i e^{-b_i u_i}$.

According to the first order Karush-Kuhn-Tucker (KKT) necessary conditions, we define the Lagrange function as $L = f(u_1, u_2, \dots, u_N) + \lambda g(u_1, u_2, \dots, u_N) + \sum_{i=1}^{N} \mu_i^\top h_i(u_i)$, which adjoins the original performance function and the constraints using the Lagrange multipliers λ and μ_i. The KKT necessary conditions for a solution $u = [u_1, u_2, \dots, u_N]$ to be locally optimal are that the constraints are satisfied, i.e., $g(u) = 0$ and $h(u) = [h_1(u_1), h_2(u_2), \dots, h_N(u_N)] \geq 0$, and there exist Lagrange multipliers λ and μ_i such that the gradient of the Lagrangian vanishes. That is,

$\frac{\partial L}{\partial u_i} = \frac{\partial f}{\partial u_i} + \lambda \frac{\partial g}{\partial u_i} + \sum_{j=1}^{N} \mu_j \frac{\partial h_j}{\partial u_i} = y_i + \lambda + \mu_i = 0$. Furthermore, μ_i satisfies the complementarity condition of $\mu_i h_i = 0$ with $\mu_i \geq 0$. This implies that when the memory allocation is optimal and pool sizes are not at the boundaries, the measured outputs of memory pool are equal ($y_i = -\lambda$, and $\mu_i = 0$ since $h_i > 0$). In the case that the memory allocation is optimal when some pool sizes are at the boundaries, the measured output from these memory pool may be smaller ($y_i = -\lambda - \mu_i$, and $\mu_i \geq 0$ since $h_i = 0$). Since f is a convex function, the optimal solution is unique in that the local optimum is also the global optimum.

We design a multiple-input multiple-output (MIMO) feedback controller to equalize the measured output. Such an approach allows us to exploit well established techniques for handling dynamics and disturbances (from changes in workloads) and to incorporate the cost of control (throughput reductions due to load imbalance and resource resizing) into the design. The feedback control system is defined as follows (where matrices are denoted by boldface uppercase letters and vectors by boldface lowercase):

$$\mathbf{y}(k+1) = \mathbf{A}\mathbf{y}(k) + \mathbf{B}\left(\mathbf{u}(k) + \mathbf{d}^{\mathbf{I}}(k)\right) \tag{7.5}$$

$$\mathbf{e}(k) = \left(\frac{1}{N}\mathbf{1}_{N,N} - \mathbf{I}\right)\left(\mathbf{y}(k) + \mathbf{d}^{\mathbf{O}}(k)\right) \tag{7.6}$$

$$\mathbf{e}_{\mathbf{I}}(k+1) = \mathbf{e}_{\mathbf{I}}(k) + \mathbf{e}(k) \tag{7.7}$$

$$\mathbf{u}(k) = \mathbf{K}_{\mathbf{P}}\mathbf{e}(k) + \mathbf{K}_{\mathbf{I}}\mathbf{e}_{\mathbf{I}}(k) \tag{7.8}$$

The first equation represents a state space model [14], which is a local linear approximation of the concave memory-benefit relationship. Although most computing systems are inherently non linear, from the local point of view, a linear approximation can be effective and rational, especially when considering the existence of system noise and the ability of on line model adaptation. The $N \times 1$ vector $\mathbf{y}(k)$ denotes the measured output (i.e., response time benefit), the $N \times 1$ vector $\mathbf{u}(k)$ represents the control input (i.e., memory pool size), and the $N \times 1$ vector $\mathbf{d}^{\mathbf{I}}(k)$ indicates possible disturbances applied on the control inputs (e.g., adjustments made to enforce the equality and inequality resource constraints). The $N \times N$ matrices $\mathbf{A}$ and $\mathbf{B}$ contain state space model parameters that can be obtained from measured data and system identification [20].

Equation (7.6) specifies the $N \times 1$ control error vector $\mathbf{e}(k)$, where $\mathbf{I} = \begin{bmatrix} 1 & \cdots & 0 \\ \vdots & & \vdots \\ 0 & \cdots & 1 \end{bmatrix}$

and $\mathbf{1}_{N,N} = \begin{bmatrix} 1 & \cdots & 1 \\ \vdots & & \vdots \\ 1 & \cdots & 1 \end{bmatrix}$ are $N \times N$ matrices. The $N \times 1$ vector $\mathbf{d}^{\mathbf{O}}(k)$ indicates possible disturbances applied on the measured outputs (e.g., measurement noises that are not characterized by the deterministic model). Implied from this equation is that we define the average measured output $\bar{y}(k) = \frac{1}{N}\sum_{i=1}^{N} y_i(k)$ as the control reference for all measured outputs, and the i-th control error $e_i(k) = \bar{y}(k) - y_i(k)$. Note that in contrast to having a static value or external signal as the reference input, we specify the reference as a linear transformation of the measured outputs. The control objective is to make $e_i(k) = 0$, that is, equalizing the measured outputs (i.e., $y_i(k) = y_j(k)$ for any i and j) so as to maximize the total saved response time.

The dynamic state feedback control law is defined in Equation (7.8), and the integral control error $\mathbf{e_I}(k)$ is the $N \times 1$ vector representing the sum of the control errors as defined in Equation (7.7). The $N \times N$ matrices $\mathbf{K_P}$ and $\mathbf{K_I}$ are controller parameters to be chosen (through controller design) in order to stabilize the closed loop system and achieve the SASO performance criteria regarding convergence and settling time.

We design the controller and choose the control parameters in a way that considers the cost of control–both the cost of transient memory imbalances and the cost of changes in memory allocations [10]. Reducing memory imbalance generally indicates an aggressive control strategy with short settling time of moving the memory from imbalance to balance. However, too aggressive control can also lead to overreacting to random fluctuations and thus incurs additional cost of allocation changes.

We handle this trade-off by exploiting optimal linear quadratic regulator (LQR) control [15]. LQR chooses control parameters that minimize the quadratic cost function

$$J = \sum_{k=1}^{\infty} \left[\mathbf{e}^\top(k) \; \mathbf{e_I}^\top(k) \right] \mathbf{Q} \begin{bmatrix} \mathbf{e}(k) \\ \mathbf{e_I}(k) \end{bmatrix} + \mathbf{u}(k)^\top \mathbf{R}\mathbf{u}(k) \qquad (7.9)$$

over an infinite time horizon as well as satisfy the dynamics defined in Equation (7.5)-(7.8). The cost function includes the control error $\mathbf{e}(k)$ and $\mathbf{e_I}(k)$, and the control input $\mathbf{u}(k)$. The former is related to the cost of transient resource imbalances, and the latter the cost of changing resource allocations. The matrices $\mathbf{Q}$ and $\mathbf{R}$ determine the trade-off. Intuitively, if $\mathbf{Q}$ is large compared to $\mathbf{R}$, the controller will make big changes in resource allocations and hence can react quickly to disturbances. On the other hand, if $\mathbf{R}$ is large compared to $\mathbf{Q}$, the controller is much more conservative since there is a high cost for changing resource allocations.

With $\mathbf{Q}$ and $\mathbf{R}$ defined, the control parameters $\mathbf{K_P}$ and $\mathbf{K_I}$ can be computed in the usual way by solving the Riccati equation [4]. Hence, the controller design problem is to select the proper weighting matrices $\mathbf{Q}$ and $\mathbf{R}$ which quantify the cost of control. We achieve this by developing a cost model, regarding to the performance impact of control, and constructing $\mathbf{Q}$ and $\mathbf{R}$ in a systematic way [10].

Although the cost model and LQR framework provides a systematic way to study the cost of control, it is more appropriate to be used off-line for analyzing the target system and designing the controller prior to operation. Further simplification is needed to facilitate real time adaptation when the workload is unknown in advance and can change overtime. This also helps to manage a large set of memory pools where the number of pools is varying.

This simplification is achieved using a distributed control architecture and adaptive pole placement techniques. The model is built and the controller is designed locally for each individual memory pool; the only connection between different pools is the control reference signal–the average measured output. Specifically, a single-input single-output (SISO) model

$$y_i(k+1) = b_i(k)u_i(k) \qquad (7.10)$$

is built on line for the i-th memory pool. This is equivalent to having $\mathbf{A} = \mathbf{0}$ and $\mathbf{B} = diag([b_1,\ldots,b_N])$ in Equation (7.5), while the disturbance term $\mathbf{d^I}(k)$ is enlarged to include the modeling uncertainty. Having a set of SISO models simplifies the model structure and parameter, so that on line modeling techniques such as recursive least squares can be effectively applied with less computational complexity [20].

The controller is also built individually

$$u_i(k+1) = u_i(k) - \frac{1-p}{b_i(k)} \left(y_i(k) - \frac{1}{N} \sum_{j=1}^{N} y_j(k) \right) \qquad (7.11)$$

The controller takes the format of integral control, a simplification from Equation (7.8) by setting $\mathbf{K_P} = \mathbf{0}$ and $\mathbf{K_I} = diag([\frac{1-p}{b_1(k)},\ldots,\frac{1-p}{b_N(k)}])$. The control parameter $\frac{1-p}{b_i(k)}$ is designed through adaptive pole placement so that it will be adapted when different model parameter $b_i(k)$ is estimated on line.

With reasonable simplifications, a distributed architecture makes the controller agile to workload and resource variations, and increase its robustness regarding to measurement uncertainties and maybe uneven control intervals. For example, although in general for a database server the system dynamics may not be negligible (i.e., an increase of buffer pool size may not immediately result in response time benefit decrease, as time is needed to fill up the added buffer space) and the cross memory pool impact does exist (i.e., an increase of sort memory will not only bring down the benefit for sort memory but also that for the buffer pool that stores temporary sort spill pages), our experimental results confirm the control performance of this distributed controller.

Figure 7.5 evaluates the performance of the feedback controller under an on line transaction processing (OLTP) workload. The OLTP workload consists of a large number of concurrent requests, each of which has very modest resource demands; we use 20 buffer pools to contain data and index for the database tables and 50 database clients to generate the load. Figure 7.5(a) shows the throughput (measured in transactions per unit time) that indicates the performance impact of buffer pool re-sizings. Figure 7.5(b) and (c) display the memory allocations and response time benefits for the controlled buffer pools (as indicated by the 20 solid lines in the plot). Initially, the database memory is not properly allocated: most of the memory has been allocated to one buffer pool, while the other buffer pools are set at the minimum size. The controller adjusts the size of buffer pools so as to equalize the response time benefits of the pools. We see that even for a large number of memory pools the controller converges in approximately 80 intervals. Further, our studies in [10] show that the controller's actions increases throughput by a factor of three.

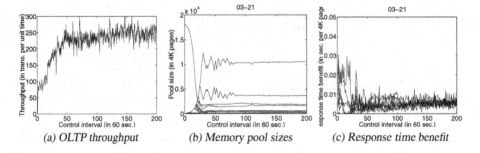

(a) OLTP throughput   (b) Memory pool sizes   (c) Response time benefit

Fig. 7.5 *Control performance under an OLTP workload.*

7.4 Application to CPU Utilization Control in Distributed Real-Time Embedded Systems

Distributed real-time embedded (DRE) systems must control the CPU utilization of multiple processors to prevent overload and meet deadlines in face of fluctuating workload. We present the *End-to-end Utilization CONtrol (EUCON)* algorithm that controls the CPU utilization of all processors in a DRE system by dynamically adjusting the invocation rates of periodic tasks. A DRE system is comprised of m end-to-end periodic tasks $\{T_i | 1 \leq i \leq m\}$ executing on n processors $\{P_i | 1 \leq i \leq n\}$. Task T_i is composed of a chain of subtasks $\{T_{ij} | 1 \leq j \leq n_i\}$ running on multiple processors. The execution of a subtask T_{ij} is triggered by the completion of its predecessor $T_{i,j-1}$. Hence all the subtasks of a task are invoked at a same rate. For example, on a Real-Time CORBA middleware a task may be implemented as a sequence of remote operation requests to distributed objects, where each remote operation request corresponds to a subtask. Each subtask T_{ij} has an *estimated* execution time c_{ij} known at deployment time. However, the *actual* execution time of a subtask may differ from c_{ij} and vary at run time. The rate of T_i can be dynamically adjusted within a range $[R_{min,i}, R_{max,i}]$. A task running at a higher rate contributes higher utility at the cost of higher CPU utilization. For example, both video streaming and digital control applications usually deliver better performance when running at higher rates.

As shown in Figure 7.6, EUCON is composed of a centralized *controller*, and a *utilization monitor* and a *rate modulator* on each processor. A separate TCP connection connects the controller with the pair of utilization monitor and rate modulator on each processor. The user inputs to the controller include the utilization set points, $\mathbf{B} = [B_1 \ldots B_n]^T$, which specify the desired CPU utilization of each processor, and the rate constraints of each task. The *measured output* is the CPU utilization of all processors, $\mathbf{u}(k) = [u_1(k) \ldots u_n(k)]^T$. The *control input* is the change to task rates $\triangle \mathbf{r}(k) = [\triangle r_1(k) \ldots \triangle r_m(k)]^T$, where $\triangle r_i(k) = r_i(k) - r_i(k-1)$ $(1 \leq i \leq m)$. The goal of EUCON is to regulate the CPU utilizations of all processors so that they remain close to their respective set points by adjusting the task rates, despite variations in task execution times at run time.

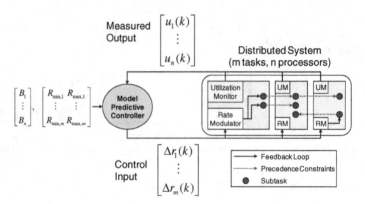

Fig. 7.6 *The feedback control loop of EUCON.*

DRE systems pose several challenges to utilization control. First, the utilization control problem is *multi-input-multi-output (MIMO)* in that the system needs to regulate the CPU utilization of multiple processors by adjusting the rates of multiple tasks. More importantly, the CPU utilization of different processors is *coupled* to each other due to the correlation among subtasks belonging to a same task, *i.e.*, changing the rate of a task will affect the utilization of all the processors hosting its subtasks because they must execute at the same rates. Therefore the CPU utilization of different processors cannot be controlled independently from each other. Finally, the control is subject to *actuator constraints* as the rate of a task must remain with an application-specific range.

To deal with inter-processor coupling and rate constraints, EUCON adopts *Model Predictive Control (MPC)* [23], an advanced control technique used extensively in industrial process control. Its major advantage is that it can deal with coupled MIMO control problems with constraints on the actuators. The basic idea of MPC is to optimize an appropriate cost function defined over a time interval in the future. The controller employs a model of the system which is used to predict the behavior over P sampling periods called the *prediction horizon*. The control objective is to select an *input trajectory* to minimize the cost subject to the actuator constraints. An input trajectory includes the control inputs in the following M sampling periods, $\triangle r(k), \triangle r(k+1|k), \dots \triangle r(k+M-1|k)$, where M is called the *control horizon*. The notation $\triangle r(k+1|k)$ means that $\triangle r(k+1)$ depends on the conditions at time k. Once the input trajectory is computed, only the first element $(\triangle r(k))$ is applied as the control input to the system. In the next step, the prediction horizon slides one sampling period and the input trajectory is computed again based on the measured output $(\mathbf{u}(k))$.

Before designing the controller for EUCON, we derive a dynamic model that characterizes the relationship between the control input $\triangle \mathbf{r}(k)$ and the measured output $\mathbf{u}(k)$. First, we model the utilization $u_i(k)$ of one processor P_i. Let $\triangle r_j(k)$ denote the change to the task rate, $\triangle r_j(k) = r_j(k) - r_j(k-1)$. We define the *estimated change to utilization*, $\triangle b_i(k)$, as:

$$\triangle b_i(k) = \sum_{T_{jl} \in S_i} c_{jl} \triangle r_j(k) \tag{7.12}$$

where S_i represents the set of subtasks located at processor P_i. Note $\triangle b_i(k)$ is based on the *estimated* execution time. Since the *actual* execution times may differ from their estimation, we model the utilization $u_i(k)$ as:

$$u_i(k) = u_i(k-1) + g_i \triangle b_i(k-1) \tag{7.13}$$

where the *utilization gain* g_i represents the ratio between the change to the *actual* utilization and the estimated change $\triangle b_i(k-1)$. For example, $g_i = 2$ means that the actual change to utilization is twice of the estimated change. Note that the value of g_i is *unknown a priori* due to the uncertainty of subtasks' execution times. A system with m processors is described by the following MIMO model:

$$\mathbf{u}(k) = \mathbf{u}(k-1) + \mathbf{G} \triangle \mathbf{b}(k-1) \tag{7.14}$$

where $\triangle \mathbf{b}(k-1)$ is a vector including the estimated change to the utilization of each processor, and $\mathbf{G}$ is a diagonal matrix where $g_{ii} = g_i (1 \leq i \leq n)$ and $g_{ij} = 0 (i \neq j)$. The relationship between the changes to the utilizations and the changes to the task rates is characterized as follows:

$$\triangle \mathbf{b}(k) = \mathbf{F} \triangle \mathbf{r}(k) \tag{7.15}$$

where the *subtask allocation matrix*, $\mathbf{F}$, is an $n \times m$-order matrix. $f_{ij} = c_{jl}$ if subtask T_{jl} (the lth subtask of task T_j) is allocated to processor i, and $f_{ij} = 0$ if no subtask of task T_j is allocated to processor i. Note that $\mathbf{F}$ captures the inter-processor coupling caused by end-to-end tasks. Equations (7.14-7.15) give the dynamic model of a distributed system with m tasks and n processors.

Based on the system model, we now design the controller. In the end of every sampling period, the controller computes the control input $\triangle \mathbf{r}(k)$ that minimizes the following cost function under the rate constraints:

$$\mathbf{V}(k) = \sum_{i=1}^{P} \| \mathbf{u}(k+i|k) - \mathbf{ref}(k+i|k) \|^2 + \sum_{i=0}^{M-1} \| \triangle \mathbf{r}(k+i|k) - \triangle \mathbf{r}(k+i-1|k) \|^2 \tag{7.16}$$

where P is the *prediction horizon*, and M is the *control horizon*. The first term in the cost function represents the *tracking error, i.e.,* the difference between the utilization vector $\mathbf{u}(k+i|k)$ and a *reference trajectory* $\mathbf{ref}(k+i|k)$. The reference trajectory defines an ideal trajectory along which the utilization vector $\mathbf{u}(k+i|k)$ should change from the current utilization $\mathbf{u}(k)$ to the utilization set points $\mathbf{B}$. Our controller is designed to track the following exponential reference trajectory so that the closed-loop system behaves like a linear system:

$$\mathbf{ref}(k+i|k) = \mathbf{B} - e^{-\frac{T_s}{T_{ref}} i} (\mathbf{B} - \mathbf{u}(k)) \tag{7.17}$$

where T_{ref} is the time constant that specifies the speed of system response. A smaller T_{ref} causes the system to converge faster to the set point. By minimizing the tracking error, the closed loop system will converge to the utilization set point if the system is stable. The second term in the cost function (7.16) represents the *control penalty*, which causes the controller to reduce the changes to the control input.

The controller minimizes the cost function (7.16) under the rate constraints based on an approximate system model. This constrained optimization problem can be transformed to a standard constrained *least-squares* problem. The controller can then use a standard *least-squares* solver to solve this problem on-line [22].

Note that the system model described in (7.14) and (7.15) cannot be used directly by the controller because the system gains $\mathbf{G}$ are unknown. The controller assumes $\mathbf{G} = \mathbf{I}$ in (7.14), *i.e.*, the actual utilization is the same as the estimation. Although this approximate model may behave differently from the real system, as proven in [22], the closed loop system can maintain stability and track the utilization set points as long as the actual $\mathbf{G}$ remains within a certain range. Furthermore, this range can be established using stability analysis of the closed-loop system.

EUCON has been implemented in FC-ORB [31], a distributed middleware for DRE systems. We now summarize the representative experimental results presented in [31]. All tasks run on a Linux cluster composed of four Pentium-IV machines. The EUCON controller is located on another Pentium-IV machine. The workload comprises 12 tasks with a total of 25 subtasks. In the first experiment shown in Figure 7.7(a), the average execution times of all subtasks change simultaneously. The execution times of all subtasks increase by 50% at 600 seconds, EUCON responds to the overload by reducing task rates, which causes the utilization of every processor to converge to its set point within 100 seconds (25 sampling periods). At 1000 seconds, the utilization of every processor drops sharply due to 56% decrease in the execution times of all subtasks. EUCON increases task rates until the utilizations reconverge to their set points. In the second experiment shown in Figure 7.7(b), only the average execution times of the subtasks on one of the processors experience the same variations as in the first run, while all the other subtasks maintain the same average execution times. As shown in Figure 7.7(b) the utilization of every processor converges to its set point after the variation of execution times at 600 seconds and 1000 seconds, respectively. These results demonstrate that EUCON can effectively control the utilization of multiple processors under varying execution times, while handling inter-processor coupling and rate constraints.

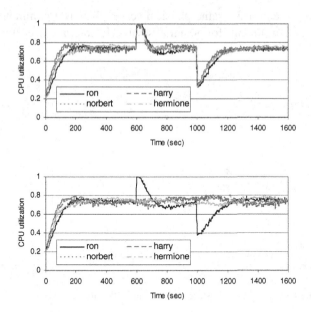

Fig. 7.7 The CPU utilization of all the processors in a Linux cluster when subtask execution times change on all four processors (top figure) and only one processor (bottom figure)

7.5 Application to Automated Workload Management in Virtualized Data Centers

7.5.1 Introduction

Data centers today play a major role in providing on-demand computing to enterprise applications supporting key business processes including supply chain, e-commerce, payroll, customer relationship management, etc. These applications typically employ a multi-tier architecture where distinct components of a single application, e.g., the web tier, the application tier, and the database tier, spread across multiple servers. In recent years, there has been wide adoption of server virtualization in data centers due to its potential to reduce both infrastructure and operational costs. Figure 7.8 shows an example scenario where multiple multi-tier applications share a common pool of physical servers. Each physical server contains multiple virtual containers, and each virtual container hosts a specific component of a multi-tier application. Here a "virtual container" can be a hypervisor-based virtual machine (e.g., VMware, Xen), an operating system level container (e.g., OpenVZ, Linux VServer), or a workload group (e.g., HP Global Workload Manager, IBM Enterprise Workload Manager). Although the grouping of application tiers can be arbitrary in general, we specifically consider the case where the same tiers from different applications are hosted on the same physical server. This is a common scenario for shared hosting environments for potential savings in software licensing costs.

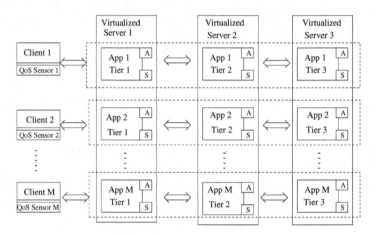

Fig. 7.8 A virtualized server pool hosting multiple multi-tier applications

When multiple enterprise applications share a common infrastructure, meeting application-level QoS goals becomes a challenge for data center operators due to the time-varying nature of typical enterprise workloads, and the complex interactions among individual tiers of the hosted applications. Existing workload management tools for UNIX systems or mainframes typically allow individual virtual containers to be dynamically sized in order to maintain a specified level of resource utilization. However, these tools can neither manage other types of containers such as virtual machines, nor provide direct guarantees for application-level QoS. In the past few years, there has been work in applying control theory to the design of automated workload management solutions that fill these gaps [34, 32, 19]. In [34], QoS-driven workload management was presented using a nested feedback controller, where the inner loop regulates the CPU utilization of a virtual container and the outer loop maintains the application-level response time at its target. In [32], a predictive controller was developed to allocate CPU resource to a virtual container proactively by exploiting repeatable patterns in an application's resource demands. This controller has been tested for managing Xen virtual machines, and a variation of it has been integrated into the latest release of the HP Global Workload Manager [8].

The work in [19] deals with the scenario where some virtualized servers are *overloaded*. This means, the aggregate demand from all the application components sharing a server exceeds its total capacity. In this case, the performance of all the applications may suffer. This is undesirable because failing to meet the QoS goals may have different consequences for different applications, depending on their respective service level agreements (SLAs). Therefore, it is desirable for a workload management solution to also provide service differentiation among co-hosted applications in order to maximize the overall business value generated by these applications.

7.5.2 *Problem statement*

Consider the system in Figure 7.8, where N ($N = 3$) virtualized servers are used to host M 3-tier applications. When one or more of the virtualized servers become overloaded, the workload management tool needs to dynamically allocate the shared server resources to individual tiers of the M applications in a coordinated fashion such that a specified level of QoS differentiation can be maintained. Next, we describe how this problem can be cast into a feedback control problem. For simplicity, we assume that only a single resource on a server (e.g., CPU) may become a bottleneck. The approach described here can be generalized to handle multiple resource bottlenecks.

Each virtual container has an actuator (box "A" in Figure 7.8) associated with it, which can allocate a certain percentage of the shared server resource to the application component running in the container. This is referred to as "resource entitlement." At the beginning of each control interval k, the *control input* $\mathbf{u}(k)$ is fed into the actuators, where $u_{i,j}(k)$ denotes the resource entitlement for tier j of application i during interval k. Since $\sum_{i=1}^{M} u_{i,j} = 1$, $1 \le j \le N$, there are a total of $(M-1) \times N$ such independent variables. Hence, $\mathbf{u}(k)$ is an $(M-1) \times N$-dimensional vector.

Each application has a QoS sensor (see Figure 7.8) that measures some end-to-end performance (e.g., mean response time, throughput) at the end of each control interval. Let $q_i(k)$ denote the QoS measurement for application i during interval $k-1$. We then define the *measured output*, $\mathbf{y}(k)$, to be the normalized QoS ratios for individual applications, where $y_i(k) = \frac{q_i(k)}{\sum_{m=1}^{M} q_m(k)}$. Since $\sum_{i=1}^{M} y_i(k) = 1$, only $M-1$ of such $y_i(k)$'s are independent. As a result, the system output $\mathbf{y}(k)$ is an $(M-1)$-dimensional vector.

The goal of the feedback controller is to automatically determine the appropriate value for each $u_{i,j}(k)$, such that each $y_i(k)$ can track its *reference input*, $r_i(k)$, the desired QoS ratio for application i when the system is overloaded.

7.5.3 *Adaptive optimal controller design*

We now describe the adaptive optimal controller we presented in [19] for the service differentiation problem. A block diagram of the closed-loop control system is shown in Figure 7.9. The controller consists of two key modules: a *model estimator* that learns and periodically updates a linear model between the resource entitlements for individual application tiers and the measured QoS ratios, and an *optimal controller* that computes the optimal resource entitlements based on estimated model parameters and a quadratic cost function.

We use the following linear, auto-regressive MIMO model to represent the input-output relationship in the controlled system:

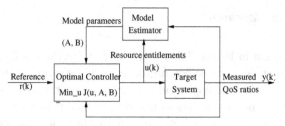

Fig. 7.9 A self-tuning optimal resource control system

$$\mathbf{y}(k+1) = \sum_{l=1}^{n} \mathbf{A}_l \mathbf{y}(k+1-l) + \sum_{m=0}^{n-1} \mathbf{B}_m \mathbf{u}(k-m). \tag{7.18}$$

Note that $\mathbf{A}_l \in \Re^{O \times O}$ and $\mathbf{B}_m \in \Re^{O \times V}$, where $V = (M-1) \times N$ is the input dimension, and $O = M-1$ is the output dimension. The use of a MIMO model allows us to capture complex interactions and dependencies among resource entitlements for different application tiers, which cannot be captured by individual SISO models. The order of the model, n, captures the amount of memory in the system. Its value can be estimated in offline system identification experiments [20]. Typically, a low-order model is sufficient for computing systems [16]. Since the linear model is a local approximation of the real system dynamics that is typically nonlinear, we estimate and adapt the values of the coefficient matrices, $\mathbf{A}_l$ and $\mathbf{B}_m$, online using the recursive least squares (RLS) estimator [4], whenever a new measurement of $\mathbf{y}(k)$ becomes available.

We use optimal control that minimizes the following quadratic cost function:

$$J = \|\mathbf{W}(\mathbf{y}(k+1) - \mathbf{r}(k+1))\|^2 + \|\mathbf{Q}(\mathbf{u}(k) - \mathbf{u}(k-1))\|^2. \tag{7.19}$$

The controller aims to steer the system into a state of optimum reference tracking, while penalizing large changes in the control variables. $\mathbf{W} \in \Re^{O \times O}$ and $\mathbf{Q} \in \Re^{V \times V}$ are weighting matrices on the tracking errors and the changes in the control actions, respectively. They are commonly chosen as diagonal matrices. Their relative magnitude provides a trade off between the *responsiveness* and the *stability* of the control system.

The optimal control law, $\mathbf{u}^*(k)$, can be derived by first explicitly expressing the dependency of the cost function J on $\mathbf{u}(k)$, and then solving the equation $\frac{\partial J}{\partial \mathbf{u}(k)} = 0$. As a result, we get

$$\mathbf{u}^*(k) = ((\mathbf{W}\hat{\mathbf{B}}_0)^T \mathbf{W}\hat{\mathbf{B}}_0 + \mathbf{Q}^T \mathbf{Q})^{-1}[(\mathbf{W}\hat{\mathbf{B}}_0)^T \mathbf{W}(\mathbf{r}(k+1) - \hat{\mathbf{X}}\tilde{\phi}(k)) + \mathbf{Q}^T \mathbf{Q}\mathbf{u}(k-1)],$$

where

$$\tilde{\phi}(k) = [0 \ \mathbf{u}^T(k-1) \ \dots \ \mathbf{u}^T(k-n+1) \ \mathbf{y}^T(k) \cdots \ \cdots \ \mathbf{y}^T(k-n+1)]^T,$$
$$\hat{\mathbf{X}} = [\hat{\mathbf{B}}_0, \ \dots, \ \hat{\mathbf{B}}_{n-1}, \ \hat{\mathbf{A}}_1, \ \dots, \ \hat{\mathbf{A}}_n].$$

Note that $\hat{\mathbf{X}}$ and $\hat{\mathbf{B}}_0$ are online estimates of the model parameters.

7.5.4 *Experimental evaluation*

Our controller design has been validated on a two-node testbed hosting two instances of the RUBiS application [1], an online auction benchmark. We use a two-tier implementation consisting of an Apache web server and a MySQL database (DB) server. Each application tier is hosted in a Xen virtual machine. The "web node" is used to host two web tiers, and the "DB node" is used to host two DB tiers. For this application, CPU is the only potential resource bottleneck. We use the credit-based CPU scheduler in the hypervisor of Xen 3.0.3 unstable branch [7] as the actuator in our control loop. It implements proportional fair sharing of the CPU capacity among multiple virtual machines.

We choose a control interval of 20 seconds, which offers a good balance between responsiveness of the controller and predictability of the measurements. For each RUBiS application i, we use mean response time per interval $(RT_i(k))$ as the QoS metric, and the normalized RT ratio, $y(k) = RT_1(k)/(RT_1(k) + RT_2(k))$, as the measured output. The reference input, $r(k)$, indicates the desired level of QoS differentiation between the two applications. Note that both $y(k)$ and $r(k)$ are scalars in this example.

In the first experiment, we varied the reference input, $r(k)$, from 0.3 to 0.5 then to 0.7. Each reference value was used for a period of 60 control intervals.

Figure 7.10(a) shows the measured per-interval throughput in requests per second (top) and the mean response time in seconds (middle) for the two applications, as well as the normalized RT ratio $y(k)$ against the reference input $r(k)$ (bottom) over a period of 180 control intervals (one hour). The vertical dashed lines indicate the two step changes in the reference input. As we can see, the measured output was able to track the changes in the reference input fairly closely. The performance of both applications also behaved as we expected. For example, a $r(k)$ value of 0.3 gave preferential treatment to application 1, where application 1 achieved higher throughput and lower average response time than application 2 did. When $r(k)$ was set at 0.5, both applications achieved comparable performance. Finally, as $r(k)$ was increased to 0.7, application 2 was able to achieve a higher level of performance than application 1 did, which was consistent with our expectation.

Figure 7.10(b) shows the corresponding CPU entitlements and resulting CPU consumptions of individual application tiers. As we can see, as $r(k)$ went from 0.3 to 0.5 to 0.7, our controller allocated less and less CPU capacity to both tiers in application 1, and more CPU capacity to application 2.

In the second experiment, we fixed the target RT ratio at $r(k) = 0.7$, and varied the intensity of the workload for application 1 from 300 to 500 concurrent users. This effectively created varying resource demands in both tiers of application 1. Experimental results showed that, the controller was able to allocate the CPU capacity on both nodes accordingly, and always maintained the normalized RT ratio near the reference value, in spite of the change in the workload.

In this section, we described how control theory can be applied to the design of automated workload management solutions for a virtualized data center. In particular, as one or more virtualized servers become overloaded, our controller can

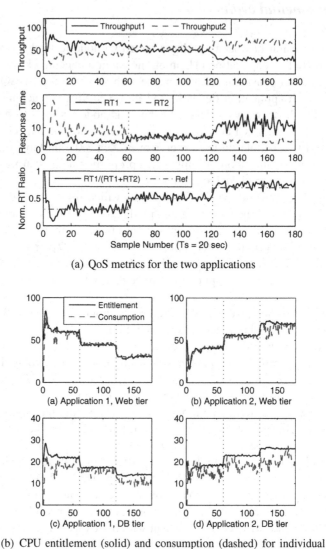

(a) QoS metrics for the two applications

(b) CPU entitlement (solid) and consumption (dashed) for individual application tiers

Fig. 7.10 Experimental results with changes in reference input

dynamically allocate shared server resources to individual application tiers in order to maintain a desired level of service differentiation among co-hosted applications. The self-tuning optimal controller we presented has been validated on a lab testbed, and has demonstrated good closed-loop properties in face of workload variations or changes in the reference input.

7.6 Application to Power and Performance in Data Centers

The following case study is motivated by the importance of energy saving in multi-tier Web server farms. In large server farms, it is reported that 23-50% of the revenue is spent on energy [13, 6]. In order to handle peak load requirements, server farms are typically over-provisioned based on offline analysis. A considerable amounts of energy can be saved by reducing resource consumption during non-peak conditions. Significant research efforts have been expended on applying dynamic voltage scaling (DVS) to computing systems in order to save power while meeting time or performance constraints [13, 6, 12, 28, 27, 33].

In this section, we describe adaptive techniques for energy management in server farms based on optimization and feedback control. We specifically illustrate the importance of *joint* adaptation. We show that in large-scale systems, the existence of several individually stable adaptive components may result in a collectively unstable system. For example, a straightforward combination of two energy-saving policies may result in a larger energy expenditure than that with either policy in isolation. We illustrate this problem by exploring a combination of a DVS policy (that controls frequency, f, of machines in a server farm given their delay D[1]) and an independently designed machine On/Off policy (that increases the number of machines m in the server farm when the delay is increased and removes machines when the delay is decreased). We then provide a solution to avoid the unstable interaction between the two policies.

Figure 7.11 shows experimental results from a three-tier Web server farm testbed. Four different energy saving configurations are compared: the On/Off policy, the DVS policy, the combination of On/Off + DVS (exhibiting adverse interaction) and finally an optimized policy that we explain later in this section. It is clearly demonstrated that when the workload increases, the combined On/Off + DVS policy spends much more energy than all other policies.

The adverse interaction is because the DVS policy reduces the frequency of a processor, increasing system utilization, which increases end-to-end delay causing the On/Off policy to to turn more machines on.

7.6.1 Design Methodology for Integrating Adaptive Policies

In this section, we describe how to design feedback control mechanisms that are free of adverse interactions, optimize energy and respect end-to-end resource and timing constraints. Our solution methodology is divided into three steps:

1. Formulate the optimization problem: Optimization is performed with respect to the available feedback control knobs subject to (i) resource constraints, and (ii)

---

[1] Observe that changing frequency of a processor also changes the associated core voltage. Therefore, we interchangeably use "changing frequency (level)" and "changing DVS (level)" throughout this paper.

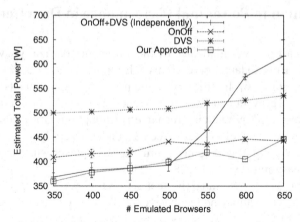

Fig. 7.11 Comparison of total system power consumption for different adaptive policies in the Web server case study.

performance specification constraints. Suppose there are a total of n different feedback control policies. For each feedback control policy i, a corresponding set of feedback control knobs is denoted as x_i, where $i = 1, \cdots, n$. We can formulate a constrained optimization problem as follows:

$$\min_{x_1,\ldots,x_n} \ f(x_1,\ldots,x_n)$$
$$\text{subject to} \ \ g_j(x_1,\ldots,x_n) \le 0, \ \ j = 1,\ldots,m, \qquad (7.20)$$

where f is the common objective function[2]; $g_j(\cdot)$, $j = 1,\ldots,m$ are the resource and performance constraints related to the application. Introducing Lagrange multipliers $v_1,\ldots,v_m$, the Lagrangian of the problem is given as:

$$\begin{aligned}
L(x_1,\ldots,x_n,v_1,\ldots,v_m) = \ & f(x_1,\ldots,x_n) + \\
& v_1 g_1(x_1,\ldots,x_n) + \\
& \ldots + \\
& v_m g_m(x_1,\ldots,x_n) \qquad (7.21)
\end{aligned}$$

2. Derivation of necessary conditions: Model inaccuracies (such as those in estimating actual computation times, exact energy consumption, or end-to-end delay in practical systems) are likely to render the expressions for functions $f(.)$ and $g_j(.)$ above inaccurate. Hence, we would like to combine optimization with feedback control to compensate for such inaccuracies.

Our approach is to derive only *approximate necessary conditions* for optimality, instead of exact necessary and sufficient conditions. This gives a locus of solution

---

[2] In this case f represents a notion of cost to be minimized. Alternatively, it could represent a notion of utility to be maximized.

points. A series of feedback loops is then used to traverse that locus in search of a maximum utility point.

The necessary conditions of optimality are derived by relaxing the original problem (i.e., where knob settings are discrete) into a continuous problem (where knob setting are real numbers and functions $g(.)$ and $f(.)$ are differentiable), then using the Karush-Kuhn-Tucker (KKT) optimality conditions [5], $\forall i : 1,\ldots,n$:

$$\frac{\partial f(x_1,\ldots,x_n)}{\partial x_i} + \sum_{j=1}^{m} v_j \frac{\partial g_j(x_1,\ldots,x_n)}{\partial x_i} = 0 \qquad (7.22)$$

Let us call the left-hand-side, Γ_{x_i}. Observe that, we have the necessary condition:

$$\Gamma_{x_1} = \ldots = \Gamma_{x_n} \qquad (7.23)$$

We then use a feedback control approach to find the maximum utility point on the locus that satisfies Equation (7.23). Our feedback control approach is described next. We find it useful for the discussion below to also define the average $\Gamma_x = (\Gamma_{x_1} + \ldots + \Gamma_{x_n})/n$. This average at time k will serve as the set point $r(k)$ for each individual Γ_{x_n}.

3. Feedback control: The purpose of feedback control is to find knob values x_i such that the condition in Equation (7.23) is satisfied. Conceptually, when some values of Γ_{x_i} are not equal, two directions are possible for fixing the deviation in the condition. One is for modules with smaller values of Γ_{x_i} to change their knobs x_i to catch up with larger ones. The other is for those with larger values of Γ_{x_i} to change their knobs to catch up with smaller ones. Moreover, more than one knob may be adjusted together. In the spirit of hill climbing, we take the combination that maximizes the increase in utility (i.e., optimizes the objective function). Hence, we define the control error, $e(k)$, at time k, as $\Gamma_x - \Gamma_{x_i}$ (we omit index k for notational simplicity) and find the set of neighboring points to the current x_i vector that reduces the error in the direction that involves a maximum increase in utility. The algorithm will dynamically guide the system toward a better configuration.

We will next briefly show how this general solution methodology can be applied to the multi-tier Web server farm case study.

1. Formulating the optimization problem: The decision variables in the optimization problem are the tuning knobs for each individual feedback control policy, namely the frequency levels of each machine (for the DVS policy) and the number of active machines at each tier (for the On/Off policy). They are optimized subject to resource and delay constraints. For simplicity, let us use a queuing-theoretic M/M/1 model for each server machine to predict delay. In this model, the system utilization, U, is expressed as λ/μ, given the arrival rate λ of the traffic and the service rate μ of the server. Assuming a load-balanced tier i of m_i machines and of total arrival rate λ_i, the arrival rate per machine is λ_i/m_i and the service rate is proportional to frequency f_i. Expressing λ_i in clock cycles, the utilization of a machine at tier i, denoted U_i, becomes $U_i = \frac{\lambda_i}{m_i f_i}$, We further approximate power consumption P_i by a function of CPU frequency f_i for each machine at tier i, namely $P_i(f_i) = A_i \cdot f_i^p + B_i$, where A_i and B_i are positive constants. In realistic systems p varies between 2.5 and 3 [12]. A_i, B_i, and p can be obtained by curve fitting against empirical measurements when profiling the system off-line. Merging the above two equations, we get $P_i(U_i, m_i) = A_i \cdot \left(\frac{\lambda_i}{U_i m_i}\right)^p + B_i = \frac{A_i \lambda_i^p}{U_i^p m_i^p} + B_i$. The total power consumption can be obtained by summing over N tiers as $P_{tot}(U_i, m_i) = \sum_{i=1}^{N} m_i \cdot P_i(U_i, m_i)$. We want to minimize the total server power consumptions subject to two functional constraints. The first constraint is that the total end-to-end delay should be less than some end-to-end delay bound, L. In the M/M/1 queuing model, this translates to $\sum_{i=1}^{N} \frac{m_i}{\lambda_i} \cdot \frac{U_i}{1-U_i} \le K$, where K is some constant. The second constraint is on the total number of machines M in the farm, $\sum_{i=1}^{N} m_i \le M$. For a 3-tier server farm ($N = 3$) and using $p = 3$, the constrained minimization problem can now be formulated as:

$$\min_{U_i \ge 0, \, m_i \ge 0} P_{tot}(U_i, m_i) = \sum_{i=1}^{3} m_i \left(\frac{A_i \lambda_1^3}{U_i^3 m_i^3} + B_i \right)$$

$$\text{subject to} \quad \sum_{i=1}^{3} \frac{m_i}{\lambda_i} \cdot \frac{U_i}{1-U_i} \le K, \tag{7.24}$$

$$\sum_{i=1}^{3} m_i \le M$$

2. Derivation of necessary conditions: To derive necessary conditions, let $x = [U_1 \; U_2 \; U_3 \; m_1 \; m_2 \; m_3]^T$ be the vector of decision variables. Observe that we could have alternatively chosen frequency f_i instead of utilization U_i for the decision variables, since utilization cannot be set directly. Since we assume an algebraic relation between utilization and frequency, the two choices are mathematically equivalent. Expressing control knobs in terms of utilization could be more intuitive in that it directly quantifies a measure of server load. Introducing the Lagrange multipliers $v_1, v_2 \ge 0$, we can write the Lagrangian function as:

$$L(x, v_1, v_2) = \sum_{i=1}^{3} m_i \left(\frac{A_i \lambda_i^3}{U_i^3 m_i^3} + B_i \right) + $$
$$+ v_1 \cdot \left(\sum_{i=1}^{3} (\frac{m_i}{\lambda_i} \cdot \frac{U_i}{1-U_i}) - K \right) + v_2 \cdot \left(\sum_{i=1}^{3} (m_i) - M \right). \tag{7.25}$$

The Karush-Kuhn-Tucker (KKT) conditions [5] associated with the optimization problem are:

$$\frac{\partial L}{\partial U_i} = -\frac{nA_i\lambda_i^3}{m_i^2 U_i^4} + \frac{v_1 m_i}{\lambda_i(1-U_i)^2} = 0 \ \forall i,$$

$$\frac{\partial L}{\partial m_i} = -\frac{2A_i\lambda_i^3}{m_i^3 U_i^3} + B_i + \frac{v_1}{\lambda_i}\cdot\frac{U_i}{1-U_i} + v_2 = 0 \ \forall i,$$

$$v_1 \cdot \left(\sum_{i=1}^{3}(\frac{m_i}{\lambda_i}\cdot\frac{U_i}{1-U_i}) - K\right) = 0,$$

$$v_2 \cdot \left(\sum_{i=1}^{3}(m_i) - M\right) = 0.$$

(7.26)

Solving for v_1 and v_2 then substituting in the first two sets of equations above, we get after some rearranging:

$$\frac{\lambda_1^4(1-U_1)^2}{m_1^3 U_1^4} = \frac{\lambda_2^4(1-U_2)^2}{m_2^3 U_2^4} = \frac{\lambda_3^4(1-U_3)^2}{m_3^3 U_3^4}. \tag{7.27}$$

To simplify the notations, we will use $\Gamma(m_i, U_i)$ to denote $\frac{\lambda_i^4(1-U_i)^2}{m_i^3 U_i^4}$ in the following discussions. Then the necessary condition for optimality is expressed as

$$\Gamma(m_1, U_1) = \Gamma(m_2, U_2) = \Gamma(m_3, U_3). \tag{7.28}$$

3. Feedback control: It can be easily seen from the necessary condition that, assuming stable changes in λ_i and m_i, the value of $\Gamma(m_i, U_i)$ will increase as U_i decreases. On the other hand, $\Gamma(m_i, U_i)$ will decrease if U_i increases. From this, we can deduce that a smaller value for $\Gamma(m_i, U_i)$ indicates that tier i is *overloaded* and, similarly, a larger value for $\Gamma(m_i, U_i)$ indicates that tier i is *underloaded*. Based on this observation, we can design a feedback loop in which the utilization and the number of machines are adjusted (using traditional control-theoretic analysis techniques described earlier in this tutorial) in the direction that reduces error (i.e., enforces Equation (7.28)) while minimizing the energy objective function.

7.6.2 Evaluation

Next, we evaluate five different energy saving approaches: a baseline (no power management), the Linux On-demand governor [25], and the three control algorithms mentioned above (the Feedback DVS, the Feedback On/Off, and the Feedback On/Off & DVS). For the baseline, we set the CPU frequency to the maximum on all machines. For each test run, 2500 seconds of TPC-W workload are applied, with a 300-second ramp-up period, a 2000-second measurement interval, and finally a 200-second ramp-down period. The TPC-W benchmark generates requests by starting a number of emulated browsers (EB). We used the shopping mix workload consisting of 80% browsing and 20% ordering, which is considered the primary performance metric by the Transactional Processing Council [30]. The user think time was set to 1.0 seconds. We used 450 ms as the delay set-point for all experi-

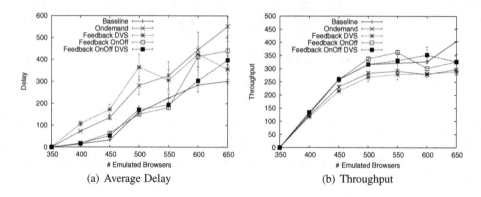

(a) Average Delay   (b) Throughput

Fig. 7.12 Other Metrics: Average Delay, Deadline Miss Ratio, and Throughput

ments. The delay set-point is computed such that if the average delay is kept around or below it, the miss ratio of the latency constraint is maintained at or below 0.1, assuming that the end-to-end delay follows an exponential distribution. Figure 7.11 shows that our approach improves energy consumption (baseline and Linux governor are not shown). Figure 12(a) depicts the average delay of the five algorithms. Figure 12(b) depicts throughput.

7.7 Conclusions And Research Challenges

Current trends in computing systems are challenging our ability to engineer systems that adapt quickly to changes in workloads and resources. Examples addressed in this paper include: self-tuning memory management in database systems that adapts to changes in queries and disk contention, dynamic control of resources in real-time embedded systems that control variations in task resource demands to meet real time objectives, adapting CPU allocations of virtualized servers in data centers in response to variations in the user requests, and addressing interactions between control loops for power management in response to workload variations. Such adaptation is usually addressed by building a closed loop system that dynamically adjusts resource allocations and other factors based on measured outputs. Control theory provides a formal approach to designing closed loop systems that is used in many other fields such as mechanical engineering, electrical engineering, and economics.

This paper provides a brief introduction to key concepts and techniques in control theory that we have found valuable in the design of closed loops for computing systems. There has been considerable success to date with applying control theory to computing systems, including impact on commercial products from IBM, Hewlett Packard, and Microsoft. However, many research challenges remain. Among these are the following.

- Benchmarks for assessing closed designs. While there are well established benchmarks for steady state workloads of web servers, database systems, and other widely used applications, assessing the ability of closed loop systems to adapt to changes in workloads and resources requires the characterizations of transients. Examples of such characterizations include the magnitude of changes in arrival rates and/or service times, how quickly changes occur, and how long they persist. Further, we need efficient ways to generate such workload dynamics that permit the construction of low cost, low noise benchmarks. Good insights into workload characteristics will allow us to incorporate more sophisticated techniques, such as model based predictive control that is discussed in Section 4.

- Control patterns for software engineering. To make control design accessible to software practitioners, we need a set of "control patterns"' that provide a convenient way to engineer resource management solutions that have good control properties. By good control properties, we mean considerations such as the SASO properties (stability, accuracy, settling time, and overshoot) discussed in Section 2. Two starting points for such patterns are contained in this paper: self-tuning memory in Section 3, which shows how to use control theory to do load balancing, and the optimal design of interacting control loops in Section 6.

- Scalable control design for distributed systems. Traditionally, control engineering deals with complex systems by building a single Multiple Input, Multiple Output closed loop. This approach scales poorly for enterprise software systems because of the complexity and interactions of components. Helpful here are decomposition techniques such as those in Section 5 that address virtualized servers for enterprise computing.

- Analysis tools to address interactions between control loops. Feedback control introduces a degree of adaptive behavior into the system that complicates the construction of component based systems. Analysis tools are needed to understand and quantify the side-effects of interactions between individually well-optimized components, as well as any emergent behavior that results from component compositions.

- Dynamic verification of design assumptions. Feedback loops make assumptions about causal relations between systems variables, such as an admission controller assuming that request rate and utilization change in the same direction. There is considerable value in dynamically verifying design assumptions. For example, one could have a "performance assert" statement that tests that system variables change in the expected direction in relation to one another. When violations of these assumptions are detected, appropriate actions must be taken.

- Control of multiple types of resources. Most of the existing applications of control theory deal with one resource type, for instance, memory in Section 3, and CPU in Sections 4 and 5. In practice, the performance of applications running in computing systems depends on multiple resources, such as CPU, memory, network bandwidth and disk I/O. From a control perspective this creates challenges with interactions between multiple controllers and target systems with different time constants, delay characteristics, and software interfaces.

- Extending the application of control theory beyond performance management. While control theory provides a systematic approach to designing feedback systems for performance management, computing solutions also involve considerations such as user interface design, security, installation, and power. To what extent can feedback control be applied to these areas? Also, to what extent can other technologies, such as machine learning, be applied to performance management?

References

1. C. Amza, A. Ch, A. Cox, S. Elnikety, R. Gil, K. Rajamani, E. Cecchet, and J. Marguerite. Specification and implementation of dynamic Web site benchmarks. In *Proceedings of WWC-5: IEEE 5th Annual Workshop on Workload Characterization*, Oct. 2002.
2. K. Astrom. Challenges in Control Education. *Advances in Control Education*, 2006.
3. K. J. Astrom. *Introduction to Stochastic Control Theory*. Academic Press, 1970.
4. K. J. Astrom and B. Wittenmark. *Adaptive Control*. Addison-Wesley, second edition, Jan. 1995.
5. D. P. Bertsekas. *Nonlinear Programming*. Athena Scientific, 1995.
6. R. Bianchini and R. Rajamony. Power and energy management for server systems. *Computer*, 37(11):68–74, 2004.
7. C. Corp. XenServer.
8. H. P. Corporation. HP Integrity Essentials Global Workload Manager.
9. Y. Diao, J. L. Hellerstein, A. Storm, M. Surendra, S. Lightstone, S. Parekh, and C. Garcia-Arellano. Using MIMO linear control for load balancing in computing systems. In *Proceedings of the American Control Conference*, pages 2045–2050, June 2004.
10. Y. Diao, J. L. Hellerstein, A. J. Storm, M. Surendra, S. Lightstone, S. Parekh, and C. Garcia-Arellano. Incorporating cost of control into the design of a load balancing controller. In *Proceedings of the Real-Time and Embedded Technology and Application Systems Symposium, Toronto, Canada*, pages 376–387, 2004.
11. Y. Diao, C. W. Wu, J. L. Hellerstein, A. J. Storm, M. Surendra, S. Lightstone, S. Parekh, C. Garcia-Arellano, M. Carroll, L. Chu, and J. Colaco. Comparative studies of load balancing with control and optimization techniques. In *Proceedings of the American Control Conference, Portland, OR*, pages 1484–1490, 2005.
12. E. N. Elnozahy, M. Kistler, and R. Rajamony. Energy-efficient server clusters. In *Power Aware Computing Systems*, pages 179–196, 2002.
13. E. N. Elnozahy, M. Kistler, and R. Rajamony. Energy conservation policies for web servers. In *USENIX Symposium on Internet Technologies and Systems*, 2003.
14. G. F. Franklin, J. D. Powell, and A. Emani-Naeini. *Feedback Control of Dynamic Systems*. Addison-Wesley, Reading, Massachusetts, third edition, 1994.
15. G. F. Franklin, J. D. Powell, and M. L. Workman. *Digital Control of Dynamic Systems*. Addison-Wesley, Reading, Massachusetts, third edition, 1998.
16. J. L. Hellerstein, Y. Diao, S. Parekh, and D. M. Tilbury. *Feedback Control of Computing Systems*. John Wiley & Sons, 2004.
17. C. V. Hollot, V. Misra, D. Towsley, and W. B. Gong. A control theoretic analysis of RED. In *Proceedings of IEEE INFOCOM*, pages 1510–1519, Anchorage, Alaska, Apr. 2001.
18. S. Keshav. A control-theoretic approach to flow control. In *Proceedings of ACM SIGCOMM*, pages 3–15, Sept. 1991.
19. X. Liu, X. Zhu, P. Padala, Z. Wang, and S. Singhal. Optimal multivariate control for differentiated services on a shared hosting platform. In *Proceedings of the IEEE Conference on Decision and Control*, Dec. 2007.

20. L. Ljung. *System Identification: Theory for the User*. Prentice Hall, Upper Saddle River, NJ, second edition, 1999.
21. C. Lu, J. A. Stankovic, T. F. Abdelzaher, G. Tao, S. H. Son, and M. Markley. Performance specifications and metrics for adaptive real-time systems. In *Proceedings of the IEEE Real Time Systems Symposium*, Orlando, 2000.
22. C. Lu, X. Wang, and X. Koutsoukos. Feedback utilization control in distributed real-time systems with end-to-end tasks. *IEEE Transactions on Parallel and Distributed Systems*, 16(6):550–561, 2005.
23. J. Maciejowski. *Predictive Control with Constraints*. Prentice Hall, 1 edition, 2002.
24. K. Ogata. *Modern Control Engineering*. Prentice Hall, 3rd edition, 1997.
25. V. Pallipadi and A. Starikovskiy. The ondemand governor. In *Proceedings of the Linux Symposium*, volume 2, 2006.
26. S. Parekh, N. Gandhi, J. Hellerstein, D. Tilbury, J. Bigus, and T. S. Jayram. Using control theory to acheive service level objectives in performance management. *Real-time Systems Journal*, 23:127–141, 2002.
27. P. Pillai and K. G. Shin. Real-time dynamic voltage scaling for low-power embedded operating systems. In *SOSP '01: Proceedings of the 18th ACM Symposium on Operating Sstems Principles*, pages 89–102, New York, NY, USA, 2001. ACM Press.
28. V. Sharma, A. Thomas, T. Abdelzaher, K. Skadron, and Z. Lu. Power-aware QoS management in Web servers. In *RTSS '03: Proceedings of the 24th IEEE International Real-Time Systems Symposium*, page 63, Washington, DC, USA, 2003. IEEE Computer Society.
29. J.-J. E. Slotine and W. Li. *Applied Nonlinear Control*. Prentice-Hall, 1991.
30. Transaction Processing Performance Council. TPC Benchmark W (Web Commerce).
31. X. Wang, Y. Chen, C. Lu, and X. Koutsoukos. FC-ORB: A robust distributed real-time embedded middleware with end-to-end utilization control. *Journal of Systems and Software*, 80(7):938–950, 2007.
32. W. Xu, X. Zhu, S. Singhal, and Z. Wang. Predictive control for dynamic resource allocation in enterprise data centers. In *Proceedings of the IEEE/IFIP Network Operations & Management Symposium*, Apr. 2006.
33. W. Yuan and K. Nahrstedt. Energy-efficient soft real-time cpu scheduling for mobile multimedia systems. In *SOSP '03: Proceedings of the 19th ACM Symposium on Operating Systems Principles*, pages 149–163, New York, NY, USA, 2003. ACM Press.
34. X. Zhu, Z. Wang, and S. Singhal. Utility driven workload management using nested control design. In *Proceedings of the American Control Conference*, June 2006.

Index